Jan Morris was born in 1926 of a Welsh father and an English mother, and when she is not travelling she lives with her partner Elizabeth Morris in the top left-hand corner of Wales, between the mountains and the sea.

Her books include *Coronation Everest*, *Venice*, *The Pax Britannica Trilogy* (*Heaven's Command*, *Pax Britannica*, and *Farewell the Trumpets*), and *Conundrum*. She is also the author of six books about cities and countries, two autobiographical books, several volumes of collected travel essays and the unclassifiable *Trieste and the Meaning of Nowhere*. *A Writer's World*, a collection of her travel writing and reportage from over five decades, was published in 2003. *Hav*, her novel, was published in a new and expanded form in 2006. Her most recent book, *Contact!*, about the people she encountered on her many travels, was published in 2009.

Praise for Jan Morris:

'Exquisite, powerful and profoundly tender, just as fresh as the time it was written . . . I first read *Coronation Everest* in a tent in Uganda, and promptly wrote to the author, astonished by the achievement - it utterly changed my life. I feel gratitude and delight each time I open its pages.' Simon Winchester on *Coronation Everest*

'Morris's imperial trilogy [are all] marvellous works of imagination and re-creation underpinned by travel and scholarship.'
Ian Jack, editor of *Granta*, on *The Pax Britannica Trilogy*

'A revelatory and moving memoir . . . Morris's wise and painfully honest writing illuminates not only the confusion of sexuality, but the mystery of life itself. In a new introduction, Morris describes the book as a period piece. She does herself an injustice. It is a classic.'
Michael Arditti in *The Times* on *Conundrum*

'In typically lyrical and vivid prose Morris uses Trieste as a metaphor for her own life as an exile, brilliantly weaving musings on love, patriotism, civility and old age with fact and personal memories. A richly introspective and satisfying book.'
Clover Hughes in the *Observer* on *Trieste and the Meaning of Nowhere*

Books by Jan Morris

HEAVEN'S COMMAND: AN IMPERIAL PROGRESS
PAX BRITANNICA: THE CLIMAX OF AN EMPIRE
FAREWELL THE TRUMPETS: AN IMPERIAL RETREAT

CORONATION EVEREST
CONUNDRUM
TRIESTE AND THE MEANING OF NOWHERE
A WRITER'S WORLD
EUROPE: AN INTIMATE JOURNEY
FISHER'S FACE
HAV
A VENETIAN BESTIARY
SPAIN
COAST TO COAST
CONTACT!

VENICE

JAN MORRIS

faber and faber

First published in 1960
by Faber and Faber Limited
Bloomsbury House
74–77 Great Russell Street
London WC1B 3DA

First published in this edition 1963
First revised edition 1974
Second revised edition 1983
Third revised edition 1993

Photoset by Wilmaset Ltd, Wirral
Printed and bound by CPI Group (UK) Ltd, Croydon, CR0 4YY

A CIP record for this book
is available from the British Library

ISBN 978–0–571–16897–2

Contents

THE LAGOON

Foreword

This is the third revised edition of a book which I originally wrote in the persona of James Morris.

It is not a history book, but it necessarily contains many passages of history. These I have used magpie-style, embedding them in the text where they seem to me to glitter most effectively; but for those who prefer their history in chronological order, at the back of the book there is a historical index, with dates and page numbers.

It is not a guide book, either; but in Chapter 21 I have listed the Venetian sights that seem to me most worth seeing, arranged for the most part topographically, and only occasionally confused by brief purple passages. The index contains map references as well as page numbers, and any building mentioned in the book can thus be at least roughly located on the map of the city.

Nor is it exactly a report. When I wrote it, in 1960, I thought it was. I was a foreign correspondent then, and I planned this book as a dispatch about contemporary Venice. When I began to prepare its first new edition, some ten years later, I thought I could simply bring the whole thing up to date, as a newspaper editor reshuffles a page. However as I wandered the canals and alleys with my own book in my hand, I was quickly disillusioned. I soon came to realize that it was not that kind of book at all, and could not be modernized, as I had supposed, with a few deft strokes of the felt-tipped pen. In the edition of 1974, and in its successor of 1983, I changed the details of the book, but hardly touched its generalities.

For it turns out to be nothing like the objective report that I had originally conceived. It is a highly subjective, romantic, impressionist picture less of a city than of an experience. It is Venice seen through a particular pair of eyes at a particular moment – young eyes at that, responsive above all to the stimuli of youth. It possesses the particular sense of well-being that comes, if I may be immodest, when author and subject are perfectly matched: on the one side, in this case, the loveliest city in the world, only asking to be admired; on the other a writer in the full powers of young maturity, strong in physique, eager in passion, with scarcely a care or a worry in the world. Whatever the faults of the book (and I do acknowledge two or three), nobody could deny its happiness. It breathes the spirit of delight.

So I had mixed feelings in preparing those successive revisions. When I first knew this city, at the very end of the Second World War, it still perceptibly retained that sense of strange isolation, of separateness, which had made it for so many centuries unique in Europe. It was a half joyous, half melancholy city, but not melancholy because of present anxieties, only because of old regrets. I loved this mixture of the sad and the flamboyant. I loved the lingering defiance of the place, bred of empire long before, the smell of rot and age which was so essential to its character, the queerness, the privacy. The neglect of Venice was part of its charm for me, as it had been for so many *aficionados* before. The very echo of a footfall in a shabby lane, the soft plash of an oar beneath a shadowy bridge, could tug my heart and shape my susceptible cadences.

By the 1970s all was different. Because of a great sea-flood in 1966, Venice had captured the concern of the world. The possibility of her extinction beneath the waters, remote though it really was, was seen as an international catastrophe, and from many nations skills and monies poured in not only to save her from drowning, but to restore all her fabrics and preserve her works of art. By the 1980s a new Venice was coming into being, protected, cherished, no longer sufficient to itself, but adopted by the world at large as a universal heritage. While I acknowledged the excitement of this new fulfilment, I could not altogether share it. For one thing, I believed the idea of Venice – my idea of Venice, anyway – to be unreconcilable with the contemporary world. For another, selfishly perhaps, foolishly even, I missed the tristesse. The sad magic had gone for me. Incomparable though Venice remained, I missed the pathos of her decline. I was out of love with her, I thought.

*

Another decade has passed, and here I am revising the book yet again. Am I in love once more? Perhaps, in a resigned, come-to-terms way. The Venice of the 1990s is yet another city, and has moved, I think, beyond nostalgia. Almost overwhelmed though it is by the pressures of mass tourism (sometimes more than 100,000 visitors in a single day), frequently addled by bureaucracy, chafing against the political control of Rome, it has found its new place in the world. All but gone is the curious, quirky Venice of long ago, the Venice of aristocrats and sea-peasants rooted so irrevocably in their own past. Today, I am told, less than 20,000 of the city's inhabitants can claim parents and grandparents born in Venice. Physically it has not greatly changed, but it is a less insular, more prosaic city, and a far more modern one – not a consummation to be sneered at, after all, for in its republican heyday Venice was an epitome of the very latest thing. Safer than any other Italian city, it has become a resort of rich Romans and Milanese, a place of second homes, not so much gentrified as plutocrified. At the same time it has discovered other functions for itself: as the most splendid of conference sites, as a centre of art studies and the techniques of conservation, as a real-estate investment, as a stage for spectacles ranging from regattas to rock concerts.

In short it has, for better or for worse, got over some kind of historical hump. It no longer even aspires to the worldly consequence it once possessed, and with the aspiration has gone the regret. Contemporary Venice is what it is: a grand (and heavily overbooked) exhibition, which can also play useful, honourable, but hardly monumental roles in the life of the new Europe. Can one be in love with such a place? Sometimes I do feel a rush of the old emotion, but it is no longer when some dappled glimpse of a backwater stirs my memories, or I smell the intoxicating fragrance of crumbling antiquity, or feel a pang of poignancy. It is rather when I see the old prodigy once more in full flush, as it were, jam-packed with its admirers, jangling its profits, flaunting its theatrical splendours, enlivened once more by that old Venetian aphrodisiac – success.

Love of another kind, then. I cannot pretend that I feel about Venice as I felt when I originally wrote this book, and so once again I find that I cannot really revise it. To refurbish my Venice would be false; to rejuvenate myself would be preposterous. The inessentials of this third new edition – the facts and figures that is – have once again been amended. The essentials – the spirit, the feel, the dream of it – I have left unchanged. Though Venice no longer compels me back quite so bemused year after year to her presence, I hope this record of old ecstasies will still find its responses among my readers, and especially among those who, coming to the Serenessima fresh, young and exuberant as I did, will recognize their own pleasures in these pages, and see a little of themselves in me.

TREFAN MORYS, 1993

Thanks

Peter Lauritzen, whose own books include *Venice: A Thousand Years of Culture and Civilization*, *Palaces of Venice* and *Venice Preserved*, has done me the honour of casting an eye through the previous edition of this book, and helping me to decide what really had to be changed, and what was best left alone.

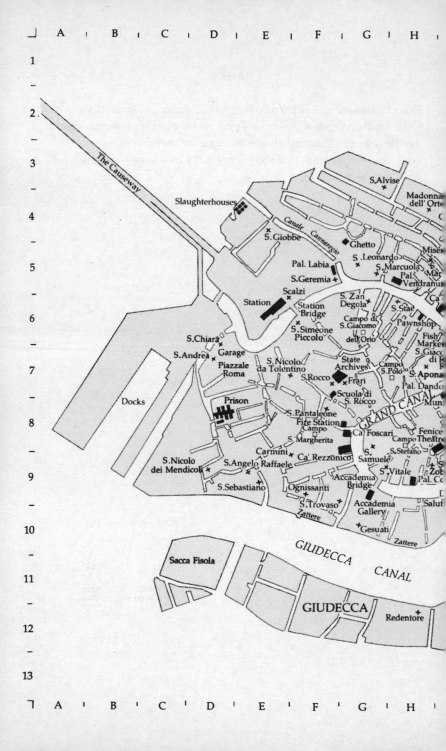

J K L M N O P Q

1

2

Venice

3

0　　　　　yards　　　　1000

Cemetery
of
San Michele

4

5

+ Gesuiti

Fondamente Nuove

6

S. Maria
i Miracoli
Hospital
+ S. Zanipolo
Gasworks ●

Office
tolómeo
vatore
+ S. Francesco
della Vigna

7

Campo S. Maria
Formosa
Scuola di S. Giorgio
degli Schiavoni

Piazzetta
Leoncini
lica
a
S. Zaccaria
Arsenal

8

Old
Prisons
La Pieta
+ S. Martino
+ S. Pietro

Doge's
Palace
Riva degli Schiavoni

9

*BASIN OF
SAINT MARK*

+ S. Francesco
di Paola

10

+ S. Giorgio
Maggiore
*ISOLA
S. GIORGIO*

+ S. Giuseppi

11

+ S. Elena

Public
Gardens
Naval
School

12

13

J K L M N O P Q

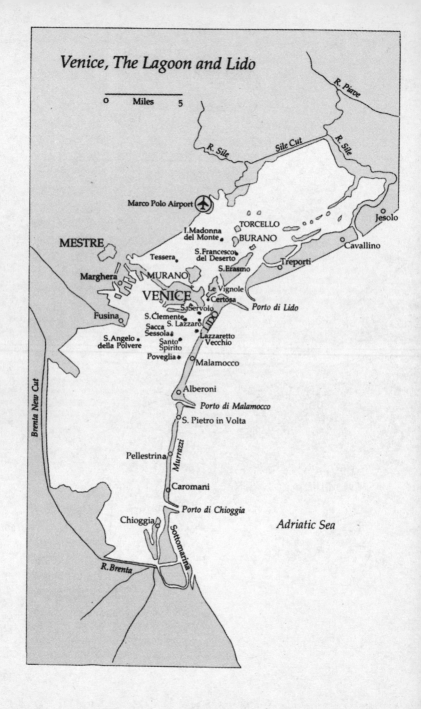

Venice, The Lagoon and Lido

0   Miles   5

R. Piave

R. Sile   Sile Cut   R. Sile

Marco Polo Airport

TORCELLO

I. Madonna del Monte

BURANO

JESOLO

MESTRE

Tessera

S. Francesco del Deserto

Cavallino

Treporti

S. Erasmo

Marghera

MURANO

VENICE

Le Vignole

Certosa

Porto di Lido

Fusina

S. Servolo

S. Clemente

Sacca Sessola

S. Lazzaro

LIDO

S. Angelo della Polvere

Santo Spirito

Lazzaretto Vecchio

Poveglia

Malamocco

Alberoni

Porto di Malamocco

S. Pietro in Volta

Pellestrina

Murrazzi

Brenta New Cut

Caromani

Porto di Chioggia

Chioggia

Adriatic Sea

Sottomarina

R. Brenta

LANDFALL

At 45°14′N, 12°18′E, the navigator, sailing up the Adriatic coast of Italy, discovers an opening in the long low line of the shore: and turning westward, with the race of the tide, he enters a lagoon. Instantly the boisterous sting of the sea is lost. The water around him is shallow but opaque, the atmosphere curiously translucent, the colours pallid, and over the whole wide bowl of mudbank and water there hangs a suggestion of melancholy. It is like an albino lagoon.

It is encircled with illusory reflections, like mirages in the desert – wavering trees and blurred hillocks, ships without hulls, imaginary marshes: and among these hallucinations the water reclines in a kind of trance. Along the eastern reef, strings of straggling fishing villages lie empty and unkempt. The shallows are littered with intricate shambling palisades of sticks and basket-work, and among them solitary men, knee-deep in sludge and water, prod in the mud for shellfish. A motor boat chugs by with a stench of fish or oil. A woman on the shore shouts to a friend, and her voice eddies away strangely, muffled and distorted across the flats.

Silent islands lie all about, lapped in marsh and mud-bank. Here is a glowering octagonal fort, here a gaunt abandoned lighthouse. A mesh of nets patterns the walls of a fishermen's islet, and a restless covey of boats nuzzles its water-gate. From the ramparts of an island barracks a listless soldier with his cap over his eyes waves half-heartedly out of his sentry-box. Two savage dogs bark and rage from a broken villa. There is a flicker of lizards on a wall. Sometimes a country smell steals across the water, of cows or hay or fertilizer: and sometimes there flutters in the wake of the boat, not an albatross, but a butterfly.

Presently this desolate place quickens, and smart white villas appear upon the reef. The hump of a great hotel protrudes above the trees, gay parasols ornament a café. A trim passenger steamer flurries southwards, loaded deep. A fishing flotilla streams work-manlike towards the open sea. To the west, beneath a smudge of mountains, there is a thin silver gleam of oil drums, and a suggestion of smoke. A yellow barge, piled high with pop bottles, springs from a landing-stage like a cheerful dove from an ark. A white yacht sidles indolently by. Three small boys have grounded their boat on a sand-bank, and are throwing slobbery mud at each other. There is a flash of oxy-acetylene from a dark shed, and a barge stands on stilts outside a boat yard. A hooter sounds; a bell booms nobly; a big white sea-bird settles heavily upon a post; and thus the navigator, round-ing a promontory, sees before him a city.

It is very old, and very grand, and bent-backed. Its towers survey the lagoon in crotchety splendour, some leaning one way, some another. Its skyline is elaborate with campaniles, domes, pinnacles, cranes, riggings, television aerials, crenellations, eccentric chimneys and a big red grain elevator. There are glimpses of flags and fretted rooftops, marble pillars, cavernous canals. An incessant bustle of boats passes before the quays of the place; a great white liner slips towards its port; a multitude of tottering palaces, brooding and monstrous, presses towards its water-front like so many invalid aristocrats jostling for fresh air. It is a gnarled but gorgeous city: and as the boat approaches through the last church-crowned islands, and a jet fighter screams splendidly out of the sun, so the whole scene seems to shimmer – with pinkness, with age, with self-satisfaction, with sadness, with delight.

The navigator stows away his charts and puts on a gay straw hat: for he has reached that paragon among landfalls, Venice.

The estuaries of three virile rivers first formed the Venetian lagoon, rushing down from the Alps with their sediments of sand, shale and mud, and falling into the north-western corner of the Adriatic. For many centuries, sheltered from the open sea by a bulwark of sandy reefs, it remained obscure and anonymous, on the edge of the Pax Romana. Scattered communities of fishermen and salt-gatherers lived among its marshes. Traders sometimes wandered through it. A few of the Roman sporting rich built villas, picnicked, idled or hunted duck on its islands. Some historians say the people of Padua maintained a port upon its outer reefs; others believe it was much less watery then, and that half of it was under the plough. Around its perimeter, on the mainland of Roman Veneto, celebrated cities flourished – Aquileia, Concordia, Padua, Altinum, all rich in the imperial civilization: but the lagoon itself stood aside from history, and remained shrouded in myth and malaria.

Then in the fifth and sixth centuries there fell out of the north, in successive waves, the Goths, Huns, Avars, Herulians and Lombards who were the scavengers of empire. The hinterland was lost in fire and vengeance. Driven by barbarism, brutality and even the threat of Christian heresy, the peoples of the Veneto cities abandoned their comforts and fled into their obvious refuge – the lagoon. Sometimes, when a phase of barbaric invasion had passed, they went home again: but gradually, over the years, their exodus became an emigration. They became Venetians in fits and starts. Some were ordered into the lagoon by direct divine command, and were led by their formidable bishops, clutching vestments and chalices. Some saw guiding omens, of birds, stars and saints. Some took the tools of their trades with them, even the stones of their churches. Some were destitute – 'but they would receive no man of servile condition', so the traditions assure us, 'or a murderer, or of wicked life'.

Many of these people went to the northern islands of the lagoon, fringed in reeds and soggy grass (where St Peter himself, for example, assigned one fertile estate to the citizens of Altinum). Others went to the outer perimeter, as far as possible from the fires of Attila. Gradually, in a movement sanctified by innumerable miracles and saintly interventions, the original humble islanders were overwhelmed, rights of property were established, the first council chambers were built, the first austere churches. Venice was founded in misfortune, by refugees driven from their old ways and forced to learn new ones. Scattered colonies of city people, nurtured in all the ease of Rome, now struggled among the dank miasmas of the fenlands (their 'malarious exhalations', as Baedeker was to call them, fussily adjusting his mosquito-net 1,400 years later). They learnt to build and sail small boats, to master the treacherous tides and shallows of the lagoon, to live on fish and rain-water. They built houses of wattles and osiers, thatched and mounted on piles.

Guided by priests and patricians of the old order, they devised new institutions based upon Roman precedents: there were governing tribunes in each settlement, slowly uniting, with bickering and bloodshed, into a single administration under the presidency of a non-hereditary Doge, elected for life – 'rich and poor under equal laws', said the first of Venice's innumerable sycophants, 'and envy, that curse of all the world, hath no place there'. The lagoon people were pioneers, like settlers in the early West, or colonials on the Veld. Crèvecoeur once wrote of 'this new man, the American': but Goethe used precisely the same phrase to describe the first of the Venetians, whose old world had died around them.

Their beginnings are distinctly blurred, and were certainly not so uniformly edifying as their early apologists would have us believe. It took many years for the lagoon to spring into life and vigour; and several centuries for these new men to stop quarrelling with each other, develop into nationhood, and build the great city of Venice proper, until they could say of themselves (as they said haughtily to the Byzantine kings): 'This Venice, which we have raised in the lagoons, is our mighty habitation, and no power of Emperor or Prince can touch us!' The early chronology of Venice is hazy and debatable, and nobody really knows what happened when, if at all.

Legend, though, is always precise, and if we are to believe the old chronicles, the foundation of Venice occurred on 25 March 421, at midday exactly. It was, according to my perpetual calendar, a Friday.

THE PEOPLE

1 Islanders

So the Venetians became islanders, and islanders they remain, still a people apart, still tinged with the sadness of refugees. The squelchy islands of their lagoon, welded over the centuries into a glittering Republic, became the greatest of trading States, mistress of the eastern commerce and the supreme naval power of the day. For more than a thousand years Venice was something unique among the nations, half eastern, half western, half land, half sea, poised between Rome and Byzantium, between Christianity and Islam, one foot in Europe, the other paddling in the pearls of Asia. She called herself the Serenissima, she decked herself in cloth of gold, and she even had her own calendar, in which the years began on 1 March, and the days began in the evening. This lonely hauteur, exerted from the fastnesses of the lagoon, gave to the old Venetians a queer sense of isolation. As their Republic grew in grandeur and prosperity, and their political arteries hardened, and a flow of dazzling booty enriched their palaces and churches, so Venice became entrammelled in mystery and wonder. She stood, in the imagination of the world, somewhere between a freak and a fairy tale.

She remained, first of all, uncompromisingly a city of the waters. In the early days the Venetians made rough roads in their islands, and rode about on mules and horses: but presently they evolved the system of canals, based on existing water-channels and rivulets, that is to this day one of the piquant wonders of the world. Their capital, the city of Venice proper, was built upon an archipelago in the heart of the lagoon. Their esplanade was the Grand Canal, the central highway of this city, which swung in a regal curve through a parade of palaces. Their Cheapside or Wall Street was the Rialto, first an island, then a district,then the most famous bridge in Europe. Their Doges rode in fantastic golden barges, and outside each patrician's house the gondolas lay gracefully at their moorings. Venice evolved an amphibious society peculiar to herself, and the ornate front doors of her mansions opened directly upon the water.

Against this extraordinary physical background, the Venetians erected a no less remarkable kind of State. At first a kind of patriarchal democracy, it became an aristocratic oligarchy of the tightest kind, in which (after 1297) power was strictly reserved to a group of patrician families. Executive authority passed first to this aristocracy; then to the inner Council of Ten; and later, more and more, to the still more reclusive and reticent Council of Three, which was elected in rotation, a month at a time. To maintain this supremacy, and to prevent both popular risings and personal dictatorships, the structure of the State was buttressed with tyranny, ruthless, impersonal, bland and carefully mysterious. Sometimes the stranger, passing by the Doge's Palace, would find a pair of anonymous conspirators hanging mangled from a gibbet, or hear a whisper of appalling torture in the dungeons of the Ten. Once the Venetians awoke to discover three convicted traitors buried alive, head downwards, among the flagstones of the Piazzetta, their feet protruding between the pillars. Time and again they learnt that some celebrated national leader, admiral or *condottiere*, had grown too big for his buskins, and had been strangled or thrown into gaol. Venice was a sort of police State, except that instead of worshipping power, she was terrified of it, and refused it to any single one of her citizens: and by these means, at once fair and ferocious, she outlived all her rivals, and preserved her republican independence until the very end of the eighteenth century.

All this was wonderful, but no less marvellous was the wealth and strength of Venice – which was, so the Venetians assiduously let it be known, divinely granted. First St Theodore, then St Mark the Evangelist supervised the destinies of the Republic, and all kinds of sacred relics and allusions gave power to the Venetian elbow. '*Pax tibi, Marce, Evangelista Meus.*' So said a heavenly messenger to St Mark, when the Evangelist was once stranded on an apocryphal sand-bank in this very lagoon: and the words became the national slogan of the Venetian Republic, a divine writ of recommendation.

She was the greatest sea-power of her day, unrivalled in tonnage, fire-power and efficiency. Her great Arsenal was the supreme shipyard of the world, its secrets as jealously guarded as any nuclear armoury; its walls were two miles round, its pay-roll numbered

16,000, and in the sixteenth-century wars against the Turks a new galley left its yards every morning for 100 days. The Venetian Navy, manned by free men until the slavers' seventeenth-century heyday, was a most formidable instrument of war, and long after the rise of Genoa and Spain as naval powers, Venetian gunnery remained incomparable.

Venice stood at the mouth of the great Po valley, facing eastwards, protected in the north by the Alps. She was a natural funnel of intercourse between east and west, and her greatness was built upon her geography. She was hazily subject first to Ravenna and then to Byzantium, but she established herself as independent both of east and of west. She became mistress of the Adriatic, of the eastern Mediterranean, and finally of the trade routes to the Orient – Persia, India and the rich mysteries of China. She lived by the eastern commerce. She had her own caravanserai in the cities of the Levant: and 'all the gold in Christendom', as one medieval chronicler querulously observed, 'passes through the hands of the Venetians'.

In Venice the Orient began. Marco Polo was a Venetian, and Venetian merchants, searching for new and profitable lines of commerce, travelled widely throughout central Asia. Decked in Oriental fineries, Venice became the most flamboyant of all cities – 'the most triumphant Citie I ever set eyes on', wrote Philippe de Commynes in 1495. She was a place of silks, emeralds, marbles, brocades, velvets, cloth of gold, porphyry, ivory, spices, scents, apes, ebony, indigo, slaves, great galleons, Jews, mosaics, shining domes, rubies, and all the gorgeous commodities of Arabia, China and the Indies. She was a treasure-box. Venice was ruined, in the long run, by the Muslim capture of Constantinople in 1453, which ended her supremacy in the Levant; and by da Gama's voyage to India in 1498, which broke her monopoly of the Oriental trade: but for another three centuries she retained her panache and her pageantry, and she keeps her gilded reputation still.

She was never loved. She was always the outsider, always envied, always suspected, always feared. She fitted into no convenient category of nations. She was the lion who walked by herself. She traded indiscriminately with Christian and Muslim, in defiance of ghastly Papal penalties (she is the only Christian city marked on Ibn Khaldun's celebrated fourteenth-century map, together with such places as Gog, Oman, Stinking Land, Waste Country, Soghd, Tughuzghuz and Empty In The North Because Of The Cold). She was the most expert and unscrupulous of money-makers, frankly dedicated to profit, even treating the Holy Wars as promising investments, and cheerfully accommodating the Emperor Baldwin of Jerusalem, when he wished to pawn his Crown of Thorns.

Venice's prices were high, her terms were unyielding, and her political motives were so distrusted that in the League of Cambrai most of the sixteenth-century Great Powers united to suppress 'the insatiable cupidity of the Venetians and their thirst for domination' (and so perversely efficient was she that the news of their resolution was brought by her couriers from Blois to Venice in eight days flat). Even when, in the seventeenth and eighteenth centuries, she stood almost alone for Christendom against the triumphant Turks, Venice was never embraced by the nations. She was like a griffin or a phoenix, on the outside of a rookery.

And as the centuries passed, and she lost her supremacies, and the strain of the merchant princes was weakened, and she sapped her energies in endless Italian squabbles and embroilments, and became a mainland Power – as she sank into her eighteenth-century degeneracy, she became another kind of prodigy. During her last century of independence she was the gayest and worldliest of all cities, a perpetual masque and revelry, where nothing was too daring, too shameful or too licentious. Her carnivals were protracted and uninhibited. Her courtesans were honoured. The domino and the Ace of Spades were her reigning symbols. The dissolute of the western world, the salacious and the mere fun-loving flocked to her theatres and gaming-tables, and respectable people all over Europe looked towards her as they might, from a safe distance, deplore the goings-on of a Sodom or a Gomorrah. No other nation ever died in such feverish hedonism. Venice whirled towards her fall, in the reign of the 120th Doge, in a fandango of high living and enjoyment, until at last Napoleon, brusquely deposing her ineffective Government, ended the Republic and handed the Serenissima contemptuously to the Austrians. *'Dust and ashes, dead and done with, Venice spent what Venice earned.'*

This peculiar national history lasted a millennium, and the constitution of Venice was unchanged between 1310 and 1796. Nothing in the story of Venice is ordinary. She was born dangerously, lived grandly, and never abandoned her brazen individualism. 'Those pantaloons!' is how a gentleman of the sixteenth-century French Court referred to the Venetians in an unguarded moment, and he was promptly slapped hard in the face by His Excellency the Venetian Ambassador. His contempt, anyway, was forced. You could not feel disdainful towards the Venetians, only resentful. Their system of government, for all its cruelties, was a brilliant success, and fostered in citizens of all classes an unparalleled love of country. Their navies were incomparable. The noblest artists of the day embellished Venice with their genius; the highest paid mercenaries competed for her commissions; the greatest Powers borrowed her money and rented her ships; and for two centuries the Venetians, at least in a commercial sense, 'held the gorgeous east in fee'. 'Venice has preserved her independence during eleven centuries', wrote Voltaire just thirty years before the fall of the Republic, 'and I flatter myself will preserve it for ever': so special was the Venetian position in the world, so strange but familiar, like Simeon Stylites on top of his pillar, in the days when Popes and Emperors sent their envoys to Syria to consult him.

Venice is still odd. Since Napoleon's arrival, despite moments of heroism and sacrifice, she has been chiefly a museum, through whose clicking turnstiles the armies of tourism endlessly pass. When the Risorgimento triumphed in Italy, she joined the new Kingdom, and since 1866 has been just another Italian provincial capital: but she remains, as always, a phenomenon. She remains a city without wheels, a metropolis of waterways. She is still gilded and agate-eyed. Travellers still find her astonishing, exasperating, overwhelming, ruinously expensive, gaudy, and what one sixteenth-century Englishman called 'decantated in majestie'. The Venetians have long since become Italian citizens, but are still a race *sui generis*, comparable only, as Goethe said, to themselves. In essence, Venice was always a city-State, for all her periods of colonial expansion. There have perhaps been no more than three million true Venetians in all the history of the place: and this grand insularity, this isolation, this sense of queerness and crookedness has preserved the Venetian character uncannily, as though it were pickled like a rare intestine, or mummified in lotions.

2 The Venetian Way

You can tell a Venetian by his face. Thousands of other Italians now live in Venice, but the true-born Venetian is often instantly recognizable. He probably has Slav blood in him, perhaps Austrian, possibly oriental tinctures from the distant past, and he is very far indeed from the stock music-hall Latin. Morose but calculating is the look in his limpid eye, and his mouth is enigmatical. His nose is very prominent, like the nose of a Renaissance grandee, and there is to his manner an air of home-spun guile and complacency, as of a man who has made a large fortune out of slightly shady dealings in artichokes. He is often bow-legged (but not from too much riding) and often pale (but not from lack of sunshine). Occasionally his glance contains a glint of sly contempt, and his smile is distant: usually he is a man of gentle reserve, courteous, ceremonious, his jacket neatly buttoned and his itchy palm discreetly gloved. The Venetians often remind me of Welshmen, and often of Jews, and sometimes of Icelanders, and occasionally of Afrikaners, for they have the introspective melancholy pride of people on their own, excluded from the fold of ordinary nations. They feel at once aloof, suspicious and kind. They are seldom boisterous or swashbuckling, and when you hear a Venetian say 'Buona sera, bellissima Signorina!' he says it without flourish or flattery, with a casual inclination of the head. The Venetian in the street can be uncompromising, and cheerfully butts you in the stomach with the tip of her loaf, or drops her laundry-basket agonizingly on your toe. The Venetian in the shop has a special muffled politesse, a restrained but regretful decorum that is part of the ambience of the city.

Observe a pair of Venetian housewives meeting, and you will see reflected in all their gestures the pungent character of Venice. They approach each other hard-faced and intent, for they are doing their shopping, and carry in their baskets the morning's modest purchases (this evidently not being their day for the weekly supermarket expedition): but as they catch sight of each other, a sudden soft gleam of commiseration crosses their faces, as though they are about to barter sympathies over some irreparable loss, or share an unusually tender confidence. Their expressions instantly relax, and they welcome each other with a protracted exchange of greetings, rather like the benign grace-notes and benedictions with which old-school Arabs encounter their friends. Their tone of voice is surprised but intimate, falling and rising with penetration through the din of the market: and they sound as though they are simultaneously sympathetic about something, and mournful about something, and a little peevish, and resigned, and reluctantly amused. ('Poor Venice!' the housewife sometimes sighs, leaning from her balcony window: but it is little more than a wry slogan, like a commuter's exorcism upon the weather, or one of those general complaints, common to us all, about the universal decline of everything.)

They talk for five or ten minutes, sometimes shaking their heads anxiously or shifting their weight from one foot to another, and when they part they wave good-bye to each other in a manner all their own, holding their right hands vertically beside their shoulders, and slightly wagging the tips of all five fingers. In a flash their expressions are earnestly mercantile again, and they are disputing the price of beans with a spry but knowing greengrocer.

The modern Venetians are not a stately people. They are homely, provincial, fond, complacent. At heart this is a very bourgeois city. The Venetians have lost the unassertive confidence of power, and love to be thought well of. There was a time when kings and pontiffs bowed before the Doge of Venice, and Titian, the most lordly of the Venetian painters, once graciously allowed the Emperor Charles V of Spain and Austria to pick up the paint brush he had accidentally dropped. But by the end of the eighteenth century the Venetians were already becoming testy of criticism, like Americans before their time of power, or Englishmen after theirs. Parochial to a Middle-Western degree was the reply sent by Giustina Renier Michiel, the last great lady of the Republic, when Chateaubriand dared to write an article unflattering to Venice ('a city against nature – one cannot take a step without being obliged to get into a boat!'). Frigid is the disapproval of the contemporary Venetian *grande dame*, if you venture to suggest that some of the city's gardens might be the better for a pair of shears.

The Venetian way is the right way, and the Venetian nearly always knows best. In the church of San Salvatore there is an Annunciation by Titian which, being a little unconventional in style, so surprised its monastic sponsors that they flatly declared it to be unfinished, or perhaps not really by Titian at all; the old artist was understandably annoyed, and wrote on the bottom of the picture, where you may see it still, the irritated double inscription *Titianus Fecit. Fecit.* I have often sympathized with him, faced with the know-all Venetians, for the true son of Venice (and even more, the daughter) is convinced that the skills, arts and sciences of the world ripple outwards, in ever-weakening circles, from the Piazza of St Mark. If you want to write a book, consult a Venetian professor. If you want to tie a knot in a rope, ask a Venetian how. If you want to know how a bridge is built, look at the Rialto. To learn how to make a cup of coffee, frame a picture, stuff a peacock, phrase a treaty, clean your shoes, sew a button on a blouse, consult the appropriate Venetian authority.

'The Venetian custom' is the criterion of good sense and propriety. Pitying, lofty but condescending is the smile on the Venetian face, when you suggest frying the fish in breadcrumbs, instead of in flour. Paternal is the man in the camera shop, as he demonstrates to you the only correct way to focus your Leica. 'It is our custom' – by which the Venetian means not merely that Venetian things are best, but that they are probably unique. Often and again you will be kindly told, as you step from the quayside into your boat, that Venetian seaweed is slippery: and I have even heard it said that Venetian water is inclined to be wet.

These are the harmless conceits of the parish pump. Foreigners who have lived in Venice for years have told me how detached they have grown to feel from the affairs of the world at large, as though they are mere onlookers: and this sense of separateness, which once contributed to the invincibility of the Republic, now bolsters Venetian complacencies. Like poor relations or provincial bigwigs, the Venetians love to ponder the glories of their pedigree, tracing their splendours ever further back, beyond the great Doges and the Tribunes to Rome herself (the Giustinian family claims descent from the Emperor Justinian) and even into the mists of pre-history, when the original Venetians are variously supposed to have come from Paphlagonia, from the Baltic, from Babylon, from Illyria, from the coast of Brittany, or directly, like nymphs, out of the morning dew. Venetians love to tell you about 'my grandfather, a man of much cultural and intellectual distinction'; or invite you to share the assumption that the opera at the Fenice is, on the whole, the best and most cultural on earth; or point out the Venetian artist Vedova as the greatest of his generation ('But perhaps you're not, shall we say, *au fait* with the tendencies of contemporary art, such as are demonstrated here in Venice at our Biennale?'). Every Venetian is a connoisseur, with a strong bias towards the local product. The guides at the Doge's Palace rarely bother to mention the startling paintings by Hieronymus Bosch that hang near the Bridge of Sighs – he was not, after all, a Venetian. The Venetian libraries concern themselves assiduously with Venice. The pictures that hang in Venetian houses are nearly always of Venetian scenes. Venice is a shamelessly self-centred place, in a constant glow of elderly narcissism.

There is nothing offensive to this local pride, for the Venetians are not exactly boastful, only convinced. Indeed, there is sometimes real pathos to it. Modern Venice is not so pre-eminent, by a half, as they like to suppose. Its glitter and sparkle nearly all comes with the summer visitors, and its private intellectual life is sluggish. Its opera audiences (except in the galleries) are coarse and inattentive, and few indeed are the fairy motor boats that arrive, in the dismal winter evenings, at the once brilliant water-gate of the Fenice. Concerts, except in the tourist season, are generally second-rate and expensive.

The celebrated printing houses of Venice, once the finest in Europe, have nearly all gone. Venetian cooking is undistinguished, Venetian workmanship is variable. The old robust seafaring habits have long been dissipated, so that the average Venetian never goes too near the water, and makes a terrible fuss if a storm blows up. In many ways Venice is a backwater. Some people say she is dead on her feet. Memphis, Leeds and Leopoldville are all bigger, and all livelier. Genoa handles twice as much shipping. There is a better orchestra in Liverpool, a better newspaper in Milwaukee, a better university in Capetown; and any weekend yachtswoman, sailing her dinghy at Chichester or Newport, will tie you as practical a knot as a gondolier.

But there, love is blind, especially if there is sadness in the family. The Venetians love and admire their Venice with a curious fervency. 'Where are you off to?' you may ask an acquaintance. 'To the Piazza', he replies: but he can give you no reason, if you ask him why. He goes to St Mark's for no definite purpose, to meet nobody specific, to admire no particular spectacle. He simply likes to button his coat, and sleek his hair a little, assume an air of rather portentous melancholy and stroll for an hour or two among the sumptuous trophies of his heritage. Hardly a true Venetian crosses the Grand Canal without the hint of a pause, however vestigial, to breathe its beauties. Our housekeeper grumbles sometimes about the narrowness of Venice, its cramped and difficult nature; but never was a lover more subtly devoted to her protector, or an idealist to his flaming cause. Venice is a sensual city, and there is something physiological about the devotion she inspires, as though the very fact of her presence can stimulate the bloodstream.

I was once in Venice on the day of the Festival of the Salute, in November, when the Venetians, to celebrate the ending of a seventeenth-century plague, erect a temporary bridge across the Grand Canal and process to the great church of Santa Maria della Salute. In the evening I posted myself at the end of the bridge, a rickety structure of barges and timber. (It was designed, so I was reassuringly told, 'according to an immemorial pattern', but one November in the 1930s it collapsed, just as Sir Osbert Sitwell was crossing it.) There, turning up my collar against the bitter sea wind, I watched the

Venetians walking to evening Mass, in twos or threes or youth groups, cosily wrapped. There was a curiously proprietorial feeling to their progress: and as each little group of people turned the corner to the bridge, and saw the lights of the quay before them, and the huge dome of the Salute floodlit in the dusk, 'Ah!' they said, clicking their tongues with affection, 'how beautiful she looks tonight!' – for all the world as though some frail but favourite aunt were wearing her best lacy bed-jacket for visitors.

This self-esteem makes for narrow horizons and short focuses. In the 1960s many poor Venetians had never been to the mainland of Italy. Even now thousands have never visited the outer islands of the lagoon. You sometimes hear stories of people who have never crossed the Grand Canal or set eyes on the Piazza of St Mark. Simple Venetians are often extraordinarily ignorant about geography and world affairs, and even educated citizens (like most islanders) are frequently poor linguists.

The Venetians indeed have a language of their own, a rich and original dialect, only now beginning to lose its vigour under the impact of cinema and television. It is a slurred but breezy affair, lively enough for Goldoni to write some of his best plays in it, formal enough to be the official language of the Venetian Republic. Byron called it 'a sweet bastard Latin'. Dazed are the faces of visiting linguists, confronted by this hairy hybrid, for its derivation is partly French, and partly Greek, and partly Arabic, and partly German, and probably partly Paphlagonian too – the whole given a fine extra blur by a queer helter-skelter, sing-song manner of delivery. Often the Venetian seems to be mouthing no particular words, only a buttery succession of half-enunciated consonants. The Venetian language is very fond of Xs and Zs, and as far as possible ignores the letter L altogether, so that the Italian *bello*, for example, comes out *beo*. There are at least four Italian-Venetian dictionaries, and from these you can see that sometimes the Venetian word bears no resemblance to the Italian. A fork is *forchetta* in Italian, but *piron* in Venetian. The Venetian baker is *pistor*, not *fornaio*. A watch is *relozo*, not *orologio*. The Venetian pronouns are *mi, ti, lu, nu, vu, lori*. When we say 'thou art', and the Italians 'tu sei', the Venetians say 'ti ti xe'. The Venetian word lovo means first a wolf, and secondly a stock-fish.

This distinctive and attractive language also specializes in queer contractions and distortions, and the street signs of the city, still often expressed in the vernacular, can be very confusing. You may look, consulting your guide book, for the church of Santi Giovanni e Paolo; but the street sign will call it San Zanipolo. The church of Sant' Alvise was originally dedicated to St Louis. What the Venetians call San Stae is really Sant' Eustacchio. San Stin is Santo Stefano. Sant' Aponal is Sant' Apollinare. The convent of Santa Maria di Nazareth, used as a leper colony, was so long ago blurred into San Lazzaretto that it has given its corruption to almost all the languages of the earth. What holy man is commemorated by the Fondamenta Sangiantoffetti I have never been able to discover, and it took me some time to realize that the titular saint of San Zan Degola was San Giovanni Decollato, St John the Beheaded. Most inexplicable of all, the church of the Saints Ermagora and Fortunato is known to the Venetians as San Marcuola, a usage which they toss at you with every appearance of casual logic, but never a word of explanation. It is, as they would say, their custom.

Venice itself, compact though the city is, remains criss-crossed with local flavours and loyalties. Each district, each clamorous market square has it own recognizable atmosphere – here harsh, here kindly, here simple, here sophisticated. Even more than London, Venice remains a collection of villages. In one you may be sure of kindly treatment, courteous shopmen and friendly women: in another, experience will teach you to be hard-skinned, for its manners may be gruff and its prices unyielding. Even the dialect varies from quarter to quarter, though only half a mile may separate them, and there are words in use at one end of Venice that are quite unfamiliar at the other. Street names appear over and over again, so independent is each section of the city: there are a dozen lanes called Forno in Venice, and thirteen named for the Madonna.

Until modern times the city was divided into two implacably rival factions, the Nicolotti and the Castellani, based upon long-forgotten animosities in the early days of settlement; and so riotous were the brawls between the two parties that the old Rialto bridge had a drawbridge in the middle, enabling the authorities to separate the mobs, by a swift tug of a rope, leaving them glaring at each other impotently across the void. This deep-rooted hostility gradually lost its venom, and degenerated into mock combats, regattas and athletic competitions, until in 1848 the old rivals were reconciled in a secret dawn ceremony at the Salute, as a gesture of unity against Austrian rule. Today the factions are dead and almost forgotten (though you might not think so from the more imaginative guide books); but there remains an element of prickly parochial pride, based upon a parish or a square, and sometimes boisterously expressed.

. None of this is surprising. Venice is a maze of waterways and alleys, crooked and unpredictable, following the courses of antique channels in the mud, and unimproved by town planners. Until the last century only one bridge, the Rialto, spanned the Grand Canal. In the days before motor boats and tarred pavements it must have been a fearfully tiresome process to move about Venice, let alone take ship to the mainland: and who can wonder if the people of Santa Margherita, satisfied with their own shops and taverns, rarely bothered to trudge all the way to Santa Maria Formosa? Sometimes a Venetian housewife announces conclusively that there are no cabbages in the city today: but what she means is that the greengrocer at the corner of Campo San Barnaba, with whom her family custom has been traditionally associated since the days of the early Crusades, has sold out of the vegetable this morning.

3 Strong Men

From this small city, though, from this very people sprang the glories of the Serenissima. It is said that at the time of the Fourth Crusade, in which Venice played a prominent and quite unprincipled part, the population of the city was only 40,000. In all the thirteen centuries of the Republic it was probably never more than 170,000. Venice was therefore a State of severely specialized talents. She produced fine administrators, seamen, merchants, bankers, artists, architects, musicians, printers, diplomatists. She produced virtually no poets, only one great dramatist, hardly a novelist, scarcely a philosopher. Her only eminent thinker was Paolo Sarpi, the monk who conducted the Venetian case in the worst of the Republic's quarrels with the Papacy, and who discovered the contraction of the iris. Her boldest generals were *condottieri*. She was pre-eminently an adapter rather than an innovator. Her vocation was commerce; her countryside was the sea; her tastes were voluptuous; her function was that of a bridge between east and west; her obsession was political stability; her consolation, when she needed it, was self-indulgence; and it is remarkable how closely her talents fitted her needs. For many centuries Venice was never short of the leaders, craftsmen, entertainers and business men she required, from astute ambassadors to diligent shipwrights, from financiers to architects, from Marco Polo to Titian to Goldoni, the merriest of minor geniuses.

The Venetians always had an eager eye for a monopoly or a quick return, and enjoyed the reputation of being willing to sell anything they possessed, if offered enough for it (though in the sixteenth century a Duke of Mantua, coveting Rizzo's famous statue of Eve in the Doge's Palace, unsuccessfully offered its own weight in gold for it). They first ventured out of the lagoon as carriers, conveying other people's produce from source to consumer, and throughout the period of the Crusades they shamelessly milched both sides. When the Fourth Crusade was launched in 1202, the Venetians were asked to ship the Frankish armies to Palestine. 'We come in the name of the noblest barons of France,' said the emissaries to the Doge Enrico Dandolo. 'No other power on earth can aid us as you can; therefore they implore you, in God's name, to have compassion on the Holy Land, and to join them in avenging the contempt of Jesus Christ by furnishing them with the ships and other necessaries, so that they may pass the seas.' The Doge returned a classic Venetian reply. 'On what terms?' he asked.

Nor did he allow any soft Christian scruples to affect the conduct of the campaign. The agreed fee for the job was 85,000 silver marks, payable in four instalments, plus a half of all booty: and for this the

Venetians were to ship 33,500 men to the Holy Land, with their horses, keep them in provisions for nine months, and contribute their own quota of soldiers and warships to the war. The Frankish army duly arrived in Venice, and was encamped upon the island of the Lido. The ships and supplies were ready as promised. The Venetians, who had some doubts about actually taking part in the holy enterprise, were encouraged in their enthusiasms by a round of liturgy and pageantry. The imperturbable old Dandolo, practically blind and almost ninety, declared his intention of leading the fleet in person. But when it came to the crucial point, the Crusaders had not the money to pay.

Old hands at unfulfilled contracts, the Venetians were undismayed. They first set a watch upon all the approaches to the Lido, to ensure that the knights-at-arms did not slip away, and they then made a proposition of their own. The Crusaders could still be shipped to the Holy Land, they said, if they would agree to stop on the way and subdue one or two rebellious Venetian colonies on the Dalmatian coast, thus securing the Republic's trade routes through the Adriatic. The Franks accepted these unorthodox terms, the great fleet sailed at last, and the Dalmatian ports were subdued one by one: but the Venetians still had further profits to exact. Dandolo next agreed with the adaptable Crusaders to make another diversion, postpone the humiliation of the infidel, and capture the Greek Christian bastion of Constantinople, with whose Emperor the Venetians were, for one reason and another, angrily at odds. Led by the old blind Doge himself, they stormed the 400 towers of the city, deposed the Emperor, loaded their ships with booty, and divided the Empire among themselves. The Crusade never did reach the Holy Land, and the temporary fall of Byzantium only strengthened the cause of Islam. But from a simple breach of contract, brilliantly exploited, the Venetians became 'Lords and Masters of a Quarter and a Half-quarter of the Roman Empire'; they acquired sovereignty over Lacedaemon, Durazzo, the Cyclades, the Sporades and Crete; they sailed home with cargoes of treasure, gold, precious gems, sacred relics, that were to make their city an enduring marvel; and they consolidated the commercial supremacy in the Levant that was to keep them comfortably in their palaces for many a long century to come.

They are sharp business men still. Venetian merchants, contractors and shippers retain a reputation for hard-headedness, if not cussedness. ('A stiff-necked and rebellious people' is how one administrator from Rome recently described the Venetians.) The Bourse of Venice, near the Piazza of St Mark, is conducted with grave and Doge-like precision: not a breath of wild speculation ruffles its notice-boards, but a strong sense of opportunism leaks from the doors of its telephone booths. The Venetian banks, whose offices still cluster evocatively about the Rialto, that old hub of fortune, are impeccably organized. The holiday industry sucks its last dollar, pound, franc, pfennig from the visiting crowds with exquisite impartiality.

The Venetians remain hard but wise bargainers. When their forebears undertook to transport an army or equip a fleet, their prices were high and their terms inflexible, but they did it in style. Their ships were the best, their trappings the most gorgeous, they fulfilled their agreements scrupulously. 'Noi siamo calculatori', the Venetians have always cheerfully admitted – 'We are a calculating people.' So it is today. The Venetians will always let you pay another time, will seldom cheat you over the odd lira, are never disgruntled if you break off a negotiation. They are business men of finesse. Nor is the old high-vaulted enterprise altogether dead. There is at least one hotelier in the city who would undoubtedly storm the walls of Byzantium, or navigate a galley around the meridian, if guaranteed a suitable commission. The Venetians believe in self-dependence. On the Accademia bridge one day a boy was hawking horoscopes, wrapped up in little yellow paper packages. A passing business man of my acquaintance paused to ask what they were, gave a toss of his head to me, and slapped his right arm (genteelly draped, as it happened, in a nice herring-bone tweed). 'That's my horoscope!' he said grandly, and stalked off towards the bank.

Such Venetian men of action, martial or commercial, have always been supported by a class of devoted administrators and functionaries, in the old days mostly patricians. The prestige of the civil servants declined with the rot of the Republic, and their morality weakened, so that at the end the administration of Venice was rancid with corruption: but the best of the aristocrats, adapting themselves to changing times, maintained the old traditions of thoughtful integrity, and became merged with the professional classes. Their successors, the lawyers, doctors and engineers of today, are still formidable: handsome and serious people, long-boned and soberly dressed, with a cool look of Rome to their features, and scarcely a trace of southern passion. The fuddy-duddy bureaucracy of Italy has long since invaded Venice: but the true Venetian servants of the State still serenely circumvent it, and conduct their affairs with all the logic, lucidity and unflustered sense of the old Republic.

To see such people at their best, you should visit the criminal law courts of Venice, in an old palace beside the Rialto bridge, overlooking the markets. Outside the windows there is a clamour of market-men and shrill-voiced women; a housemaid singing adenoidally at her chores; a roar of boat-engines on the Grand Canal; sometimes the wet thud of a steam-hammer driving a pile into the mud. The building is crumbling a little, but is still sombrely dignified, with high shaded passages, and heavy dark doors, and a smell of wax, age and documents. At the back of the panelled court-room a few spectators stand respectfully, holding their hats and whispering. Beside the door the usher, in a dark grey suit, meditatively toys with a pencil at his desk, as the clerk to the council might have played ominously with a quill, before the grimmer tribunals of the Republic. And high at the dark mahogany dais, beneath a carved slogan of justice – *La Legge E Uguale Per Tutti* – sit the Venetian magistrates. Their robes are gloomy and the tabs of their collars very white. Their faces are clever and cryptic. They sit there at the bench in attitudes of indolent but potentially menacing attention, sprawling a little like parliamentarians, some young, some middle aged; and as they examine the next witness, a cross-eyed laundry-woman who sits crookedly on the edge of her chair, squirming mendaciously, every inch a liar, from Paisley head-scarf to grubby high heels – as they put their points, in turn, with a cold piercing courtesy, they seem the very essence of the old Venice, a hard but brilliant organism, whose disciplines were known to all, and applied without favouritism. (And you can see plausible portraits of all those jurists, painted 300 years before their time, in the pictures of the Magistrates and Supervisors of the Mint that hang in the Ca' d'Oro.)

The Republic was sustained, too, by a stout company of artisans, denied all political responsibility, but never without self-respect. The rulers of Venice, though they held the working classes well under control, did their cunning best to keep them contented, partly by feeding them upon a diet of ceremonial, partly by fostering their sense of craft and guild. When the fishermen of the Nicolotti faction elected their leader each year, the Doge himself was represented at the ceremony – first by a mere doorkeeper of the Doge's Palace, later by a more senior official. So important to the State were the sixteenth-century glass-blowers, masters of one of the Venetian monopolies, that they were given a patrician status of their own, and excused all kinds of impositions. (As a cold corollary, it was publicly announced that if any glass-blower emigrated with his secrets, emissaries of the State would instantly be dispatched to murder him: legend has it that the two men who made the famous clock in the Piazza of St Mark, with its intricate zodiacal devices, were later officially blinded, to prevent them making another for somebody else.) The great Venetian artists and architects were nearly all of the craftsmen class, rich and celebrated though they became, and the painters usually subscribed to the Guild of House Painters. Hale old characters they were, living robustly and dying late – Venice was a State of Grand Old Men: Tintoretto died at 76, Guardi at 81, Longhi and Vittoria at 83, Longhena at 84, Giovanni Bellini at 86, Titian and da Ponte at 88, Sansovino at 91. Above all, Venice depended upon her men of the sea. The city Venetians soon gave up crewing their own ships, relying upon Dalmatians and people of the outer lagoon: but the Republic was always well supplied with sea captains, fishermen, boatbuilders, and artisans at the great naval base of the Arsenal, the first dockyard of the world.

By and large it is still true. Modern Venice is rich in conscientious craftsmen, people of strong and loyal simplicity, such as one imagines in the sea-ports of early Victorian England. The specialist workmen of Venice are still impressive, from the men at the garage at the Piazzale Roma, who skilfully steer cars by manipulating the two front wheels, to the myriad picture-framers of the city, whose hearts must sink at the very thought of another sunset Rialto. Splendid horny craftsmen work in the sawdust shambles of the boat-yards – in Venetian, *squeri* – where the tar cauldrons bubble and stink, and they caulk the boats with flaming faggots. Crusty old men like London cabbies, holding antique hooks, stand beside the canals in long flapping greatcoats looking rheumily for gondolas to help alongside. Even the drivers of grand motor boats sometimes hide an agreeable heart behind a pompous exterior: and there are few kindlier police-men than those who patrol the canals in their little speedboats, or solemnly potter about, buttoned in blue greatcoats, in flat-bottomed skiffs (an activity dramatically described in one guide book as 'controlling the water-ways from swiftly moving punts').

And among them all, the very image of Venice, straight-descended from Carpaccio, moves the gondolier. He is not a popular figure among the tourists, who think his prices high and his manner sometimes overbearing: and indeed he is frequently a Communist, and no respecter of persons, and he often shamelessly pumps the innocent foreigner with inaccurate information, and sometimes unfairly induces him to disregard the tariff ('Ah, but today is the feast of San Marcuola, *signor*, and it is *traditional* to charge double fares on this holy day'). I have grown to like and admire him, though, and I can forgive a few peccadillos among men who live on a four-months' tourist season, and scrape the winter through as part-time fishermen and odd-job workers. The gondoliers are usually highly intelligent: they are also tolerant, sardonic, and, with some grumpy and usually elderly exceptions, humorous. They are often very good-looking, too, fair and loose-limbed – many of their forebears came from the Slav coast of Istria and Dalmatia – and they sometimes have a cultivated, worldly look to them, like undergraduates punting on the Cherwell, naval officers amusing themselves, or perhaps fashionable ski instructors.

The gondoliers still have a strong sense of guild unity. Their co-operative is a powerful force in Venice, and in the past they even had their own communal banks, run on a system of mutual risk. Not long ago each *traghetto*, or gondola ferry-station, was organized in its own assertive guild (they still maintain the protocol, though the officials are now municipally appointed). Nowadays, though nearly every gondolier is still affiliated to a *traghetto*, they are all members of one co-operative. Each gondola is privately owned – your gondolier is not necessarily the owner, possession often running in families – and profits go to the proprietor, the co-operative being merely a negotiating agency, a system of social security, and a common convenience – and sometimes a political organ too. Competition between gondoliers is, nevertheless, strictly governed, and the celebrated gondoliers' quarrels, dear to generations of travel writers, often have a distinctly stagy air to them. Nor are other classes of watermen welcomed at their stands. Only fifty *sandoli*, the smaller passenger boats of Venice, are officially licensed: all the others you see, blandly stealing custom from the gondolas, are darkly described as being 'outside the law'.

Yet for all this protectionism, an old Venetian practice, the gondoliers are generally broad-minded men, and are unexpectedly sympathetic to amateurs and aliens. Never a testy word will you hear from them, when your craft zigzags in a flurry of indecision across their path: and when at last you stagger to the quayside, wet from the lagoon, with your ropes trailing and your engine seized, a broken gunwale and a torn trouser-leg, they will welcome you with amusement, explain to you again (for they are whole-hog Venetians) about salt getting into the carburettor, and send their kind regards to the children.

Now and then they have regattas, partly impelled by the power of tradition, partly by the Tourist Office. In many a smoky *trattoria* you will see, carefully preserved behind glass, the trophies and banners of a regatta champion, or even his portrait in oils – it is customary to commission one: and there is still a lingering trace of popular enthusiasm to these races, a faint anthropological echo of folk rivalries and ancestral feuds. Fiercely and intently the competitors, sweatbands to match their colourful oars, pound down the Grand

Canal, or swing around the marker buoy beside the public Gardens. A raggle-taggle fleet of small craft follows their progress, speedboats and rowing-boats and tumble-down skiffs, half-naked boys in canoes, big market barges, elegant launches, yachts, all tumbling hilariously along beside the gondolas, with their ferry steamers swerving precariously towards the quay, and a fine surge of foam and clatter of engines, as in some nightmare University Boat Race, half-way to a lunatic Putney.

But the best moment of the regatta comes later, in the evening. Then the new champions, pocketing their prize-money or grappling with their sucking-pig (the traditional fourth prize) are fêted by their fellow-gondoliers: and you will see them, gaily-hatted and singing jovially, parading down the Grand Canal in a large grey barge, with a row of bottles on a neatly spread table, a cheerful impresario playing an accordion, a string of fluttering pennants, and a radiation of fun, *bonhomie* and satisfaction.

Under the Republic none of these working men had any share in the running of the State. A small hereditary aristocracy, enumerated loftily in the Golden Book, preserved all power for itself. Only occasionally was the Book opened for the inclusion of a newly elevated patrician, honoured for prowess in war, for particular fidelity to the State, or for a suitable (but of course purely symbolic) fee. Thirty families were ennobled for service in the wars against Genoa, and sometimes rich commoners from the mainland bought their way into the Venetian aristocracy, as you might buy yourself membership at Lloyds. It took generations, though, for such parvenus to be accepted by the old aristocrats, who often thought so highly of themselves, not without reason, that they shuddered at the very thought of going abroad and being treated like ordinary folk.

The working people, in return for their labour and loyalty, were governed fairly and often generously, but they had not one iota of political privilege, and could only occasionally alter the course of events by a riot or a threatened mutiny. Generally they remained astonishingly faithful to the system. There were only three serious revolutions in the history of the Serenissima, all in the fourteenth century, and none of them was a proletarian eruption. The most serious, the Tiepolo rising of 1310, was mounted by aristocrats: and it was baulked, so tradition tells us, by 'an old woman of the people', who dropped a stone mortar smack on the head of the rebellious standard-bearer, and plunged the rest into confusion (she is still doing it, in stone, in a plaque on the site of her house in the Merceria, the principal shopping street of Venice, while a tablet inserted in the pavement below indicates the point of impact). Throughout the protracted decline of Venice the people remained pathetically proud of their Republic, and when at last the leveller Napoleon arrived, it was liberal patricians, not disgruntled plebs, who were his most vociferous supporters – the Countess Querini-Benzoni, Byron's celebrated 'blonde in a gondola', danced round a Tree of Liberty in the Piazza of St Mark, wearing only an Athenian tunic, and hand-in-hand with a handsome revolutionary poet.

Like England, another marine oligarchy, Venice was given stability and cohesion by a sense of common purpose. The English felt themselves 'a happy breed of men', a 'band of brothers', for all the disparities between earl and labourer: and the Venetians, too, in their great days, had this sense of shared fortune, and considered themselves to be first of all, not rich men or poor men, privileged or powerless, but citizens of Venice. Since Venice was never feudal, she was never hamstrung by private armies or serfly obligations, like the cities of the Italian mainland. Beneath the patrician crust, the merchant classes and working men had carefully defined rights of their own, and the Venetian aristocrats, though terribly complacent, do not seem to have treated their social inferiors with crudity or contempt. Venetians of all kinds revelled in the wild days of Carnival, and the young blades of the seventeenth and eighteenth centuries, with their riotous clubs and fanciful costumes, appear to have been regarded with the same kind of half-envious tolerance that readers of the London newspapers may reserve for the King's Road gallants.

Some observers consider that the Venetians' complete dependency upon aristocratic condescensions bred a servility still apparent in the city. I do not find this to be so. There is, it is true, a degree of social sycophancy in Venice. Venetians are considered more docile than most Italians, and used to be more easily exploited abroad, in the days when Italy provided cheap labour for half Europe. Sometimes a retainer will speak to you of his employers in a hushed and respectful whine, as though he were talking in church. Venetians now, as always, have a healthy respect for the moneyed – more, perhaps, than for the well-bred.

But generally a sturdy sense of equality pervades Venetian life. It is still, like the rest of Italy, a place of domestic servants, trim-uniformed housemaids, motherly cooks, soft-footed men-servants: but they have a sensible hail-fellow-well-met approach to the problems of the household, with few traces of oily subservience. With a friendly familiarity your housekeeper sits down beside you at the breakfast table, for a rambling discussion of the day's prospects, or a kind word of correction about how to bring up the children. Many, beaming, and unidentified are the friends and relatives who may appear on your terrace, when a regatta or a serenade goes by: and there is no nicer welcome in the world than the one the babysitter gives you, with her sister beside her at the wireless, when you come home at midnight from a Venetian celebration, blurred but apologetic. A certain child-like simplicity may have been fostered by the old system, and is still evident among the Venetians; there is a suggestion of submissiveness to their character still; but they never feel in the least down-trodden.

At the other end of the scale there remain the aristocrats and plutocrats of Venice. Some are the descendants of the old Venetian patricians, a few families still inhabiting their ancestral palaces on the Grand Canal, just as they maintain their estates on the mainland. One dowager, I have been told, recently overheard a gondolier pointing her out as the widow of the last Doge – a suggestion which, though possibly flattering to her Venetian pride, assumed her to be rather more than 180 years old. Most of the families of the Golden Book, though, have vanished. There were 1,218 names in it at the fall of the Republic, but many of the old houses were in mortgage to the monasteries, and when Napoleon abolished the Orders he effectively abolished the families too. The ancient oligarchy disintegrated: a community of feckless and indigent patricians, called the Barnabotti, already existed in the quarter of San Barnaba, and by 1840 more than a thousand members of the old nobility were receiving State charity.

The modern Venetian aristocracy is thus of mixed origins. Some of its members are rich merchants, who long ago crossed the gulf between impotence and privilege. Most are not Venetians by blood at all, but are Romans or Milanese who have houses in the city, and who spend the summer commuting between Harry's Bar and the Lido beaches. A few are foreigners. Titles are no longer awarded by the Italian Republic, but there are still many Counts in Venice, permitted by custom to retain their rather forlorn distinctions; and not a few Princesses or Baronesses, with Slavonic names, or Russian coronets upoon their visiting cards; and many whose names are preceded by the honorific 'Nobile Homine' – 'N.H.' for short. There is also much money in the city, supported largely by land ownership. Its grandest apartments are still very, very grand. Its most luxurious motor boats are palatial. Its opera audiences, though thick-set, are sumptuously dressed. A few families still maintain their private gondolas, and are to be seen sweeping down the Grand Canal in a glitter of brasswork, rowed by two oarsmen in blazing livery.

I once passed an idle breakfast looking through the Venice telephone directory to see which of the names of the Doges were still represented in the city. Most of the early incumbents have understandably vanished into the mists of legend. Of the first twenty-five, according to the chroniclers, three were murdered, one was executed for treason, three were judicially blinded, four were deposed, one was exiled, four abdicated, one became a saint and one was killed in a battle with pirates. (Seventy-five of the first seventy-six, all the same, are confidently portrayed in the Great Council Chamber of the Doge's Palace.) The later names are still mostly on the telephone. There were 120 Doges in all, between the years 697 and 1797. They bore sixty-seven different names, the honour often running in families, and thirty-nine of these appear in the book. Sometimes there are two or three representatives of the name. Sometimes there are ten or twelve. A surprising number seem to be either Countesses or horse-butchers. A good many are probably descended from servants of the old families, rather than from the families themselves. The name of the first Doge does not appear; nor does the name of the last; but there is one impressive subscriber, Count Dottore Giovanni Marcello Grimani Giustinian, who bears three ducal names at a go.

Family pride was immensely strong among the old Venetian aristocrats, as you may see from a visit to the museum in the Ca' Rezzonico: there somebody has gone to the trouble of producing a family tree in which every member is represented by a little wax portrait, mounted behind glass. The Venetians were so keen on genealogy that in the Basilica of St Mark's there is even a family tree, done all in mosaic, of the Virgin Mary. Whole quarters of the city were named for the major clans, and it was considered a public tragedy when one of the great names died out. The story is still told with regret of the extinction of the Foscaris, the family whose ill-fated forebear, the Doge Francesco Foscari, was the subject of Byron's tragedy. Their name still appears in the telephone book, but they are supposed to have petered out at the beginning of the last century: the last male representative died an obscure actor in London, and his two surviving sisters both went mad, and were exhibited to tourists by unscrupulous servants as the very last of the Foscaris.

One of the greatest of all the Venetian houses was the family of Giustinian; but during the twelfth-century wars every male member of the family, bar one, was killed in battle or died of the plague. The single exception was a Giustinian youth who had become a monk, and lived an austere life in a convent on the Lido. All Venice was distressed at the possible extinction of the Giustinians, and a public petition was sent to the Pope, asking him to release the monk from his vows. Permission was granted, the reluctant layman was hastily married to a daughter of the day's Doge, and they dutifully produced nine boys and three girls. When their job was done, and the children were grown up, the father returned to his monastery and the mother founded a convent of her own, in a distant island of the lagoon. As for the House of Giustinian, it flourished ever after. A Giustinian was almost the only Venetian to maintain the dignity of the Republic in the face of Napoleon's bullying; and today there are still eleven

Giustinian palaces in Venice, a striking memorial to monkly self-denial.

The purposes of aristocracy were firmly defined in the iron days of the Republic, and all these patrician families had their duties to perform. There were no orders of nobility. You were either a patrician, with your name in the Golden Book, or you were not (when the Austrians took over, any patrician who wished could become a Count). Every Venetian nobleman was in effect an unpaid servant of the State. His life was circumscribed by strict rules – even ordaining, for example, what he might wear, so that impoverished aristocrats were sometimes to be seen begging for alms in tattered crimson silk. Voltaire was shocked to discover that Venetian noblemen might not travel abroad without official permission. If a Venetian was chosen to be an Ambassador, he must maintain his embassy largely at his own expense, sometimes ruining himself in the process; one old gentleman served the Serenissima in this way for eleven years without a penny's recompense, and asked as his sole reward the particular privilege of keeping a gold chain presented to him by one of the European monarchs, a gift which would in the ordinary way have gone instantly into the coffers of the State.

The patrician was not allowed to refuse an appointment: and at the same time it was essential to the Venetian system that any citizen showing signs of self-importance or dangerous popularity should at once be humiliated, to prevent the emergence of dictators and *pour encourager les autres*. If you refused a command, you were disgraced. If you lost a battle, you were impeached for treason. If you won it, and became a public hero, you would probably be charged, soon or later, with some trumped-up offence against the State. The fifteenth-century general Antonio da Lezze, for example, defended Scutari for nearly a year against Turkish assaults so ferocious that a cat, stealing out one day across an exposed roof-top, was instantly transfixed by eleven arrows at once, and so sustained that afterwards the expended arrow-shafts kept the place in firewood for several months: but when at last he surrendered the city to overwhelmingly superior forces, and returned honourably to Venice, he was immediately charged with treason, imprisoned for a year and banished for ten more. In Venice a great commander was always a bad risk, and he was seldom left for long to enjoy his gouty retirement.

Worse still, ignominy was often immortalized in stone. Above the central arch of the Basilica there is an unhappy turbaned figure on crutches, biting his finger-nails. He is said to be the architect of the great church, condemned to perpetual contempt because he boasted that his work would be absolutely perfect, when it wasn't. He is only the first of such victims. A tablet in the pavement of the Campo Sant' Agostin permanently commemorates the punishment of Bajamonte Tiepolo, the aristocratic rebel of 1310. An iron lion clamped to a house in the Campo Santa Maria Mater Domini signifies that the place was sequestered by the State when its owner was thrown into prison. Beneath the arcade of the Doge's Palace there is a plaque recording the banishment of Girolamo Loredan and Giovanni Contarini, members of two famous Venetian clans, for having abandoned the fortress of Tenedos to the Turks, 'with grievous injury to Christianity and their country'. The one Doge whose face does not appear among his fellows in the Great Council Chamber is Marin Faliero, who was beheaded after a conspiracy to make him absolute ruler. His place there is a black vacancy, and beneath it is the cold inscription: *Hic est locus Marini Falethri decapitati pro criminibus.*

Once the Venetian Government did erect a tablet of remorse, exonerating the patrician Antonio Foscarini from the charge of treason for which he had been executed: but it is tucked away so high among the family monuments in the church of San Stae that hardly anybody notices it. Generally, though shame was perpetuated, distinction was muffled. Historians complain about the dearth of personal information on prominent Venetians, and until 1866 and the florid enthusiasms of the Risorgimento the only outdoor public monument in Venice was the statue of the *condottiere* Colleoni at San Zanipolo. Amends are sometimes made nowadays – there is a steamboat named for the brave general Bragadino, and a dredger for the dashing admiral Morosino: but ask any educated Londoner to name a distinguished Venetian, and he may perhaps murmur Marco Polo, Goldoni, Sarpi, or a tentative Foscari, but he will probably stick fast at Titian and Tintoretto.

All these rules applied most forcibly to the Doge himself, the unhappiest of the Venetian patricians. He was the most obvious aspirant for dictatorial glory, so to keep him helpless his powers were so persistently whittled away, over the centuries, that in the end he was almost a parody of a constitutional monarch, a gilded puppet, who was forbidden to talk to foreigners without supervision, and could not even write an uncensored letter to his wife. The only presents he might legally accept were rose-water, flowers, sweet-smelling herbs and balsam, than which it is difficult to conceive a more milk-sop selection; and after 1494 the Doge of Venice might only be represented on his own coinage kneeling humbly at the feet of St Mark. The most elaborate methods were devised to keep him impotent – methods, as the British Ambassador Sir Henry Wotton once observed, that did 'much savour of the cloister'. The Doge was elected by his fellow-members of the Great Council, the general assembly of aristocrats, but choosing him was a tortuous process. First nine members of the council were picked by lot to elect forty electors, who had to be approved by a majority of at least seven. Twelve of the forty were then chosen by lot to elect twenty-five more, again by a majority of seven. Nine of the twenty-five were chosen by lot to elect forty-five by a majority of seven. Eleven of the forty-five were chosen by lot to elect another forty-one; and these forty-one, thus sifted in four stages from the entire Venetian aristocracy, had to elect a doge by a majority of at least twenty-five.

Yet despite all these disciplines, restrictions, penalties and expenses, leaders of quality were always available to the Venetian Republic in its great days, and the patricians were, by and large, wonderfully conscientious in performing their duties – one man whose life has been carefully recorded only missed a single weekly meeting of the Grand Council in thirty years of membership. Proud, romantic and often honourable were the names that sprang at me across the cornflakes, as I thumbed the telephone directory that morning – Grimani and Morosini, Pisano and Mocenigo, Bembo, Barbarigo and Gradenigo: but I saved the best of all till last.

The great-heart of the Doges was Enrico Dandolo, a rascally giant, who stormed the bastions of Constantinople at the age of 88, and held those Frankish grandees in the palm of his wrinkled hand. He was one of four Dandolo Doges, and you may see the remains of his palace, a smallish Gothic house, standing among the coffee shops near the Rialto bridge. *'Oh for an hour of old blind Dandolo!'* Byron wrote of him, *'th'octogenarian chief, Byzantium's conquering foe!'* His figure stumps through the chronicles like a Venetian Churchill, and when he died they buried him as magnificently as he lived, in the basilica of Santa Sofia above the Golden Horn. (The Sultan Mohamet II destroyed his tomb: but Gentile Bellini, who spent some years in Constantinople as court painter to His Sublimity, brought home to Venice the old warrior's sword, helmet and breastplate.) There was only one Dandolo left in the telephone directory, and hastily finishing my coffee and rolls, I set off that morning to visit him.

He was not, I should judge, a rich man, and he worked in the municipal department called the Magistracy of the Water, which supervises the canals and waterways of Venice. His wife and daughter (he had no son) were fresh-faced, kindly women, like a country vicar's family in England. His apartment near San Zanipolo was pleasantly unpretentious. But when Andrea Dandolo leaned from his window to wave me good-bye, across the dark water of the side-canal, a gleam of old battles seemed to enter his eye, his deep voice echoed down the centuries, and all the sad pride of Venice was in his smile.

4 The Truth Not to Everyone

Venice is a complicated place, physically and spiritually, and it is extraordinarily difficult to establish Venetian facts. Nothing is ever quite certain. Life is enmeshed in contradictions and exceptions, and the most painstaking and persistent enquirers, the ones who *always* know what time the trains go, are often hopelessly misled.

The past of Venice, like the present, is thus shrouded in dubious fancies and deceits, and there are several alternative versions of almost every tradition. No guide book will make clear to you the significance of St Theodore and the crocodile, who stand together, one on top of the other, upon a pillar in the Piazzetta beside St Mark's – for the good reason that nobody is quite certain what their significance is: most writers hazard a brief conjectural biography of the saint, but evade the crocodile altogether. The body of St Mark, which was seized by two Venetian adventurers from its tomb in Alexandria in the ninth century (they covered the mummified corpse with pickled pork, to keep curious Muslims away), is always said to be preserved beneath the High Altar of the Basilica: but all the odds are that it was destroyed in a fire in 976, and was artificially resuscitated for reasons of prestige. Why is the Campo dei Mori so called? Because the warehouse of the Moors was near-by, because of the Moorish figures that stand upon its walls, because its presiding family came from Morea, because their name was Moro – take your choice, nobody can contradict you. There are several different authoritative versions of the capture of Venice by the Allies in 1945, as you will discover by comparing the various unimpeachably official reports in the War Office library. Five modern reference books I have consulted give five different figures for the area of the Venetian lagoon. Napoleon, when he seized Venice, ordered an inquiry to be made into the character of the Venetians, rather on his Egyptian pattern – what were their prejudices, their political views, their tastes, their manners? The report was never completed, for the scholars assigned to the task confessed themselves incapable of establishing the truth.

No wonder the books seem inconsistent. In Venice you can never be quite sure. The odd thing is that though the information may be distinctly uncertain, the informants are usually dogmatic: for there is to Venetian manners something of the spurious conviction of the outsider. The Welshman tells a half-truth with insuperable assurance. The Afrikaner explains his preposterous principles with an air that is positively statistical. The Israeli finds it painful indeed to admit an error. The Venetian's weakness is that he hates to confess ignorance. He always has an answer. You can never stump him, and hardly ever disconcert him, and if you ask him the way somewhere, through the tangled wilderness of the Venetian back-streets, he will summon a wise and helpful look, consider the situation carefully, take you kindly by the arm and usher you to the nearest vantage point; and pointing a finger through the labyrinth of medieval lanes that lies before you, entangled in canals, archways, dead ends, unexpected squares and delusive passages, '*Sempre diretto!*' he will say courteously – 'Straight ahead!'

This is no more than *politesse*, but sometimes the imprecision of the Venetians is deliberate. Sarpi once remarked to a friend: 'I never, never tell a lie, but the truth not to everyone.' There is little serious crime in Venice, but there runs through the affairs of the place a niggling note of amorality. It is rarely blatant. The hotels are expensive, the gondolas and water-taxis ruinous, the porters, shouldering your fibre-glass bag from one alley-way to the next, extortionate: but they generally work to a legal tariff, and are all too ready to discomfort the quibbler by producing it. The Venetians are never crude. They are a meditative people, who know just how far they can squeeze a victim without sending him away to Majorca, and their charm often outweighs their cupidity. The system of the Venetian Republic presupposed the worst in everyone, from the Doge downwards – during the last decades of independence, when corruption was rampant, enough bundles of wood disappeared annually from the Arsenal to build ten complete warships. The modern Venetian is similarly cynical, and assumes that you are too. 'We Venetians,' they say, 'we're just like anyone else: some of us are honest, and some of us are not.' On a dungeon wall in the Doge's Palace somebody has scratched, in dialect, the sad tag: 'From the man I trust may God defend me. From the man I trust not I will defend myself.'

Violent crime is rare in Venice, but this is a city of petty thieves. In the eighteenth century pick-pockets who took their haul to the city guards were allowed to keep a percentage of its value: a traveller who enquired the purpose of this iniquitous system was told that it 'encouraged an ingenious, intelligent, sagacious activity among the people'. When Titian was dying of the plague in 1576, robbers entered his house and pillaged it while he was still on his death-bed, some say before his very eyes. In the fifteenth century a house-

breaker even succeeded in boring a hole into the Treasury of the
Basilica, and getting away with an immense booty (he was hanged, at
his own wry request, with a golden noose). Venetian burglars are
sometimes equally impudent today. They are skilled at climbing
through the windows of canal-side houses, stealing a handbag or a
necklace, and drifting away in a silent boat, so that the big hotels
have watchmen on the canals, the private houses are heavily
shuttered, and the summer newspapers are full of burgled Finns,
disillusioned Americans and spluttering Englishmen. 'What can you
expect', say the Venetians cheerfully, 'if they *will* sleep with their
windows open?'

More casual pilferers haunt the water-buses or patrol the side-
canals, picking up what they can. Everything movable was filched
piece by piece from my own boat, lying in the Rio della Toletta: first a
bollard, then a seat, then the ropes, then the very floorboards, until at
last she rode there, chained to the wall, stripped, ravaged and
forlorn. The front doors of Venice are secured with an extraordinary
variety of locks, triple-turn Yales, antique padlocks, bolts, chains and
bars: and if you are a little amused by this assortment when you first
come to live in the city, after a few months you begin to see the point.

There is often a taste of sharp practice to the everyday transactions
of the Venetians. This is perhaps a historical phenomenon. There
were ulterior motives behind nearly everything the old Venetians
did. '*Venus* and *Venice* are Great Queens in their degree,' sang a
seventeenth-century English poet; '*Venus* is Queen of Love, *Venice* of
policy.' In particular the Venetians, like the Afrikaners, presented
themselves as the chosen and guided of God, and skilfully adapted
religious symbolisms to their own gauntly secular purposes. When
the first leaders of the lagoon announced that St Peter had personally
granted them the island of Torcello, with instructions to build a
church upon it, theirs was no mere pious fancy: the divine gift of land
established the rights of the Venetians over the hapless fishermen
who lived in the island already, and the command to build a church
was an earnest of permanence, a political declaration.

And when those brave Venetians stole the body of St Mark, in 829,
they almost certainly did so under State orders. The Venetians, till

then under the patronage of the obscure St Theodore and his crocodile, urgently needed the particular care of some more eminent divine – they were busy freeing themselves from the overlordships of the Eastern and Western Empires, and wanted an overpowering talisman of independence. The legend of St Mark's shipwreck in the lagoon was invented; the body was stolen; and from that day to this Venice and the great Evangelist have been inseparable. The glittering Basilica was, to begin with, no more than a reliquary for the corpse, and for many centuries Venice went to war beneath the banners of St Mark, shouting *'Viva San Marco!'*, holding aloft his open book, and emblazoning everything with his winged lion (who ought to have, according to the Book of Revelation, six wings about him, and be full of eyes before, behind and within).

When the Basilica was burnt, and the precious body lost, a special miracle was devised: for it was put about that the 'whereabouts of the corpse had been forgotten', and during a service of intercession to ask for divine guidance, there was a crumbling noise from a nearby pillar, a flaking of stone, a shaking, and first the hand, then the arm, then the entire saintly body was miraculously revealed! Heartfelt were the songs of praise and thanksgiving, as priests and people crowded around the relic; complacent the smile on the face of the Doge, we may reasonably conjecture, as he swept out of the great church into his palace. The people of Bari, who had acquired the body of St Nicholas and were becoming distinctly uppity, were instantly discomfited by the news: and a little red tablet on the pillar in the Basilica, beside the Altar of the Holy Sacrament, still commemorates the point of emergence.

The old Venetians could be very sly. When Antonio Grimani was impeached for treason in 1500 (he had lost a battle) he put forward one touching ground for clemency: had not his son, Cardinal Grimani, faithfully revealed to the Republic all secret matters dealt with at Papal Consistories, so that the Venetians 'with their accustomed prudence might provide for their own needs'? Even Tintoretto, entering a competition for the decoration of the Scuola di San Rocco, cheated by bringing a completed panel to the contest, when the rules demanded cartoons. The great pageantries of State, religious and secular, were intended largely to muffle the grievances of the working people. The Venetians were the first to organize pilgrimages to the Holy Land on a strictly commercial basis. The carnivals of the Venetian decadence were seen from the start as a useful tourist attraction – and the more decadent they became, the more people flocked to enjoy them. When the great mercenary Colleoni died in 1484, he left his entire fortune of nearly half a million ducats to the State (which badly needed it) on condition that a statue was erected to him in 'the Piazza before St Mark's'. The signory gratefully accepted the cash, but could not stomach the notion of a monument in the great Piazza, so reached a characteristic compromise with the truth. They commissioned the statue all right, and erected it in a piazza before St Mark's – but it was the *School* of St Mark's, not the Basilica, and the memorial stands there still in the square outside San Zanipolo.

So the Venetian moves through history surrounded by a thin miasma of dishonesty, like a cricketer with an odd tendency towards no-balls, or a golfer who can find no partners. Today the agreement of a rent is similarly tinged with chicanery, designed to delude the tax inspectors, or keep the truth from a sister-in-law. Ludicrous are the statements you will be invited to approve, assuring the authorities that you are (for example) accepting your new refrigerator as a gift from the dealer; or that you have promised the Signora to lend her your cottage in Kingston Seymour for the winter, with use of the neighbour's bathroom, in return for the absolutely free use of her apartment on the Grand Canal throughout the summer season.

But nowadays there is something rather innocent and touching to these subterfuges, for the Venetian is usually quite transparent in his small deceits, and is endearingly delighted when he has misled you. He cherishes no grudges, and he never minds losing. An air of childlike mystery surrounds his dealings, much concerned with dark and nameless go-betweens, off-stage confidants, grandmothers' funerals. There is a wood-carving by the seventeenth-century sculptor Francesco Pianta, in the Scuola di San Rocco, which beautifully illustrates these tendencies. It is called *The Spy, Or Curiosity*, and it represents a conspirator so theatrically shrouded in cloaks, so hungrily peering between his slouch hat and his raised forearm, so slung with bombs and secret documents that the kindest old lady in Cheltenham or New Hampshire, finding him destitute on her doorstep, might be tempted to refuse him a cookie. I often think of this beguiling image, when my insurance agent telephones me with a little proposition about the premium.

He might also represent the Venetian Nosey Parker, a ubiquitous character. The Venetians were encouraged to be busy-bodies by the system of denunciations which supported the autocracy of their Republic. In several parts of the city you may still see the stone boxes or lions' mouths – *bocche di leone* – that received citizens' complaints. Some, like the one on the Zattere, were merely for grumbles about the neighbours' sanitary habits, or charges of blasphemy and foul language. ('*Bestemmiate no più*', says an inscription near the Campo dei Mori, '*e date gloria a Dio*' – 'Swear no more, and give glory to God'.) Some were for more terrible accusations, of treason or conspiracy, that might well lead to a man's execution. In the later days of the Republic a note in one of these boxes could result in immediate punishment without trial, and nothing is more evocative of the ruthlessness of old Venice than these benign stone figures: the lions, whiskered and smiling, do not look at all ferocious, and the eeriest receptacle of all was a box beside a comical statue, known as Signor Antonio Rioba, which still stands, heavily patched with ironwork, at the corner of Campo dei Mori. There was a period when the *bravos* or bandits of Venice could buy immunity from the law simply by murdering one of their colleagues and producing satisfactory evidence: and it is no coincidence that the Venetians invented income-tax.

Perhaps it is not fanciful to imagine two surviving consequences of the system, which indeed had a new lease of life under the Fascists. One is that Venetians like to preserve their privacy, shuttering their flats and locking their back doors, so that you can live on one floor of a palace for weeks without catching a glimpse of the people downstairs. Nowadays they have warning mirrors attached to their window-sills; in earlier times there used to be grilles in the drawing-room floor, enabling the householder to see in good time what monumental bore was arriving at the water-gate (there is still one in Goldoni's house, near the church of the Frari).

The second consequence, a corollary, is that the Venetians have a habit of minding other people's business. Many a fussy citizen loves to interfere, if you let your children wander down the water-steps. Many a know-all will give you the benefit of his advice, if you carry more passengers in your boat than the law allows. The Venetians have an insatiable interest in your movements and purposes, and can never resist telling you how mistaken you are, or advising you how to do it better. If the luggage is stolen from your car, as it stands in the Piazzale Roma, the first reaction of Venetians is not to find the missing suitcase, or apprehend the thief, but to give you a short lecture on the evils of carelessness – and the next is to say, with a judicious raising of the eyes, 'Ah, these Italians, they'll do anything!' as if to make it absolutely clear that no proper Venetian ever stole a hat-box.

For all the blank doors of its apartments (distorted television voices seeping through their hinges, as you toil up the echoing stairs) Venice is a gossipy provincial city, where your movements are eagerly observed and your visitors adroitly analysed. If you take a picnic lunch to a far corner of the lagoon, somebody is sure to have seen your boat steal out, and when you come home at night through the empty garden a surreptitious chink of light, momentarily appearing in the shuttered mass of the palace, testifies to the alertness of the second floor. Somebody once told me that Venice used to be an important clearing-station for the British Secret Service. Certainly its ear-to-the-ground propensities are catching, and nobody is a better Venetian than I am myself, when it comes to curiosity.

5 On Women

The women of Venice are very handsome, and very vain. They are tall, they walk beautifully, and they are often fair (in the sixteenth century Venetian ladies used to bleach their hair in the sunshine, training it through crownless hats like vines through a trellis). Their eyes are sometimes a heavy-lidded greenish-blue, like the eyes of rather despondent armadillos. Rare indeed is a dishevelled Venetian woman, and even the Madonnas and female saints of the old masters are usually elegantly dressed. The most slovenly people to be seen in the city are nearly always tourists – cranks and water-colour artists apart.

The Venetians are not, by and large, rich: but they have always spent a large proportion of their money on clothes and ornaments, and you will hardly ever see a girl dressed for pottering, in a sloppy sweater and a patched skirt, or in that unpressed dishabille that marks the utter emancipation of the Englishwoman. The girls at the University, who are either studying languages, or learning about Economics and Industrial Practices, look more like models than academics: and the housemaids, when they walk off in scented couples for their weekend pleasures, would hardly seem out of place at Ascot, or at a gala convention of the Women Lawyers' Association.

This love of dress is deep-rooted in the Venetian nature. The men are very dapper, too, and until quite recently used to cool themselves with little fans and parasols in the Public Gardens – 'curious', as Augustus Hare observed austerely in 1896, 'to English eyes'. As early as 1299 the Republic introduced laws restricting ostentation, and later the famous sumptuary laws were decreed, strictly governing what people might wear, with a special magistracy to enforce them. They were never a success. When the Patriarch of Venice forbade the use of 'excessive ornaments', a group of women appealed directly to the Pope, who promptly restored them their jewellery. When the Republic prohibited long gowns, the Venetian women caught up their trains in intricate and delicious folds, fastened with sumptuous clasps. When it was announced that only a single row of pearls might be worn, with a maximum value of 200 ducats, the evasions of the law were so universal, so ingenious and so brazen that the magistracy gave up, and turned its disapproving eyes elsewhere. In the eighteenth century Venetian women were the most richly dressed in Europe, and it took an Englishwoman, Lady Mary Wortley Montagu, to observe that since everybody wore masks at the opera anyway, there was consequently 'no trouble in dressing'.

Among the patrician ladies of old Venice, as among the women of Arabian harems, there was nothing much to think about but clothes and babies. Venetian *mores* were bred out of Byzantium, and respectable women were closely guarded and carefully circumscribed. Clamped in their houses out of harm's way, they were little more than tools or playthings, western odalisques: even the Doge's wife had no official position. No item of dress was more popular among Venetian aristocrats than the absurd towering clogs, sometimes twenty inches high, which obliged their wives to totter about with the help of two servants (and which, since they made great height socially desirable, have perhaps left a legacy in the unshakeable determination of modern Venetian women to wear the highest possible heels in all circumstances).

Only two women have played parts of any prominence in Venetian history. The first was Caterina Cornaro, who married the King of Cyprus in 1472 and was officially adopted as a 'daughter of the Republic' in order to ensure Venetian control of the island: her husband died a year after their marriage, the Venetians took over, and poor Caterina languished away in gilded exile at Asolo, signing herself to the last as 'Queen of Cyprus, Jerusalem and Armenia, Lady of Asolo'. The second was Bianca Cappello, daughter of a noble house, who ran away with a Florentine clerk in 1564: she was condemned to death *in absentia*, such was the disgrace of it all, but presently rose in the world to become Grand Duchess of Tuscany, and was promptly reclasped to the Venetian bosom as another 'daughter of the Republic'. She died of poisoning in 1587, but the Republic did not go into mourning, just in case it was the Grand Duke who had poisoned her.

It was only in the eighteenth century that the upper-class Venetian woman came into her own, and even now a cloistered feeling of anachronism often surrounds her. Sometimes a beautiful young blonde is to be seen in Venice, gracefully rowing her own boat: but the gondoliers do not even consider the possibility that she might be Venetian, and airily point her out as English, American or German, according to the nationality of their passengers. With her maids, her always exquisite clothes, her waiting gondolier, and the almost insuperable difficulty she has in getting out of one cushioned gondola and into another, the Venetian lady is scarcely the kind to go messing about in boats. She is often rich and often influential ('the flat downstairs', I was once told by a house agent, 'is occupied by a lady, with her husband'): but there are few professional women in the city, and one sometimes pines, in an ambience so perfumed and cosseted, for a hard-boiled New York career woman, with her heart – or part of it, anyway – deep in the propagation of soap flakes.

Other classes of Venetian women were not so sheltered under the Republic. Burghers' wives and daughters were always freer and often better educated. Poor women lived a life of rugged equality, and Venetian working women today are often jolly gregarious characters, like figures from a Goldoni comedy, throwing hilarious ribaldries across the post-office counter, or sitting plumply at their knitting on the quaysides. Courtesans, in sixteenth-century Venice, were not only celebrated and honoured, but often people of cultivation, with a taste for art and poetry (though the law at one time decreed that each such girl must carry a red light at the prow of her gondola). In earlier centuries there was a celebrated brothel, the Casteletto, at the end of the Rialto bridge, famous throughout Europe for the beauty and skill of its girls. Later, when Venice was beginning her decline, the prostitutes became courtesans, increased in wealth and respectability, burst the confines of the bordels, and gave the city its lasting reputation for lascivious charm. At the end of the sixteenth century there are said to have been 2,889 patrician ladies in Venice, and 2,508 nuns, and 1,936 burgher women: but there were 11,654 courtesans, of whom 210 were carefully registered in a catalogue by a public-spirited citizen of the day, together with their addresses and prices – or, as the compiler delicately put it, 'the amount of money to be paid by noblemen and others desirous of entering their good graces'. The cheapest charged one *scudo*, the most expensive thirty, and the catalogue reckons that the enjoyment of them all would cost the intemperate visitor 1,200 gold *scudi*.

A scholarly Venetian once remarked that his city had fostered three bad practices hitherto unknown in Italy – adulation, Lutheranism and debauchery: but he did not sound altogether censorious. Venice in her heyday, despite a streak of salty puritanism in her character, was tolerant about sex. A favourite subject of the Venetian masters, it has been observed, was Christ Defending the Woman Taken in Adultery, and even the established church was fairly easy-going with libertines: it was only with reluctance and after long delay that the administration of the Basilica, in the seventeenth century, closed the chapel of San Clemente because of the scandalous things that were known to go on behind the altar. Gay young nuns were seen on visiting days in habits distinctly *décolletés*, and with clusters of pearls in their virginal hair. In the wildest days of carnival even the Papal Nuncio used to wear a domino. Family chaplains looked benignly upon the Venetian institution of the *cicisbeo*, the handsome young man who, in the dying years of the Republic, used to stand in constant attendance upon each great lady of Venice, even sometimes helping her maids to dress her. 'The only honest woman in Venice', a wry husband remarked to a friend one day, 'is that one there' – and he pointed to a little stone figure carved on a wall above a bridge: Venice took his point, and to this day the bridge, near the Frari church, is called The Bridge of the Honest Woman.

Today all is changed. Except at the more sophisticated levels of hotel society, sin is hard to come by in modern Venice. Brothels – 'houses of toleration' – are no longer permitted by Italian law, and the police deal severely with harlots. When some modest bordel is uncovered, the newspapers make a great fuss about it – 'an operation brilliant, delicate and complete', glowed the *Gazzettino* when the police recently pounced upon a backstairs stew in Dorsoduro. One distinguished foreign diplomat, it is true, discovered not long ago that his cook had been running a small but profitable brothel on the third floor of his consulate; but there is no red-light district in Venice. The sailors who wander through the city from their ships often look uncharacteristically lost and ill at ease, and you sometimes overhear disgruntled American business men trying to obtain guidance from reticent barmen ('My score so far is precisely zero, and I don't like it that way, see? *Comprenez, amico*? Hey?').

Venice nowadays is a regenerate city, free of public vice and aberrations, where a politic eye is still winked at the idiosyncrasies of foreigners, but where men are generally men, and women usually marry. The convent of the Penitents, reserved for remorseful harlots, has long since closed its doors – it stands on the Cannaregio, nearly opposite the slaughter-house, and offered a five-year reform course for its inmates. So has the home for fallen women, near San Sebastiano, that was founded by the most famous and cultured of all the courtesans, the prostitute-poetess Veronica Franco. This is not one of your smoky, hole-in-corner, juke-box cities, and here the Italo-American culture, that garish cross-breed, is kept at bay by water and tradition. A notice appeared on the walls of the city one recent summer day, sponsored by the Society for the Protection of Youth in Venice, begging citizens and visitors to wear garments 'in accordance with the propriety of our city, which, being proud of its traditional standard of high morality, cannot approve of scanty or unbecoming clothes'. I thought of the whoopee days of carnival as I read this sober appeal, of the masked Nuncio and the simpering *cicisbei*, the harlots and the hedonists, and '*O Tempora*,' I breathed as I hitched my trousers up, '*O Mores!*'

But for all its reformation, Venice remains a sexy city still, as many a ravished alien has discovered. It is a city of seduction. There is sex and susceptibility in the very air of the place, in the mellow sunshine stones of its pavements, the shadows of its courtyards, the discretion of its silent black gondolas (which sometimes, as Byron remarked, 'contain a deal of fun, like mourning coaches when the funeral's done'). In the summer evenings symmetrical pairs of lovers, neatly balanced, occupy each water-side seat of the Public Gardens: and the steps that lead down to the Grand Canal from the Courtyard of the Duke Sforza are worn with moonlight ecstasies.

6 Minor Venetians

The Venetians love their children, sometimes with a sickly intensity. Venetian fathers carry their babies with unashamed delight, and Venetian mothers show signs of instant cardiac crisis if little Giorgio ventures within six feet of the water. Venetian children are exquisitely, if sometimes rather ludicrously dressed: the minutest little baby girls have pocket handkerchiefs tied under their chins, as head-scarves, and even the waxen Christ-children of the churches, lapped in tinsel tawdry, sometimes wear lace-embroidered drawers.

It is not altogether an easy city for children to live in. It has no dangerous traffic and few unspeakable rascals; but Venice is inescapably urban, and only lucky children with gardens, or with parents indulgent enough to take them to the distant park, have somewhere green to play. Blithe but pathetic are the groups of urchins to be found entertaining themselves, in hot dry squares or dripping alleyways, with their inexplicable Venetian games – the most popular is governed by the accuracy with which a child can thrown the old rubber heel of a shoe, but is so hedged about with subtleties and qualifications that for the life of me I have never been able to master the rules. The State schools of Venice are excellent and lavishly staffed, but they generally occupy tall, dark, overheated buildings, heavily decorated with potted plants. There are no playing fields or yards, and even the mid-morning break (or so my own children lugubriously assure me) is celebrated indoors, with a biscuit or an orange at a blank brown desk.

And in the afternoons, when school is over – children under ten only go in the mornings – and their mothers take them for a breath of air along the quayside, dauntingly spotless are those infants' clothes, unscuffled their polished shoes, neat their gloves and impeccable their hair, as they stroll sedately along the quay, beside the dancing lagoon. In the winter months there is a fair on the Riva degli Schiavoni, near St Mark's, with the usual assembly of roundabouts, bumper-cars, swings and candy-floss men, revolving colourfully against a background of ships' funnels and riggings. All the apparatus of gaiety is there, with a tang of the sea as well, but I have never wandered through that fairground without being struck by the pathos of it all, so restrained do the children seem to be, so ardently delighted by every bump of the merry-go-round. Many Venetians seem to work their children very hard, loading them with homework, foreign languages and mathematics, to sustain the family honour, or get them into universities, and keeping them up late at night. Little Venetians often seem old beyond their years, and frighteningly well-informed. When the Doge's Palace was burnt in 1479, the only record left of Petrarch's inscriptions upon the walls was the notebook of Marin Sanudo, who had taken the trouble to copy them down when inspecting the palace at the age of eight. (He went on to write a history of the world in fifty-five volumes.)

But not all Venetian children are solemn or scholastic, and many are unusually attractive. Venetian working-class women often raise their children with a bluff common sense: a single open-handed smack on the face from a benevolent washer-woman instantly and permanently cured my elder son of the unpleasant habit of spitting. In the summer dog-days a stream of mudlarks, as in an old-fashioned Hollywood musical, throw themselves contrapuntally across your path into the canals, and some beguiling tomboys can be seen most afternoons up to their thighs in the mud-flats of the inner lagoon. Rumbustious gangs of boys parade the Zattere, fighting each other with great wooden bludgeons or rapiers, or racing about on roller-skates; and I remember with affection a group of children who climbed one afternoon to the canvas roof of a water-bus stop on the Grand Canal, and who were tumbling about in the sunshine on its taut elastic surface like so many small acrobats, to the bewilderment and consternation of the passengers waiting underneath. The little girls of Venice are over-dressed but often adorable; and the more bedraggled the urchin, the more familiar he will be to the English visitor, for as you clamber down the social ladder, away from the grand palaces towards the tenements, so the children get scruffier, and more at ease, and less subdued, and more rough-and-tumble, until at last, among the shabby homes of the poor districts, you find boys and girls so blue-eyed, fair-haired, cocky, friendly and unkempt that you may imagine yourself home in your own garden, hopelessly summoning Henry to wash his hands for tea, or disengaging Mark from his collection of earthworms.

Even more, I sometimes think, do the Venetians love their animals. I have never seen one ill-treated in Venice. Even in Roman days the people of the Veneto were so kindly to their beasts that they were repelled by the bloody circus spectacles of their day, and preferred chariot races. There are very few mortal children in the pictures of the Venetian masters, but nearly every painter has portrayed birds and beasts, from the budgerigars of Carpaccio's *Two Courtesans* to the fine big retriever who stands in the foreground of Veronese's *Feast in the House of Levi*. A multitude of little dogs prances through Venetian art, a menagerie of lions, camels, dragons, peacocks, horses and rare reptiles. I once went to an exhibition in Venice that consisted of some fifty portraits, all by the same artist, all meticulously executed, all very expensive, and all of the same cat.

Venice is one of the world's supreme cat-cities, comparable in my experience only with London and Aleppo. It is a metropolis of cats. Now and again the sanitary authorities have conducted a cat-hunt, to sweep away vagrants and scavengers: but so fond are the Venetians of their cats, even the mangiest and scabbiest of them, that these drives have always ended in ignominious failure, and the animals, spitting and scratching, have been hidden away in back yards and boxes until the hygiene men have gone. The population of cats thus increases each year. Some lead an eerily sheltered existence, and are rarely allowed out of doors, only appearing occasionally, like nuns, upon confined and inaccessible balconies. Many more are only half-domesticated, and live on charity, in old drain-pipes from which sympathetic citizens have removed the grilles, under the seats of laid-up gondolas, or in the tangled recesses of overgrown gardens. You may see them any morning wolfing the indigestible entrails, fish-tails and *pasta*, wrapped in newspapers, which householders have laid down for them: and on most winter afternoons an old lady arrives to feed the cats of the Royal Gardens, near St Mark's, while a man in a sweeping overcoat so manipulates the flow of a nearby drinking fountain that a jet of water is projected into a declivity among the paving-stones, forming a cat's basin or bath.

They are odd and sometimes eccentric animals. Although they are constantly eating, and often turn up their whiskers fastidiously at a mess of spaghetti lying on a doorstep, they seldom grow fat: the only fat cats in Venice (except at Christmas, when they all seasonally swell) are the rat-catchers of the churches. They are never harshly treated, and are often positively molly-coddled, but they are usually very timid. They hardly ever climb trees. They do not answer to 'puss, puss', but if you go to the statue of Giuliano Oberdan, at the end of the Public Gardens, and make a noise something like 'chwirk, chwirk', there will be a threshing of tails among the shrubbery, as of fishes flailing in a net, and a small multitude of cats will bound out of the bushes to greet you. At a *trattoria* on the Rio del Ponte Lungo, on Giudecca, there used to be a small white cat with one yellow eye, and one blue: this may remind otologists, so I learnt from a letter in *The Lancet*, of the white forelock and heterochromia of Wardenburg's syndrome, and the cat was probably deaf, and a reluctant hunter. It was very probably of Saracen descent, born of a Crusader's booty, for such asymmetrical cats are particularly common in the Levant.

Venetian cats often lead a kind of communal life, uncharacteristic of the species, lazing about in each other's company, and sometimes dashing down a back-alley with four or five companions, like soft grey wolves, or greyhounds. Sometimes a brave nonconformist, swept off his feet by such a pack, dares to express the opinion that the hygiene men were right – there are too many cats in Venice. In 1947 Daniele Varè, 'the laughing diplomat', put a complaint about them into one of the old denunciation boxes. 'There Are' (so said his deposition) 'Too Many Cats In The *Sestiere* Of Dorsoduro': but there the paper remains, for nowadays those old receptacles are not emptied from one century to another.

One Venetian cat became an international celebrity. He lived in the 1890s at a coffee shop opposite the main door of the Frari church, and until recently, if you had a cup of coffee among the frescoes of its front room, you would find that he was still not forgotten. Nini was a white tom who was so skilfully exploited by his owner, partly in the interests of trade, partly of charity, that it became the smart thing for visitors to Venice to call upon him: and if you asked the barman nicely he would bring out a big album from beneath his espresso machine, dust it reverently down, and let you look at Nini's visitors' book. Among his callers were Pope Leo XIII, the Tsar Alexander III, the King and Queen of Italy, Prince Paul Metternich, the Negus Menelik Salamen, and Verdi, who scribbled a few notes from Act III of *La Traviata* (first performed, disastrously, at the Fenice). When Nini died, in 1894, poets, musicians and artists all offered their fulsome condolences, now stuck in the book, and a sculptor did a figure of the animal, which used to stand on the wall beside the shop. '*Nini!*' said one obituary tribute. 'A rare gem, most honest of creatures!' Another spoke of 'an infinite necessity for tears'. He was 'a gentleman, white of fur,' said a third, 'affable with great and small'. There was a gloomy funeral march in the book, and a long Ode On The Death of Nini: and Horatio Brown, the English historian of Venice, who spent much of his time in the State Archives of the Frari, around the corner, ended a poem with the lines:

> *Yours was indeed a happy plight,*
> *For down the Frari corridors,*
> *The ghosts of ancient senators*
> *Conversed with you the livelong night.*

It was all done in a spirit of dead-pan satirism that was essentially Venetian, and you had to look very hard in the eye of the barman, as he wrapped the book in brown paper and put it carefully away, to detect a distant thin flicker of amusement.

For myself, I love the cats of Venice, peering from their pedestals, sunning themselves on the feet of statues, crouching on dark staircases to escape the rain, or gingerly emerging into the daylight from their fetid subterranean lairs. Shylock defined them as 'necessary and harmless', and Francesco Morosini, one of the great fighting Doges, thought so highly of them that he took one with him on his victorious campaigns in the Peloponnese. There are few more soothing places of refuge than a Venetian garden on a blazing summer morning, when the trees are thick with green, the air is heavy with honeysuckle, and the tremulous water-reflections of the canals are thrown mysteriously upon the walls. The rear façade of the palace before you, with its confusion of windows, is alive with gentle activity. On the top floor an elderly housekeeper lowers her basket on a string, in preparation for the morning mail. From a lower window there issues the harsh melody of a housemaid's song as she scrubs the bathroom floor. In the door of the ground-floor flat a girl sits sewing, in a black dress and a demure white apron, with a shine of polished pans from the kitchen lighting her hair like a halo. From the canal outside comes a pleasant buzz of boats, and sometimes the throaty warning cry of a bargee. On a neighbouring roof-garden an artist stands before his easel, brush in one hand, coffee cup in the other.

And dotted all about you in the grass, in attitudes statuesque and contented, with their tails tucked around them and their eyes narrowed in the sunshine, one licking his haunches, one biting a blade of grass, one intermittently growling, one twitching his whiskers – all around you sit the cats of the garden, black, grey or obscurely tabby, like bland but scrawny guardians.

There used to be many horses and mules in Venice – so many in the fourteenth century that they were compelled by law to wear warning bells. In the fifteenth century Michel Steno, a rip-roaring playboy Doge, had 400 horses, their coats all dyed yellow: it is said that one ingenious foreign diplomat asked him from what region of Italy this distinctive breed sprang. One of the bells of St Mark's Campanile was called the *Trottoria*, because when it sounded the patricians used to trot to the Council Chamber on their mules. According to some theorists the Bridge of Straw, beside the Doge's Palace, is where they used to tether their mounts with a comforting nosebag during legislative sessions. Later there was a celebrated riding-school near the church of San Zanipolo, with stabling for seventy-five horses: and beside the Frari there was a successful coach-builder, whose firm went on building carriages so long after the disappearance of the Venetian horse, shipping them to customers on the mainland, that most eighteenth-century pictures of the Campo dei Frari show a specimen outside the workshop.

The advent of the arched bridge in Venice turned the canals into highways, and ousted the horse. The last man to ride along the Merceria is said to have been a convicted procurer, condemned to be dressed up in yellow clothes and driven through the streets on a donkey, with a huge pair of horns on his head. By the eighteenth century a horse was such a rarity that Mrs Thrale reported seeing a queue of poor people paying to examine a stuffed carcase in a side-show. The horselessness of Venice became an international joke, and the Venetians became notorious as appalling horsemen, just as they have a reputation for atrocious driving today. One old tale tells of a Venetian who kept his spurs in his pocket, instead of on his heels, and who was once heard murmuring to his mare: 'Ah, if you only knew what I had in my pocket, you would soon change your step!' Another Venetian, having trouble with a cantankerous horse, is said to have produced his handkerchief and spread it in the wind. 'So *that's* why he goes so slowly,' he exclaimed. 'He's got the wind against him!' A century ago, though you could still go riding in the Public Gardens, a contemporary observer noted the curious fact that the only people who did so seemed to be 'young persons of the Hebrew persuasion'. Fifty years ago one old horse still spent the summer months in the gardens, pulling a rake and a lawn-mower: and I am told that when, each autumn, he was floated away in a scow to Mestre the children jeered him on his way, the gondoliers reviled him, and even the passengers on the passing ferries threw their cat-calls and cigar-butts in his wake. Today there is not a single live horse left in the city of Venice, and if you feel like a canter you must go to the resort island of the Lido, and take a turn along the sands.

There are, however, some gorgeous artificial horses. The equestrian statue of the *condottiere* Sforza, which figures in Dürer's *The Knight and the Death*, has long since vanished from Venice. There remain the excellent horseback figure of King Victor Emmanuel, on the Riva degli Schiavoni; the incomparable Colleoni statue at San Zanipolo; and, tucked away in a museum room within the Basilica, the four bronze horses which stood for 700 years upon its façade, and which so impressed Goethe that he wanted to get the opinion of 'a good judge of horseflesh' on them. No pampered thoroughbred, no scarred war-horse has enjoyed so romantic a career as these. Their origins are lost – some say they are Greek, some Roman: but we know that they were taken from Trajan's Arch in Rome to Constantinople, where they were mounted on the tower of the Hippodrome. There Enrico Dandolo found them, and shipped them home to Venice: a hoof of one was broken on the way, and the ship's captain, named

Morosini, kept it as a souvenir, later mounting it above the door of his house in Campo Sant' Agostin. The horses were repaired in Venice, and mounted at first outside the Arsenal: but presently they were elevated to their grand eminence upon St Mark's, and became so symbolic of Venetian pride and glory that the Genoese, when they were at war with Venice, used to boast that they were going to 'bridle the horses of St Mark' – as much as to say that they intended, before very long, to hang out their washing on the Siegfried Line. Napoleon's engineers removed them laboriously from the Basilica (they weigh 1,700 lb each) and took them to Paris, where they stood for thirteen years in the Place du Carrousel. The Austrians removed them again, after Waterloo, and restored them to St Mark's in a grand ceremony which, owing to the political fevers of the time, the Venetians themselves silently boycotted. In the First World War they were shipped away in a barge for safety: through the lagoon and down the dismal tributaries of the Po, watched all along the route by sad groups of villagers, and eventually to the garden of the Palazzo Venezia in Rome, once the seat of Venetian Ambassadors (where they were joined by the Colleoni, and by Donatello's great Gattamelata from Padua). In the Second World War they were taken down from their gallery again, and packed away safely in a warehouse.

Now they have left their belvedere for good, victims of conservationism – they were alleged to be suffering from the pollution of the air – to be replaced above the Piazza by dull replicas. I am not alone in thinking they would have been better left where they were, as the grandest of all trophies and the noblest symbols of Venetian independence. I can hardly bear to think of them shut away out of the sunshine, because they always seemed to me, as to generations of Venetians, truly living creatures, animated by the genius of their unknown creators. For all their wanderings, they used to seem, up there on their proud pedestals, ageless and untired. I often saw them paw the stonework, at starlit Venetian midnights, and once I heard a whinny from the second horse on the right, so old, brave and metallic that St Theodore's crocodile, raising its head from beneath the saintly buskins, answered with a kind of grunt.

*

There are many dogs in Venice. You will often meet examples of the fluffy white breed, all wispy tail and alertness, immortalized in the paintings of Carpaccio (the most famous of them all gazes, with an appealing mixture of impatience and affection, at the preoccupied St Jerome in the Scuola di San Giorgio degli Schiavoni). There are many poodles, and many rather nasty Alsatians, whose muzzling, compulsory under Italian law, makes them figures of impotent fun to the more impertinent cats of the place. There is a pair of Tibetan terriers in a palace on the Grand Canal, and I once saw a young business man, sitting on his haunches in the Via 22 Marzo, fanning an exhausted bull terrier with his briefcase. Best of all, there are countless dogs of indeterminate breed, tough, black, self-reliant animals, who guard the boats and boatyards of Venice, and are often to be seen riding down the Grand Canal on the prows of barges, tails streaming, heads held high, in attitudes marvellously virile and conceited.

Thousands of crabs scuttle about the water-lines of Venice. Millions of ants exude from its paving-stones. Mice proliferate, and their beastly black silhouettes often scurry away from your feet down the crumbling corridors of a palace, dart from the stagnant water of a gutter, or disappear beneath the refrigerator. More than once, according to the records of St Mark's, the nibblings of mice have silenced the great organ of the Basilica. I once found a mouse on my pillow in the middle of the night, and another was once fool enough to immure itself in my bath. The Venetians seal up mouse-holes with cement, hopelessly moving from room to room, like Dame Partington with her mop: and they call mice by their diminutive, *topolini*, as if to demonstrate that they aren't scared; but the mice of Venice are a scourge and a horror, all the same, and are no doubt one reason why Shylock, who hardly sounds an animal-lover, tolerated the cats. There are also rats, as in every port. They sometimes eat the breadcrumbs we put out for the pigeons, on the balcony of our third-floor apartment: but generally they keep to the edges of the canals, or slink, grim and emaciated, from one stinking cavity to another, or end their ghastly lives floating pink-bellied down the Grand Canal.

At one time people kept lions as pets in Venice; fifty years ago a well-known hawker used to tow a floundering dolphin up and down the Grand Canal, while people threw coins from their windows; and in 1819 an elephant, escaping from a visiting menagerie, took refuge in the church of Sant' Antonin, and was 'only despatched', so contemporary records inform us respectfully, 'by a shot from a piece of ordnance'.

Most people, though, will remember Venice as a city of birds. Birds are inextricably entangled in her legend, as they are pictured everywhere in her art. It was a flight of birds, so we are told, that inspired the people of Altinum to move into the lagoon; and birds played a picturesque part in the series of visions that inspired the founding fathers to build the first churches in the city – one must be built where they should find 'a number of birds together', another 'where twelve cranes should be in company'. Birds are still conspicuous in Venetian lore, from the swallows which arrive with a flourish in the middle of June (and which used to be, before the new antidotes, the principal destroyers of mosquitoes) to the big white seagulls of the lagoon (which are often driven into the city canals by bad weather, and are even to be seen, humiliatingly plucked, hung up for sale in the Rialto market – excellent boiled, I am told, but only in the winter season). Sometimes you see a homely sparrow looking lost among the rooftops, or pecking among the green water-growths at low tide. In a few secluded gardens of the city a vivid goose struts exotically, or a bright tame pheasant preens itself. Thousands of canaries sing in the houses of Venice, their massed cages sometimes blocking entire windows: and there is a shop near the Frari church, a dark and cavernous place, through the shuttered doors of which you can always hear, even in the depth of the night, the rustle of small caged wings and the clicking of beaks. Sometimes a wild swan flies over, with an imperial rhythm, towards the fastnesses of the lagoon or the marshes of Ravenna – and in a fifteenth-century miniature from *The Book of Marco Polo* lordly white swans are swimming past St Mark's itself.

Finally there are the pigeons, most celebrated of the Venetian fauna. They are, by tradition, honoured and protected, and to have a roast pigeon lunch you must go down the road to Padua, or better still find yourself a musty trattoria among the Euganean Hills. Some say this is because Dandolo, when he stormed Constantinople, sent back the news of victory by carrier pigeon. Others believe that it arises from an old Palm Sunday custom, when a flock of pigeons was released in the Piazza, those that were caught by the populace being promptly eaten, those that escaped guaranteed permanent immunity – a ceremony that led in the long run, one pigeon looking very like another, to a safe conduct for them all. Whatever the truth, the pigeons have prospered. They survived some violent epidemics of pigeon-plague, picked up from carrion crows in the Levant, and nowadays never actually die, but merely go out into the lagoon and sink themselves.

They are mostly a drab grey colour, only occasionally relieved by a semi-albino with a white head, and they seem to me to have a verminous flavour to them. Their headquarters is the Piazza. There the stones of the Basilica are thick with generations of their droppings, and near the porphyry lions of the northern Piazetta stands their private bird-bath, beside an antique well-head. There, at the right time of day, they assemble in their shiftless thousands, gobbling and regurgitating on the pavement, a heaving mass of grey, riding on each others' backs, pushing and swelling and rustling in an obscene frenzy to get at the maize and breadcrumbs: and only a few old world-weary doves, wedged among the pillars, or propped cynically beside a chimney-pot, prefer to watch this gluttony from a fastidious distance.

7 Pageantries and Panaceas

The Venetians grew rich on silks, spices and other exotics conveyed by their merchant ships from eastern bazaars: and just as they love fineries, so they have an Oriental taste for pageantry and display. This was encouraged by the wise men of the Republic, on the old assumption about bread and circuses. The Venetian calendar was lavish with feasts, shows and exhibitions, from the grand ceremony of the Doge Wedding the Adriatic to the manifestations of St Mark's Day, when every husband gave his wife a red rose of undying loyalty. Brilliant were the pageant-fleets that used to escort the Doge on his ceremonial duties, and the Carnival which became, in the end, the prime fact of Venetian life was one long gaudy night.

Until 1802 there used to be bull-baitings in the Venetian squares, in which snarling dogs were pitted against tethered bulls: they were astonishingly ill-organized, if we are to go by one seventeenth-century painting, which depicts the entire square of San Polo in a condition of chaos, bulls charging in all directions, women scattering, hats flying, dogs barking, and only a few masked beauties, in virginal satins, stalking through the turmoil disdainfully serene. There were hilarious public fist fights, sublimating the old vendettas between factions, and degenerating into glorious free-for-alls: you can still see on the Ponte dei Pugni (Bridge of Fists), or on the bridge beside the church of Santa Fosca, the footprints, cemented in the pavement, that formed the touchline of the game. There were magnificent regattas, and gymnastic competitions, and religious processions, and even, in earlier times, knightly jousts. There were ceremonial gun salutes in the Piazza, until it was found that their vibrations were loosening the precious mosaics of the Basilica. Sometimes the Republic mounted an official display of whole-hog extravagance, to celebrate some distant and often illusory victory, forestall an incipient subversion, or impress a visiting dignitary: and it was these chimerical affairs that gave Venice her legendary aura of gold and grotesquerie.

The most memorable of all such galas was arranged for the visit of Henry III of France, in 1574 – an event which, though it had no particular political consequences, so engraved itself upon the Venetian memory that it is included in most lists of significant Venetian dates. Triumphal arches of welcome were designed by Palladio and decorated by Tintoretto and Veronese, and Henry (aged twenty-three) was conveyed to the city in a ship rowed by 400 Slav oarsmen, with an escort of fourteen galleys. As this fleet sailed across the lagoon, glass-blowers on a huge accompanying raft blew objects for the King's amusement, their furnace a gigantic marine monster that belched flame from its jaws and nostrils: and presently it was met by a second armada of curiously decorated boats, fanciful or symbolic, elaborate with dolphins and sea gods, or draped in rich tapestries. At Venice the palace called Ca' Foscari, on the Grand Canal, had been especially prepared for the visitor. It was embellished with cloth of gold, carpets from the East, rare marbles, silks, velvets and por-phyry. The bed-sheets were embroidered in crimson silk. The pictures, specially acquired or commissioned, were by Giovanni Bellini, Titian, Paris Bordone, Tintoretto and Veronese. For the principal banquet, in the gigantic Great Council Chamber of the Doge's Palace, the sumptuary laws were temporarily suspended, and the most beautiful women of Venice appeared all in dazzling white, 'adorned', as one historian tells us, 'with jewels and pearls of great size, not only in strings on their necks, but covering their head-dresses and the cloaks on their shoulders'. There were 1,200 dishes on the bill of fare, the 3,000 guests all ate off silver plate, and the tables were decorated with sugar figures of Popes, Doges, Gods, Virtues, animals and trees, all designed by an eminent architect and fashioned by a pharmacist of talent. When Henry picked up his elaborately folded napkin, he found that it was made of sugar, too. Three hundred different kinds of *bonbon* were distributed, as the meal sank to a conclusion, and after dinner the King saw the first opera ever performed in Italy. When at last he went out into the night, he found that a galley, shown to him earlier in the evening in its component parts, had been put together during the banquet on the quay outside: it was launched into the lagoon as he emerged from the palace, complete with a 16,000 lb cannon that had been cast between the soup and the soufflé.

According to some historians the poor young King, who dressed very simply himself, and liked to wander around cities incognito, was never quite the same again, and lived the rest of his life in a perpetual daze. Many other visitors were similarly staggered by the colour and luxury of Venice. Thomas Coryat from Somerset wrote wildly in 1610 that he would deny himself four of the richest manors in his county, rather than go through life without seeing the city. A fifteenth-century Milanese priest was shown the bedroom of an eminent Venetian lady, decorated with blue and gold to the value of 11,000 ducats, and attended by twenty-five maids, loaded with jewellery: but when he was asked what he thought of it, 'I knew not how to answer' (says he convincingly) 'save by the raising of my shoulders.' 'I have oftentimes observed many strangers', wrote one old Englishman, 'men wise and learned, who arriving newly at *Venice*, and beholding the beautie and magnificence thereof were stricken with so great an admiration and amazement, that they woulde, and that with open mouth, confesse, never any thing which before time they had seene, to be thereunto comparable.'

Venice is not quite so sumptuous nowadays, but she still enjoys her round of pageants, her almanac of festivals. Some are natural and popular, some blatantly touristic, but none are without fun or beauty. There is the great feast of the Redentore, when a bridge is thrown across the wide canal of the Giudecca to the church of the Redemption on the other side, and the night is loud and bright with fireworks. There are starlight concerts in the courtyard of the Doge's Palace, and band performances in the Piazza. There are regattas still, and candle-lit sacred processions, and the great art festival of the Biennale. There is the annual Film Festival, a thing of minks and speedboats, to which the world's exhibitionists flock as dazzled moths to lamplight. Every night in summer there are serenades on the Grand Canal, when tremulous sopranos and chesty tenors, enthroned in fairy-lit barges, lurch uncomfortably down the water-way among the *vaporetti*, introduced over a loud-speaker in unctuous American English, and sometimes closely pursued, in a dissonance of arias, by a rival fleet of troubadours.

The municipal department of tourism, which pleasantly defines one of its activities as 'organizing traditional festivals', diligently maintains the old celebrations and sometimes launches new ones: and there seems scarcely a day in the Venetian summer without its own ceremonial, a procession of clergy around St Mark's, a Festival of Lights, a Traditional Custom or An Old Venetian Fête, the Century Regatta (for elderly gondoliers), an Artistic Floodlighting of the Palaces, a Romantic Moonlight Serenade. When the image of Our

Lady of Fatima was brought to Venice in 1959, it was landed at St Mark's by helicopter. Modern Venetian ceremonies usually begin half an hour late, and there is a strong taste of the travel agency to their arrangements ('and this, you see, is the very same traditional festival followed by the ancient Doges, from time immemorial, according to old-hallowed custom'): but somewhere among their sham and tinsel glitter you can still sometimes fancy a glow of old glory, and imagine King Henry watching, with his guard of sixty silk-dressed halberdiers, through the taffeta hangings of his palace.

The Venetians still love a show, and do not care about its stage management – they used to be enthusiastic followers of that most frankly artificial art, puppetry. When that ghastly serenade floats by each evening, there are always Venetians leaning tenderly from their balconies to hear the music, and watch the undeniably romantic bobbing of the gondola prows in the half-light. Given half a chance, they would climb aboard the barge and join in the chorus themselves. I once helped to make a television film in Venice, and it was wonderful with what ease and pleasure the Venetians in the street performed before our cameras (except those who, following an irrepressible instinct, asked us how much we were planning to pay them). Beside the Riva degli Schiavoni, away from the hotels, there are two long tunnel-like tenements, strung with washing, which run away from the sea into a huddle of houses. Here our Roman cameraman deployed the local inhabitants for the scene we wanted, poised beside their washing-boards, frozen in gossip, precariously balanced on doorsteps, immobilized in archways, static in windows. There they stood for two or three minutes, patiently waiting. The exposure was estimated; the producer approved the arrangements; the script-writer had a look through the viewfinder; the sun shifted satisfactorily; the steamer in the background was nicely framed through the washing; and suddenly the cameraman, pressing his key, bawled 'Via!' In an instant that tenement was plunged in frantic activity, the housewives scrubbing furiously, the gossips jabbering, the passers-by vigorously passing, the old ladies leaning energetically from their windows, and a multitude of unsuspected extras, never seen before, precipitately emerging from back-doors and alley-ways – an old man in a black hat, sudden coveys of youths, and a clown of a boy who, abruptly appearing out of a passage, shambled across our field of vision like a camel, till the tears ran down the script-writer's face, and the whole community dissolved in laughter. The Venetians are not an exuberant people, but they have a long comical tradition, and they love acting. Eleanora Duse herself was born in a third-class railway carriage as her father's Venetian dialect troupe puffed from one performance to the next, and Harlequin, like Pantaloon, was invented in Venice. The very word '*zany*', as the cameraman reminded me that morning, comes from a Venetian theatrical character – his name was Giovanni, and he acted crazy.

Now and then the Venetians still arrange a grand spectacle outside the usual tourist round, and recapture some of the old spontaneity. In 1959 there was returned to the city, to lie in state for one month, the body of Pope Pius X, one of the few canonized pontiffs of recent times. This holy man had been Patriarch of Venice for seven years, until his elevation to the papacy in 1903, and he is still venerated in the city. Scores of churches contain his effigy, and many an elderly lady will tell you, with a look of respectful affection in her eye, tales of his simplicity and goodness. He was a man of poverty – he wore his predecessor's robes, to save buying new ones, and towards the end of the month he sometimes had to make a visit to the Monte di Pieta, the pawnshop of Venice. He scorned convention, pretence and stuffiness, and was thus more popular among the common people than among the aristocrats. He once demonstrated to a lady, in private audience at the Vatican, the steps of a Venetian dance. When a nun asked for a pair of his old stockings, as a remedy for her rheumatism, and later pronounced herself entirely cured, the Pope declared it very odd – 'I wore them myself far longer than she did, and they never did me any good!'

All Venice mourned when this good person left the city for the consistory that was to elect him Pope. There is a moving photograph that shows him stepping into his gondola for the last time, to go to the railway station. In the foreground an elderly gondolier stands solemn and bareheaded, holding his oar; a bald man kneels to kiss the old priest's hand; a small boy, clutching a pillar, stares pale-faced from the background; and the scene is framed with groups of anxious, silent, sad women. It was almost certain that he would be the next Pope: but he cheerfully bought a return ticket to Rome, and he said to the crowds, in a phrase that has become famous: 'Never fear, I shall come back. Dead or alive, I shall return to Venice!' – 'O vivo o morto ritornerò!'

Half a century later another Patriarch of Venice became Pope: and one of the first acts of Giovanni XXIII, a man of much the same kind, was to fulfil his predecessor's promise, and return to the city the embalmed body of Saint Pius X. A marvellous procession conveyed it down the Grand Canal to the Basilica. First came the countless gondolas of the clergy, each rowed by a white-clad gondolier: a melange of crosses, surplices, purple cassocks, stout bishops and stooping monks, Armenians with bushy beards, Dominicans in white, rosy country parsons, foxy-faced thinkers, tremulous old saints and pallid novices, all smiling and cushioned deep in their seats. Then came the dream-like barges of the Venetian tradition, their crews in vivid medieval liveries, silver or blue castles at their prows and sterns, heavy draperies trailing in the water behind (supported by corks, to keep them ponderously afloat). The bells of Venice rang. Plainchant issued from a hundred loudspeakers. Flags, bunting and an occasional carpet flapped from the windows of the canal-side palaces. Thousands of school children, massed upon the quays and bridges, threw rose petals into the water. Police boats scurried everywhere, and by the Accademia Bridge a reporter in a speedboat spoke a purple commentary into his walkie-talkie.

Thus, in a blaze of gold, there appeared beneath the Rialto bridge the barge called the Bucintoro, successor to the magnificent State vessels of the Doges (the last of which was turned into a prison hulk at the fall of the Republic, and later broken up for firewood). A crew of young sailors rowed it, in a slow funereal rhythm, each stroke of the oar summoned by a single drum-beat from a ferocious major-domo in the well of the ship – a man who, glaring angrily from oarsman to oarsman, and striking his drum with ritual dedication, looked like an old slave-driver between decks on a galley. Slowly, heavily, eerily this barge approached us along the canal, its gold gleaming, a vast crimson textile streaming from its high stern into the water, until at last, peering down from our balcony, we could see beneath its carved gilded canopy into the ceremonial chamber beneath. There lay the corpse of the great Pope, embalmed in a crystal coffin, in a splendour of vestments, rings and satin, riding calm and silently towards St Mark's.

They took Pope Pius to the Basilica, and laid him upon the High Altar, and a multitude of pilgrims filed around his coffin, touching the glass with reverent fingers, or kissing the panelling. But when the ceremonies were over that day I took out my boat and followed those rich fantastic barges away from the Piazzetta. They plunged across the choppy Giudecca Canal, their duties done, like so many Viking long-ships. Their high poops were engraved against the sunset, their crews sweated in silhouette, their pennants fluttered in a rising wind, and their draperies trailed heavily against the tide. Past a hulking British freighter they laboured, down the shore of the Giudecca; past the Lido car-ferry; past the disused flour-mill at the end of the island; past the cranes on Sacca Fisola; until as the light began to fail they reached their destination, the crews took off their brilliant costumes and lit their cigarettes, and those peacock craft were pulled from the water, stripped of their fabrics, and put away in corrugated-iron sheds until the next festivity.

Behind all this Renaissance veneer, the splendour of the Venetian façades, the beautifully dressed women and the pomaded men, there remains a layer of squalor. There are still drab slums in Venice, despite housing programmes that have transformed whole areas of the city, and there are still many people whose simplicity borders upon the primitive. Less than a century ago Venice was a city wreathed in folk-lore, as a glance at almost any nineteenth-century description will confirm – 'in Venice the omens of death are many and various', 'the belief in witches is chiefly confined to women', 'the different factions of Venice each have their bombastic songs', 'the best place to hear a traditional story-teller is among the plane trees of the Public Gardens, whither the Venetians of the lower orders make their way for the beguilement of their summer evenings'. Most of these picturesque beliefs and customs have, so far as I can discover, died. No folksy costumes are worn in Venice, and a characteristic demonstration of contemporary taste is the silent crowd which, through the dreary winter evenings, sits spellbound before the television set in every city café.

Occasionally, though, to this very day, a quaint tale or a kitchen quirk will remind you of the knotty medieval roots of Venice, a city of water-peasants. Venetians still point to the lamps that burn before the Madonna on the Piazzetta façade of the Basilica, and tell you the story of the baker's boy, who was wrongly executed for murder, and in whose memory (so they have wrongly supposed for several centuries) the lights flicker remorsefully night and day. A few Venetians still believe a hunchback to be a symbol of good luck. They still paint great eyes on the bows of their boats – or more often euphemistic stars – to keep away ill fortune. They still invest their religion with a particular aura of magic and necromancy.

I was once filming inside the courtyard of a disused convent, now inhabited by a myriad squatter families. Washing hung dismally across the old cloisters, and was draped about the ancient well-head (clamped together with wires, to keep it from disintegrating); and there were pots and pans in the derelict dormitory windows, and ramshackle partitions and privies in the remains of the refectory. The place was cold and dirty, and a few raggety children played among its debris. A young woman was hanging up sheets in the yard, and we asked if we might photograph her, to inject some animation into an otherwise torpid scene: but as she walked obligingly towards our cameras, a searing cry came from a window directly above us. There, propped witch-like on a window-sill, was a dreadful old woman all in black, with a face that was withered and blotchy, and a voice of curdling severity. 'Don't let them do it!' she screeched. 'It's the evil eye! They did it to my poor husband, only last year, the same wicked thing, and within a month he died! Send them away, the evil ones! Send them away!' The young woman paled at these horrific words; the cameraman gaped; and as for myself, I was out of the courtyard on the quay before the last cracked echoes of her indictment had died away amongst the washing.

Venice used to be a great place for love potions, alchemists, fumigations, salivations of mercury, vapour baths, quacks and wise women. Casanova's earliest memory was of a Venetian witch, surrounded by black cats, burning drugs and pronouncing incantations over him, for the cure of a nose-bleed. (He was inclined that way himself: when the Venetians eventually arrested him, it was, so they said, partly for his Voltairean notions, and partly because of his interest in sorcery.) In 1649 a Venetian doctor offered the State an 'essence of plague' to be spread among the Turks by infusing it into textiles sold in enemy territory: the Republic did not use his invention, but to prevent anyone else getting hold of it, instantly locked the poor man up in prison. The well that gave fresh water to the Arsenal, we are told, was always pure because two rhinoceros horns had been thrown into it. Even now, you sometimes see medical mountebanks successfully promoting their cures in Venice. Outside the church of San Francesco di Paola I once came across a man who claimed to produce miraculous unguents from the juices of marmots, two of which animals sat despondently on a table in front of him. He was surrounded by skins, bottles and testimonials, like a medicine man. He guaranteed instant relief for rheumatism, arthritis, stiffening in the joints, colds in the nose, appendicitis, old age, warts, dry skin, falling hair and vertigo; and he was doing a brisk trade among the morning shoppers.

In the Middle Ages no sensible visitor to Venice left without a bottle of Teriaca, a celebrated potion that cured practically everything (except, its brewers had to admit, the plague). This panacea contained gum arabic, pepper, cinnamon, fennel, rose petals, opium, amber, aromatic leaves from the East and more than sixty kinds of medicinal herbs. It was brewed at certain times of the year, under strict State supervision, in great cauldrons beside the pharmacies – outside a chemist's shop in Campo Santo Stefano you can still see indentations in the ground, where the feet of the cauldrons used to rest. An emasculated version of the medicine is still sold in Venice, at the Pharmacy of the Golden Head, beside the Rialto bridge. A fine and secretive cat, sustaining the spirit of the thing, sits upon the counter of this shop, and the Teriaca is kept in a big glass jar on a shelf against the wall. The wrapper has a golden head upon it, crowned with laurels, and the instructions say that the mixture will be found useful in dealing with afflictions 'intestinal, nervous, verminous and stomachic'. A layer of coarse brown paper follows, and the Teriaca is contained in a cylindrical metal container, like a fat cartridge case. A brown treacly fluid oozes from the lid of this receptacle: but whether this is actually the mixture, or whether it is merely some sealing substance, I am unable to say; for to tell the truth I have never had the courage to take the top off.

With the primitive goes the filthy. Venice is a dirty city, for all its grand façades and its well-swept alleys. There are strict laws against the throwing of rubbish into the canals – punishable, if the offence is repeated, by imprisonment: but a vile mass of refuse is thrown in anyway, and the Venetian housewife thinks nothing of emptying her rubbish-basket and dust-pan out of the open window, where its miscellaneous muck can be blown by the winds across the city, into the neighbour's garden, up and down the back-alleys. After a night or two in a side canal, my boat is hideous with rubbish, from orange peel to torn letters, and odious is the flotsam that swirls and gurgles past you if you sit beside the water for a moment of meditation. This is partly because the Venetian drainage system is simplicity itself, usually consisting of pipes out of houses into canals; and partly because the Venetians have only rudimentary instincts of hygiene. For several hundred years Venetian officialdom has worried itself about the civic sanitation, but the average citizen pours her slops into the canal as blithely as ever she did in the Middle Ages. This was, I am told, the last big Italian city to revive the Roman practice of baths in houses: and though the poor woman's parlour is usually spick and gleaming, her back yard is often horrible. The canals of Venice are lined with accumulations of garbage, and nothing is more strongly worded, in the whole range of travel literature, than Herr Baedeker's warning against Venetian oysters.

Dirty, too, is the unsuspected pall of smut which falls through this pellucid atmosphere in winter, and keeps the laundry ever a little short of perfection. This is, though, the fault not of the Venetian housewife, but of the old Venetian architects. Their chimneys are charmingly inconsequential in appearance (somebody once wrote a book about them) and were specifically designed to prevent flying sparks in a city that was often ravaged by fire. With their complicated double flues and inner chambers, however, they are confoundedly difficult to clean. The Venetian chimney-sweep works from the top, lowering bundles of twigs on cords and then pulling them out again. This entails endless scrambles across rickety roof-tops, clutching antique cornices, swarming over tottering balconies. I once chanced to look out of my bedroom window to see the jet-black face of one of these men hanging almost upside-down from the roof above. He had a bundle of sticks in his hand, and a rope around his shoulders, and behind him were all the pinnacles, towers and curious weather-vanes that form the setting of his labours: but there was nothing really unfamiliar about him, for when he smiled I recognized him instantly as a member of that prime and splendid fraternity, the universal brotherhood of sweeps, whose cheerful sooty attitudes have so endeared themselves to the world that even the most aloofly unsuperstitious of brides, swathed in silk and clouded in Chanel, is pleased to see one at her wedding.

8 'Poi Cristiani'

The Venetians are not quite so religious as you might suppose from their multitude of churches and their mystical origins. 'About the same as the Romans,' an official at the Patriarchate once told me, after judicial thought, 'perhaps a bit better than the Milanese' – and these were, he seemed to imply, scarcely celestial standards of judgement. The great force of popular faith, which sustained the Republic through many trials, and was apparently still potent half a century ago, has lost its dominance. Today the great religious festivals are often ill attended, and the supreme summer services at the Basilica generally attract more tourists than Venetians. In some parts of the city, in the Italian manner, religion is laced with politics, so that Catholic and Communist slogans angrily confront each other on shop walls: but there is no sense of priestly power in Venice, and democratic though its Christian Democrats may be, they are not always very profoundly Christian.

The texture of the city, of course, is shot through with Christian symbols, and there are well-known miracles for every quarter. At the ferry station of Santa Maria Zobenigo a devout virgin, denied the use of the ferry to the church, walked across the Grand Canal instead. In the Basilica there is a wooden crucifix which, struck by a blasphemer, gushed forth blood. An angel once broke the fall of a workman who slipped from St Mark's Campanile, catching him in mid-fall and gently restoring him to his scaffolding. From the Riva degli Schiavoni a fisherman sailed on a voyage across the lagoon commissioned by Saints Mark, Nicholas and George, in the course of which they exorcized a shipload of demons (the fisherman asked anxiously which of the saints was going to pay him). In 1672 an old and simple-minded sacristan fell from the campanile of Santi Apostoli, but was miraculously caught by the minute hand of the clock, which, slowly revolving to six o'clock, deposited him safely on a parapet. In the Piazzetta dei Leoncini, beside the Basilica, a slave was rescued from judicial blinding by the intervention of St Mark, who projected himself upside-down into the assembly and, as a famous Tintoretto demonstrates, froze the burning brand in mid-air. There are miracle-working Madonnas in the churches of Santa Maria dei Miracoli and Madonna dell' Orto, and the figure of the Virgin in San Marziale came to Venice of its own accord by sea from Rimini.

The celebrated Nicopeia Madonna in the Basilica, one of many such ikons supposed to have been painted by St Luke, is still reverenced; a picture said to be by Giorgione, formerly in the church of San Rocco, was long believed to have miraculous powers; and in all parts of the city there are curative relics, shrines and statues. The silver hearts of votive offerings decorate almost every Venetian church. One grateful supplicant to the Giorgione picture, whose misery we do not know, had a marble cast of the painting made in thanksgiving – and this was prophetic, for presently the picture was removed from the church and placed in the neighbouring Scuola di San Rocco, and now only the votive copy remains. Another grateful worshipper hung a rifle beside a picture of the Madonna near the chapel of the Mascoli in the Basilica: it hangs there still, but nobody seems to know its story.

There are 107 churches in the city proper – one for every 2,000 inhabitants – of which some 80 are still in use. Venice, including its mainland suburbs and its islands, houses 24 men's convents and about 30 women's, from at least 13 different Orders. There are some 230 priests in Venice, under a Patriarch who is nowadays nearly always a Cardinal, and who shares his title, in the Western countries, only with the Patriarchs of Lisbon and the West Indies. There have been 51 Bishops of Venice, and 144 Patriarchs, and between them they have produced 3 Popes and 17 Cardinals. More than 100 saints are represented in the street names of the city, from St Julian the Martyr, who is now thought never to have existed at all, to San Giovanni in Olio – St John the Evangelist, who is said to have emerged unharmed from a vat of boiling oil into which the Emperor Domitian had plunged him. There are churches of St Moses and St Job, and the Madonna is honoured in a series of exquisite eponyms – St Mary of the Lily, of Consolation, of Health, of Grace, of The Garden, of the Friars; St Mary the Fragrant, St Mary the Beautiful, St Mary the Processional, St Mary the Mother of the Lord.

But it seems a dying order that is represented by these pieties. Only the guides speak of the Venetian miracles with much air of conviction, and the young Venetians tell the old stories, often enough, with a fond but patronizing smile. Rome, indeed, has never maintained an easy hold over Venice. *Veneziani, poi Cristiani*, is how her people used to describe themselves – Venetians first, Christians afterwards. 'Redeem us, O Christ!' sang the choir of St Mark in the Middle Ages. 'O Christ, reign! O Christ, triumph! O Christ, command!' The response, though, was not so orthodox, for the other half of the cathedral would answer: 'To the Most Serene and Excellent Doge, Health, Honour, Life and Victory Perpetual!'

'Are you a Venetian?' I once asked a saintly Dominican in the church of San Zanipolo. 'No, thank God!' he replied, in a genuinely grateful tone of voice. This is a citizenry more hard-boiled, sceptical and sophisticated than the peasantry of the mainland countryside.

The 'Show Me State' is an old sobriquet for Missouri, implying a tendency to look gift horses attentively in the mouth; it would do equally well for Venice. The Republic was never feudal, and its political system was never amenable to clerical intimidation. There was a time, early in the seventeenth century, when Venice hesitated on the brink of Protestantism (with Sir Henry Wotton, the British Ambassador, energetically trying to push her over). Several times in her history she was indicted or excommunicated by the Pope; during Paolo Sarpi's period of office as theological adviser to the Doge, in the first decade of the seventeenth century, the quarrel with the Holy See was so profound that Venice became the champion of secular State rights, and two bishops languished in the prisons of the Doge's Palace.

Her painters were sometimes notable for an almost pagan profligacy and riot of imagination. Veronese, indeed, was summoned before the Inquisition of the Holy Office for including 'dogs, buffoons, drunken Germans, dwarfs and other such absurdities' in a picture he had painted of the Last Supper. He replied that he had allowed himself 'the same licence as poets and madmen', and this the inquisitors seemed to accept, not without humour. They ordered him to 'correct' his picture, but instead he simply altered its title, and today it hangs in the Accademia as the *Feast at the House of Levi*, dwarfs, Germans, dogs and all. ('What signifies the figure of him whose nose is bleeding?' asked the inquisitors during the hearing. 'He is a servant', replied the artist blandly, 'who has a nose-bleed from some accident.')

For in her heyday Venice was subservient to the Papacy only when she found it convenient. Her parish priests were elected by a ballot of parishioners, under State direction, and the Pontiff was merely notified of their appointment. Bishops were nominated in the Senate, and even the Patriarch could not convene a synod without the permission of the Doge. All priests had to be of Venetian birth, and they could never be sure of their customary privileges: in the fifteenth century clerics convicted of various immoralities were hung in cages high on the side of St Mark's Campanile, sometimes living there for a year on bread and water, sometimes allegedly starving to death, and providing one of the principal tourist attractions of the city. The Grand Council of Venice met pointedly on Sundays and feast days, and time and again its policies on the slave trade, and on intercourse with Muslims, were in direct defiance of Papal decrees. A party of fifteenth-century Christian missionaries, lost in the Balkan hinterland, eventually turned up for sale in the Venetian slave market: and when da Gama found the sea route to India, the Venetians openly incited the Sultan of Egypt to make war upon the Portuguese, offering to find timber for the necessary warships, and to provide shipwrights, caulkers, cannon-founders and naval architects. In the Venetian priorities, Venice came unmistakably first.

The true cathedral of the city (until 1797) was San Pietro di Castello, on the eastern perimeter: but its practical spiritual centre was the Basilica of St Mark's – the Doge's private chapel. During the period of the great interdict, in 1606, one priest, wary of Venetian pride but not wishing to disobey the Pope, announced that he was waiting for the Holy Ghost to tell him whether to celebrate Mass or not: the Republican Government replied that the Holy Ghost had already inspired them – to hang anyone who refused. 'Will you kindly kneel?' said an eighteenth-century Venetian senator to a visiting Englishman, as the congregation in the Basilica fell on their knees before the Host. 'I don't believe in transubstantiation,' the Englishman replied. 'Neither do I,' said the senator, 'but either kneel down or get out of the church!'

The churches of Venice have thus had their ups and downs. The blackened chapel of the Rosary in the church of San Zanipolo, which was burnt in 1867, was deliberately destroyed, so the monks tell you darkly, 'by Anti-Religious'. The church of San Gerolamo once became a brick factory, and had smoke belching from its bell-tower. The church of Sant' Elena was used as an iron-foundry. The church of San Bartolomeo, in the fifteenth century, was used as a civil service school. The church of Santa Marina, in the nineteenth, was used as a tavern, and a visitor reported that its servants, hurrying between customers and bar, used to be heard shouting: 'A jug of white in the Chapel of the Madonna! The same again at the Altar of the Sacrament!' Madonna dell' Orto has been, in its time, a stables, a straw store and a powder magazine. The church of San Vitale is now an art gallery, its frenzied abstracts supervised in serene splendour by a Carpaccio above the old high altar. The church of San Leonardo is the practice-room of the municipal band, heavily decorated with photographs of whiskered long-dead maestros. There is a church used as a factory on Giudecca, and another provides some of the galleries of the Accademia, and a third is a cinema in Campo Santa Margherita. San Basso is a lecture hall. San Vio only opens on one day each year – its saint's day. Santa Maria Maggiore is part of the prison.

Some of the finest Venetian churches – San Zanipolo, San Marcuola, San Lorenzo, San Pantaleone – have never been finished, as their brick façades show. Many others have disappeared. Four churches were demolished, at Napoleon's orders, to make the Public Gardens. One, by Palladio, vanished beneath the foundations of the railway station. The remains of one lie beneath the great red mills at the western tip of Giudecca, and the wreck of another still lingers beside the docks. Sant' Aponal was once put up for auction; so was San Paternian, but as nobody bought it they pulled it down instead to make way for the statue in Campo Manin. A Byzantine column near the station bridge is all that remains of the church of Santa Croce, which still gives its name to one of the Venetian postal districts. As long ago as 1173 the Venetians were placed under papal interdict for altering the church of San Geminiano without the Pope's permission – they wanted to improve the appearance of the Piazza; in the end Napoleon demolished it altogether, but it is said to have looked, in its final version, exactly like the church of San Maurizio, near the Accademia bridge. In the 1860s there were serious demands for the demolition of St Mark's Basilica itself, made by those Italian icono-clasts who, sick to death of being treated as curators in a national museum, wanted to knock all of old Italy down, and start afresh.

Today the worst is probably over. The priest at the Patriarchate may tell you, with a meaning sigh, that Venice is a religious city *by tradition*: but at least there is not much active hostility to the faith. Religious processions are no longer derided, as they were, so Wagner tells us, as recently as 1858 (partly, no doubt, because many priests collaborated with the Austrian overlords). The church suffers no ignominies in Venice. Its buildings are usually immaculate, and you will find little of that damp rot and neglect so deliciously apparent to the old Protestant guide books. Several disused churches have been restored, and the activities of the church, from youth clubs to magazines, are inescapable. The Patriarch is one of the great men of Venice, and most citizens, even the agnostic, have strong feelings about him. Cardinal Sarto, who became Pope Pius X, is remembered with real affection, especially among the poorer people. One of his successors is less happily recalled. 'We Venetians, we like *sympathetic* people,' you will be told, 'we like simple people, kind people' – and here your informant, looking up from her washing, will give you a long sickly smile, intended to indicate compassion, understanding, humility. 'But this Cardinal So-and-So, he was not at all like that, he was always *cosi – urgh!*' – and with this sharp guttural expletive she will look up again, this time her face congealed in a condition of unutterable hauteur, its eyes drooping contemptuously, its chin compressed. 'Ah, no, no, no, we did not like him – but then, *guarda*, along came Cardinal Roncalli, Pope Giovanni XXIII – ah, ah, *so different . . .!*' And so intense will be the sickly smile this time, so brimming the eyes with admiration, so limp the entire body under its load of commiseration, that she is quite unable to finish the sentence, wipes her face with the corner of her apron, and returns to the sink speechless. The Patriarchs of Venice do not go unremarked.

Much of the colour and richness of the city still comes from the church – its myriad wonderful buildings; its processions and festivals and treasures; its incense and organ music, billowing through curtained doors into dim-lit squares; its thousands of monks, biting their lower lips in self-deprecation as they make their rounds of mendicancy, or swarming athletically up dizzy wires to attend to the lamps of the Frari. Priests are ubiquitous in Venice, and I remember with particular delight walking towards the Zattere on the morning of Palm Sunday, and meeting on the quayside a column of cheerful chattering nuns, all pink, black and wimpled white, scurrying home to lunch with their palms held high and joyful. On Sunday afternoons the churches are full of ill-disciplined children's classes, the cracked voices of youths, the high tinny catechisms of little girls: and almost every Venetian water-bus has a small crucifix on the wall of the steersman's cabin.

The church in Venice, though, is something more than all things bright and beautiful. It is descended from Byzantium, by faith out of nationalism: and sometimes to its high ritual in the Basilica of St Mark there is a tremendous sense of an eastern past, marbled, hazed and silken. St Mark's itself is a barbaric building, like a great Mongolian pleasure pavilion, or a fortress in Turkestan: and sometimes there is a suggestion of rich barbarism to its services too, devout, reverent and beautiful though they are.

In Easter week each year the Patriarch and his clergy bring from the vaults of the church treasury all its most sacred relics, and display them ceremonially to the people. This ancient function is heavy with reminders of the Orient. It takes place in the evening, when the Piazza is dark, and the dim lights of the Basilica shine mysteriously on the gold mosaics of its roof. The congregation mills about the nave in the half-light, switching from side to side, not knowing which way to look. A beadle in a cocked hat, with a silver sword and the face of a hereditary retainer, stands in a peremptory eighteenth-century attitude beside a pillar. The organ plays quietly from its loft, and sometimes there is a chant of male voices, and sometimes a sudden hubbub from the square outside when the door of the church is opened. All is murmurous and glinting.

A flash of gold and silver from an aisle, a swish of stiff vestments, the clink of a censer, and presently there advances through the crowd, clouded in incense, the patriarchal procession. Preceded by flurrying vergers, clearing a way through the congregation, it sweeps slowly and rheumatically up the church. A golden canopy of old tapestry sways and swings above the mitred Patriarch, and around it walk the priests, solemn and shuffling, clasping reverently the celebrated relics of St Mark's (enclosed in golden frames, jewelled caskets, crucifixes, medieval monstrances). You cannot see very well, for the crowd is constantly jostling, and the atmosphere is thick; but as the priests pass slowly by you catch a queer glimpse of copes and reliquaries, a cross set with some strange sacred souvenir, a fragment of bone in a crystal sphere, weird, ornate, elaborate objects, swaying and bobbing above the people as the old men carrying them stumble towards the altar.

It is an eastern ceremonial, a thing of misty and exotic splendour. When you turn to leave the great church, all those holy objects are placed on the rim of the pulpit, and all those grave priests are crowded together behind, like so many white-haired scholarly birds. Incense swirls around them; the church is full of slow shining movement; and in the Piazza outside, when you open the door, the holiday Venetians stroll from café to café in oblivion, like the men who sell Coca-Cola beneath the sneer of the Sphinx.

If the Venetians are not always devout, they are usually kind. They have always had a reputation, like other money-makers, for generosity to the poor. The five Great Schools of Venice, of which the Scuola di San Rocco is now the most famous, were charitable associations set up to perform 'temporal works of mercy': and even Baron Corvo, in his worst years of disillusionment, had to admit that when it came to charitable causes the Venetians were extraordinarily generous. The indigenous beggars of the city are treated with indulgence, and are seldom moved on by the easy-going police. There is a dear old lady, bundled in shawls, who sits in the evenings at the bottom of the Accademia bridge, and has many faithful patrons. There is a bent old man who haunts the alleys near Santo Stefano, and who is often to be seen, pacing from one stand to another, plucking a neat little melody upon his guitar. On Sunday mornings a faun-like couple of countrymen materialize on the quayside of Giudecca with a set of bagpipes and a wooden whistle. A well-known comic figure of the Zattere is a man in a cloth cap and a long blue overcoat who suddenly appears among the tables of the outdoor cafés, and planting himself in an uncompromising posture on the pavement, legs apart, head thrown back, produces a sheet of music from his pocket and throws himself into a loud and quite incomprehensible aria, tuneless and spasmodic, but delivered with such an air of informed authority that there are always a few innocents to be seen following the melodic line with rapt knowledge-able attention. I once asked this man if I could see his music, and discovered it to be a specimen page from a score of Beethoven's Ninth Symphony, held upside-down and close to the stomach.

I suspect the Venetians, who still have a strong clan feeling, may sometimes be less forbearing towards unfamiliar loafers. Now and then you see gypsies who have penetrated the city from the mainland in their colourful long-skirted dresses, and who whine their way from square to square with babies in their arms and skinny hands outstretched. I myself have a weakness for gypsies, but the Vene-tians are evidently not addicts, and you hardly ever see a Romany beggar rewarded. I was once a beggar in Venice myself. One bleak winter evening my boat engine broke down, and I needed a few lire to take the ferry-boat home. Providence, I assured myself, in a city so divinely founded, would certainly provide: and sure enough, pres-ently there approached me a monk from one of the mendicant orders, whom I had often seen carrying sacks from household to household, and who was now returning to his nearby convent. I stopped him and asked him for the loan of 100 lire until the next day: but chill and suspicion was the response I got; and cold the doorstep upon which, at the entrance to the monastery, my family and I were left in lonely hope; and tortuous were the channels through which the consent of the Abbot was vainly sought; and gruff was the porter who told us to go and wait in the adjacent church; and low-voiced the consultation of friars which reached us sibilantly as we stood in the nave; and hasty and off-hand were the manners of the monk who at last approached me sidelong, as if unwilling to come too close, and thrust the coin into my hand as you might offer a bone to an unreliable terrier; and irritating was my conviction, when I returned to repay the loan next morning, that the doorman who casually accepted it, beneath the grinning *memento mori* decorating his portal, almost certainly pocketed the money for himself.

But if I was cynical then, I am less so today, for now I know Venice better, and have no doubt that if I had entered some slatternly dockside tavern that evening, and put my case to the ill-shaved sinner behind the bar, he would have lent me the money in a trice, and thrown in a glass of sour white wine as a bonus. Compassion really is a powerful emotion among the simpler Venetians. In the eighteenth century the idea of pain was so insufferable to them that even characters in a play, if they happened to be killed, had to take a quick posthumous bow, to reassure the anxious audience, and accept its sympathetic cries of '*Bravo i morti!*' This is a melancholy city at heart, and its inhabitants are constantly shaking their heads in pity over some pathetic new evidence of the world's sadness. When a visitor from Bologna was drowned in the Grand Canal one evening, my housekeeper was almost in tears about him next day; and when a funeral goes by to the cemetery of San Michele, you may hear the onlookers muttering to themselves in condolence: 'Oh, the poor one, oh, dead, dead, poor thing – ah, away he goes, away to San Michele, *il povero!*'

Bad weather, too, is a subject for tender distress; and the fate of poor Venice herself, once so powerful; and sometimes a stroke of international ill fortune, a train accident in Uruguay, the failure of a conference, a princess unmarried or a sportsman discarded, summons a brief gleam of poignancy into the Venetian eye. Searing indeed is the sorrow that lingers for months, even years, after the death of a second cousin, so that the very mention of the cemetery is enough to send a mask of mourning fleeting across the bereaved features: and whenever the Venetian woman mentions her dear Uncle Carlo, who passed to a higher realm, as you will have long ago discovered, on 18 September 1936 – the mere thought of Uncle Carlo, and the whole business of the day must be momentarily suspended.

There is a trace of the morbid to this soft-heartedness. Venetians are fascinated by dead things, horrors, prisons, freaks and malformations. They love to talk, with a mixture of heartburn and abhorrence, about the islands of hospitals and lunatic asylums that ring Venice like an incantation, and to demonstrate with chilling gestures the violence of some of the poor inmates. Fierce was their disappointment when the corpse of their beloved Pius X, laid in state in its crystal coffin, turned out to have a gilded mask for a face (he had been dead for forty years, and they were curious about his condition).

There is something Oriental, too, about the predictability of their emotions. A sort of etiquette or formality summons the tears that start so instantaneously into the eyes of Maria, when you mention her poor relative, as if her affliction were no more than an antique ritual, like the wailing of hired mourners at an Egyptian funeral. It is a custom in Venice, as elsewhere in Italy, to announce deaths by posting notices in shops and cafés, often with a photograph; and elaborate is the sadness of the people you may sometimes see distributing these announcements, and extraordinary its contagiousness, so that for a few moments after their departure the whole café is plunged in gloom, and the very hiss of the espresso machine is muffled.

. A streak of sentimentality runs through Venetian life, surprising in a city of such stringy fibre. A Venetian crowd usually has a soft spot for the under-dog, and the last competitor in the regatta always gets a kindly cheer. I once saw the aftermath of a fight between two youths, beside the Rialto bridge. One was a willowy, handsome young man, who had placed a tray of packages on the stone steps beside him, and was engulfed in tears; the other a bronzed, tough and square-cut fish-boy, a Gothic boy, with a stentorian voice and a fist like iron. The slender youth was appealing to the crowd for justice, his voice breaking with grievances, now and then hoisting his shirt from his trousers to exhibit his bruises. The fish-boy was pacing up and down like a caged lion, sporadically pushing through the spectators to project an insult, now spitting, now giving his opponent a contemptuous shove or a grimace of mockery. My own sympathies were whole-heartedly with this uncouth ruffian, a Venetian of the old school: but the crowd clustered protectively about the other, and a woman ushered him tearfully towards the Rialto, out of harm's way, amid murmured commiserations on all sides. One man only held himself aloof, and seemed to share my sympathies. He was a dwarf, a little man dressed all in black, with a beret on his head, who stood on tiptoe at the back of the crowd, peering between its agitated shoulders: but I was mistaken, for when I caught this person's eye, and offered him a guilty and conspiratorial smile, he stared back at me balefully, as you might look at an unrepentant matricide, or a man with a well-known penchant for cruelty to babies.

There are many such dwarfs and hunchbacks in Venice, as observers have noted for hundreds of years, and they too are treated with kindness (though there used to be a superstition to the effect that you must keep thirty paces away from a lame man, which perhaps contributed to Lord Byron's well-known reluctance to appear in the Piazza in daylight). Many are given jobs as sacristans or cleaners in churches, and flit like smiling gnomes among their shadowy chancels. There are also many and varied originals, women a-flutter with scarves and anachronistic skirts, men talking angrily into the night from the parapets of bridges. Artists are really artists in Venice, and meet jovially to eat enormous meals in taverns. In the spring evenings a group of apparently demented girls used to dance beside the Grand Canal outside my window, and sometimes in the middle of the night you will hear a solitary opera-lover declaiming Tosca into the darkness from the poop of a water-bus. Foreigners of blatant individualism have always frequented Venice, from George Sand in tight trousers at the Danieli to Orson Welles massively in Harry's Bar: but they have never disconcerted the Venetians, long accustomed to the extremes of human behaviour. At the height of the Venetian autocracy, in the fifteenth century, a well-known exhibitionist used to parade the canals in a gondola, shouting abuse at the régime and demanding the instant obliteration of all aristocrats everywhere. He was never molested, for even the stern Council of Ten had a soft spot for the eccentric.

You may also be drunk in Venice, oddly enough, without antagonizing the town. Though most proper Venetians have lost their taste for the bawdy, and are a demure conventional people, nevertheless their evenings are frequently noisy with drunks. Often they are visitors, or seamen from the docks, but their clamour echoes indiscriminately through the high walls and water-canyons of the place, and sometimes makes the midnight hideous. In Venice you may occasionally see a man thrown forcibly from a bar, all arms and muddled protests, just like in the films; and rollicking are the songs the Venetian students sing, when they have some wine inside them. I once heard a pair of inebriates passing my window at four o'clock on a May morning, and looking out into the Rio San Trovaso I saw them riding by in a gondola. They were sitting on the floor of the boat, drumming on its floor-boards, banging its seats, singing and shouting incoherently at the tops of their thickened voices: but on the poop of the gondola, rowing with an easy, dry, worldly stroke, an elderly grey-haired gondolier propelled them aloofly towards the dawn.

9 Minorities

The practical tolerance of Venice has always made it a cosmopolitan city, where east and west mingle, and where (as Shakespeare rightly said) 'the trade and profit of this State consisteth of all nations'. Settlers of many races contributed to the power and texture of the Republic, as you can see from the paintings of the masters, which often picture turbaned Moors and Turks among the crowds, and sometimes even negro gondoliers. Venice in its commercial prime was like a bazaar city, or a caravanserai, where the Greeks, the Jews, the Armenians and the Dalmatians all had their quarters, and the Germans and the Turks their great emporia. One of the pillars of the Doge's Palace illustrates this diversity: for there, side by side upon a column-head, are the faces of a Persian, a Latin, a Tartar, a Turk, a Greek, a Hungarian, a bearded Egyptian and a surprisingly inocuous Goth. (We need not suppose, though, that the old Venetians had many illusions about equality. Around the corner there are eight more faces, on another capital: seven are hideous, one is handsome, and this 'thin, thoughtful and dignified portrait', says Ruskin, 'thoroughly fine in every way', is meant to express the 'superiority of the Venetian character over that of other nations'.)

Of all these alien residents the most resilient have been the Jews, who enjoyed a position in medieval Venice half-way between protection and persecution. They first came to the city in 1373, as refugees from the mainland, and were originally forced to live (or so most historians seem to think) on the island of Giudecca, which may be named after them, or may come from the word 'judicato', implying that it was 'adjudged' a suitable place for Jews, vagabonds and rogues. In the sixteenth century the first of all the Ghettos was instituted for them, in the north-western part of the city. It was on the site of a disused ironworks – the word 'ghetto' is thought to have been medieval Venetian for a foundry – and all the Jews, now suddenly supplemented by fugitives from the wars of the League of Cambrai, were forced to live in it.

They had to wear a special costume (first a yellow hat, later a red); they were relentlessly taxed on every conceivable pretext; they had to pay through the nose for permission, frequently renewable, to remain in the city at all. Their Ghetto was windowless on its outside walls, to cut it off entirely from the rest of the city, and its gates were locked at sunset. Christian guards (paid, of course, by the Jews) prevented all entry or exit after dark. Yet though the Jews were so harshly circumscribed, and squeezed for all financial advantage, they were physically safer in Venice than almost anywhere else in Europe. The Venetians found them useful. Once or twice there were the usual canards about Jewish baby-burners; in 1735 the official commissioners appointed to govern the affairs of the Jews had to report that the Ghetto was bankrupt; but over the centuries the Venetian Jews, protected against public violence or religious fanaticism, enjoyed periods of high prosperity and prestige.

In the seventeenth century the ladies of the Ghetto were described as 'gorgeous in their apparel, jewels, chains of gold and rings adorned with precious stones . . . having marvellous long trains like Princesses that are borne up by waiting women serving for the same purpose'. Henry VIII consulted a learned Venetian Jew when he was planning his divorce suit against Katherine of Aragon. Some of the rabbis of Venice were celebrated throughout Europe, and it became a fashionable practice for visitors to attend a sermon in a Ghetto synagogue. Napoleon abolished the Ghetto in 1797: and when, in 1848, the Venetians rebelled against their Austrian masters, their leader was half-Jewish, and Jewish brain-power gave the revolutionary Republic its astonishing financial stability.

People have often observed an affinity between Venetians and Jews – a common aptitude for money-making, a similar sense of wry humour, a shared feeling of national exclusion. One Edwardian visitor wrote of the 'Hebrew bearing' of the priests of St Mark's.

Somebody else has mentioned the conviction with which Venetian painters depicted Old Testament patriarchs. Today it is very difficult to tell who is a Jew in Venice. Lord Fisher, who had British Israelite sympathies, used to say that the faces of the Lost Tribes were obviously different from those of the other Jews, 'otherwise they wouldn't be lost': but often the male Venetian face, grave and meditative, has a striking Jewish cast to it, redolent of Venice's Eastern commerce, and the infusions of Oriental culture (and blood, too) that have enriched the city down the centuries.

There are still about 800 Jews in Venice. Some still live in the three sections of the Ghetto, *Vecchio, Nuovo, Nuovissimo* – Old, New and Newest: the story goes that when Napoleon's soldiers threw open the gates, the inmates were so debilitated that they had not the strength to move, and have stayed there ever since. Many more live in other parts of the city. They are mostly middle-class citizens and professional men – only a few are very rich – and they retain a strong sense of community. The tall teeming houses of the Ghetto are still poor, and the canal behind them, upon which the guards used to float watchfully about in scows, is usually thick with slime and refuse: but there is a comfortable Jewish old people's home, and a well-endowed meeting hall, and an interesting little museum. The Jewish cemetery on the Lido island, once Byron's riding-ground and a playing field for ribald adolescents, is now handsomely maintained. Of the five Ghetto synagogues – one originally for Levantine Jews, one for Spaniards, one for Italians and two for Germans – two are still used for services (another is part of the museum, and the rest are high and inaccessible in tenement blocks).

If you visit one on the day of the Passover, you may see how trim, bright and gregarious the Venetian Jews are today. The Rabbi stands hunched and scholarly on his high dais. The usher wears his tall top-hat at a rakish angle. A few well-dressed women peer down from the oval gallery, high in the ceiling of the synagogue. On the men's side of the floor the congregation sits placid or devout: on the women's side there is a flurry of bright dresses and floral hats, a bustle of starched children, a cheerful buzz of gossip and a veil of perfume (*Ca' d'Oro*, perhaps, named for a palace on the Grand Canal, or *Evenings in*

Venice, with a blue gondola and a pair of lovers on the package). All seems vigorous and uninhibited, and it is moving to remember, as the porter at the door ushers you politely into the sunshine, that you are standing in the middle of the very first of all the sad Ghettos of the world.

On the walls outside, though, two inscriptions are worth reading before you leave the place. One is a sixteenth-century notice declaring the intention of the Republican magistrates to repress the sin of blasphemy, as committed both by Jews proper and by converted Jews. 'They have therefore ordered this proclamation to be carved in stone in the most frequented part of the Ghetto, and threaten with the cord, stocks, whip, galleys or prisons all who are guilty of blasphemy. Their Excellencies offer to receive secret denunciations and to reward informers by a sum of a hundred ducats to be taken from the property of the offender under conviction.'

The other inscription is a modern one. It records the fact that of the 8,000 Italian Jews who lost their lives in the Second World War, 200 were Venetians. From the first plaque the Jews, presumably at the fall of the Republic, have roughly removed the image of the Lion of St Mark, symbol of their servitude: but the second plaque they put up themselves.

At the other end of the city, beyond the Piazza of St Mark, stood the Greek quarter of Venice, once thriving, rich and assured. Only a century ago the Greek colony lent a familiar splash of colour to the city, and had its own meeting-places and restaurants, and even its own café in the Piazza. Venice once paid hazy allegiance to the Byzantine Emperors, and though the Venetians later quarrelled violently with Constantinople, and engineered the temporary downfall of the Greek Empire, nevertheless the Serenissima was always close to the world of the Greeks, and deeply influenced by its ways. The Greeks, grocers and money-lenders to the Levant, were money-lenders here too, and flourished in many a minor business in the days before visas and import licences. For several centuries they fluctuated in religious loyalty between Rome and Constantinople, one bishop playing a double game with such conspicuous ineptitude that he was simultaneously excommunicated both by the Pope and by the Oecumenical Patriarch. The Government did not often press the issue, for it welcomed the presence of the prosperous Greek merchants, and until 1781 the Greek Church in Venice maintained a precarious communion with Rome, only becoming frankly schismatic when Napoleon proclaimed liberty of conscience throughout conquered Venetia.

In the heyday of the colony there were 10,000 Greeks in Venice. They established a school, the Phlangineion, which became one of the great centres of Greek culture abroad, when the Turks overran the homeland. Longhena designed a building for it, which still stands, and Sansovino built the adjacent church of San Giorgio dei Greci. Many of the most brilliant Venetian courtesans were Greeks. In the sixteenth and seventeenth centuries Greek wines were drunk at all the best Venetian tables. Many Greeks of great wealth came to Venice after the fall of Constantinople, and Venetians sometimes owned, when the political winds were blowing right, villas and gardens in the Morea.

Even now you are never far from Greece in Venice. Not only are there the Byzantine treasures of the city, and the Greek overtones to its history and culture: almost any summer day you may see a sleek white Greek steamer, a breath of the Aegean, sailing in with the morning tide, or embarking its befurred and portly passengers for an archaeological cruise. There is a Greek Consul in Venice, and a Greek institute of Byzantine studies: and sometimes in the season one of the prodigious Greek magnates will land at St Mark's from the tender of his yacht, with his dazzling mistress or his complacent wife, his immaculate captain and his sleek secretaries, bringing to these severe porticoes a full-blown vision of the merchant-venturers.

The colony itself survives, though it has dwindled to about fifty members. You can see it almost in its entirety, supplemented by a few resident Russians, at a feast-day service in San Giorgio dei Greci, now unashamedly Orthodox. The ceremonials there are beautifully calm and mysterious, set against a background of dim shimmering ikons and golden crosses. Much of the service, in the Greek way, is conducted at an inner altar, invisible to the congregation: but in the body of the church the people observe their own devotions with an impressive lack of self-consciousness, walking up the nave all alone with elaborate crossings and genuflections, to kneel before a crucifix; entering the sanctum, apparently unannounced, to receive the personal blessing of the priest; singing the canticles in a style by no means flippant or irreverent, but oddly detached. When the priest emerges from the curtains of the altar, black-hatted and heavily bearded, and passes gravely down the nave with his censer, all those Greeks bow gracefully at his passing, allowing the incense to flow around their heads, as the Arabs use it to sweeten their beards.

There are still Armenians in Venice, too. They have a famous monastery on one of the islands of the lagoon, and they have a church, Santa Croce degli Armeni, tucked away in the Alley of the Armenians, near San Giuliano. The Armenians formed the oldest of the foreign communities in Venice. They were firmly established at the beginning of the twelfth century, and their position was consolidated when a Doge who had made a fortune in their country left part of it to establish an Armenian headquarters in Venice. The Armenians were merchants, shopkeepers, financiers, money-lenders, pawnbrokers (they paid depositors partly in money, but partly in watered white wine, just as the coloured labourers of the Cape used to be paid in tots). It is said that the plague first came into Venice with Armenian immigrants, but they were never harried or victimized: in Venice, as a sixteenth-century Englishman observed, it signified nothing 'if a man be a Turk, a Jew, a Gospeller, a Papist or a believer in the Devil; nor does anyone challenge you, whether you are married or not, and whether you eat flesh and fish in your own home'.

A few Armenians still live in the Alley of the Armenians, and any Sunday morning you will find seven or eight people, mostly women, attending Mass in the church (the Armenian Church, the oldest Established church in the world, is nowadays split between Catholics and Orthodox: the Armenians in Venice are in communion with Rome). It is a strange little building. Its campanile, now silent, is so surrounded by tall buildings and chimneys that you can hardly see it: its façade is unobtrusively hidden away in a row of houses, and only the cross on the door shows that it is a church at all. Inside it is shabby but brightly decorated, and the floor of the vestibule is covered with memorial slabs, extolling the virtues of eminent Venetian Armenians – 'He lived as a Lion', says one, 'Died as a Swan, and will Rise as a Phoenix.' The congregations are usually poorly dressed: and though the priest has splendid vestments, and conducts the services with lordly grace, his solemn young acolyte will probably be wearing blue jeans and a pullover. A sense of ancient continuity informs the proceedings, for the church of Santa Croce stands on the very same site that was given to the Armenian community by that indulgent Doge, eight centuries ago.

The Germans, whose links with Venice are old and profitable, also have their church in the city: the chapel of the Lutherans, which has, since 1813, occupied a comfortable first-floor room near the church of Santi Apostoli. Its congregations are small but extremely well dressed; its lighting is discreetly subdued; and on the door a notice says: 'The service is conducted in German: do not disturb.'

For a taste of Venetian Englishry, go on a summer morning to the Anglican Church of St George, which is a converted warehouse near the Accademia bridge. Its pews are usually full, and the familiar melodies of Ancient and Modern stream away, turgid but enthusiastic, across the Grand Canal. The drone of the visiting padre blends easily with the hot buzz of the Venetian summer, and when the service ends you will see his surplice fluttering in the doorway, among the neat hats and tweedy suits, the white gloves and prayerbooks, the scrubbed children and the pink-cheeked, tight-curled, lavender-scented, pearl-necklaced, regimentally brooched ladies that so admirably represent, year in, year out, east and west, the perennial spirit of England abroad.

The English have always been familiar to the Venetians (and there are astonishing parallels between the histories of the two peoples). There was a regular service of fifteenth-century galleys between Venice and Southampton; each rower was a business man himself, and took a little private merchandise under his seat, to peddle in the Hampshire lanes on his own account. Venetian ships also put in at

Rye, Sandwich, Deal, and the other south coast ports of England, now almost as dead as the Serenissima herself. The private Church of England chapel maintained by Sir Henry Wotton, the English Ambassador, was one of the causes of Venice's worst quarrels with the Holy See. Petrarch, describing a Venetian festival in the fourteenth century, says that among the honoured guests were some English noblemen, 'comrades and kinsmen of their King', who had come to Venice with their ships on a navigational exercise. English captains and soldiers often fought in the Venetian cause, and the English, in return, sometimes hired Venetian ships and sailors.

In the nineteenth century, when Venice was in the doldrums, it was the complacent English who founded her romantic cult: Browning among the splendours of the Ca' Rezzonico (as it says in a plaque on the wall: *'Open my heart and you will see, Graven inside of it, Italy'*); Byron swimming home along the Grand Canal after a *soirée*, with a servant carrying his clothes in the gondola behind; Shelley watching the sun go down behind the Euganean Hills; Cobden fêted at a banquet on Giudecca, with an ear of corn in every guest's button-hole; Ruskin, for fifty years the arbiter of taste on Venice, and still the author of the most splendid descriptions of the city in the English language. In Victorian times the English community even had its own herd of seventeen cows, kept in a Venetian garden in imperial disregard of the rules, and providing every subscribing member with a fresh pint daily.

The Americans, too, were soon well known in Venice. W. D. Howells wrote a charming book about the place a century ago, before he turned to novel-writing: he was United States consul in the city, an agreeable sinecure granted him as a reward for writing an effective campaign biography of Abraham Lincoln. Another consul, Donald Mitchell, wrote a once-popular book called *Reveries of a Bachelor*, under the pseudonym of 'Ik Marvel'. Henry James wrote hauntingly about the city, and lived for a time in a house on the Grand Canal. Rich Americans, following the English fashion, took to buying or renting old palaces for the season, and one generous lady, when she died, left a house to each of her gondoliers. In the days when Americanism was synonymous with all that was free, generous, and sensible, the prestige of the United States was very high in Venice. The sculptor Canova was honorary President of the Philadelphia Academy of Fine Arts, and when a team of gondoliers took their craft to the Chicago World Fair, so I am told, they came home to Venice as heroes, and lived comfortably on the experience for the rest of their lives.

Nowadays the Venetian summer blazes with affluent visitors, but only a minority of foreign plutocrats prefers a rented palace to an air-conditioned hotel suite. In the winter there are very few foreign residents at all, apart from students at the University and at various language schools – probably less than a hundred, most of them from English-speaking countries. Gondoliers will sometimes tell you, to make you feel at home, that the palace you are passing is owned by an English lady (very beautiful) or an American diplomat (very wealthy); but they are generally years out of date with their information, and picked it up in childhood from the reminiscences of retired predecessors.

10 Melancholia

In Venice the past and the present are curiously interwoven, as in the minds of very old ladies, who are apt to ask if that dullard Mr Baldwin is still Prime Minister, and sometimes complain petulantly about the ill-treatment of cab-horses. The Venetians have never quite re-covered from their loss of glory, and have perhaps never quite accepted it, so that somewhere in the backs of their minds their city is still the Serenissima, the Bride of the Adriatic, the Eye of Italy, Lord of a Quarter and a Half-Quarter of the Roman Empire – dignities which seem to have varied in gender, but never in magnificence. This combination of resignation and persistence gives the people their quality of melancholy, a lagoon-like sadness, unruffled and dry. Melancholia contributes strongly to the Venetian atmosphere, whether it is expressed in overgrown gardens or nostalgic verse: and a Venetian once even wrote a play about 'the fundamental melan-choly of sexual passions'.

A century ago, when the Republic was still alive in the world's mind, the spectacle of Venice subdued was a good deal more poignant than it is now, and Englishmen, in particular, took a chill pleasure in examining the ruins of the Serenissima from the pinnacle of British success. 'In the history of mankind', observed one Victorian writer, 'three peoples have been pre-eminently great and powerful – the Romans in ancient times, the Venetians in the Middle Ages, the English in modern days.'

Men are we [said Wordsworth magnanimously], *and must grieve*
   when even the Shade
Of that which once was great is passed away.

The Victorian celebrants of Venice loved to draw sententious conclusions from her humiliation, and saw in the downfall of the Republic either a vindication of their own political system, or an awful portent of things to come.

Today it is too old a story. The world has forgotten the mighty fleets of Venice, her formidable commanders and her pitiless inquisitions. The dungeons of the Doge's Palace have lost their horror, to the generation of Auschwitz and Hiroshima; and even power itself seems too frail and fickle a commodity to waste our lyrics on. The Venetians may still half-mourn their vanished empire, but to the foreigner the sadness of Venice is a much more nebulous abstraction, a wistful sense of wasted purpose and lost nobility, a suspicion of degradation, a whiff of hollow snobbery, the clang of the turnstile and the sing-song banalities of the guides, knit together with crumbling masonries, suffused in winter twilight.

For a time this people constituted the first Power of the western world. Such a tremendous experience in the life of a community can never be expunged, except by physical destruction, and everywhere in Venice there are still reminders of her political prime, like India Offices in Whitehall, or the great Imperial Square of Isfahan.

The Republic sent its ambassadors to the capitals of the earth, and in return the Powers maintained missions of high importance in Venice, with elaborate fleets of diplomatic gondolas, and splendid crested palaces. The ghosts of these establishments have not yet been thoroughly exorcized. The old Austrian Embassy, on the Grand Canal, is still called the Palace of the Ambassadors. The Spanish Embassy is remembered in the Lista di Spagna, near the station (I have been told that any Venetian street called a *lista* has old diplomatic connotations). The palace of the Papal Legates, near San Francesco della Vigna, has given its name, agreeably corrupted, to the Salizzada delle Gatte – the Paved Alley of the Female Cats. The English Embassy, in Wotton's time, was in a palace near Santa Maria dei Miracoli. The Russian Embassy was in a house at the junction of Rio San Trovaso and the Grand Canal, around which there still hangs (at least to the imaginative) a faint evocation of sables and sledges. Rousseau was once secretary to the French Ambasssador; Wotton kept an ape in his palace, and collected lutes and Titians; the Venetians just had time, before their downfall, to exchange letters with the infant United States. (One of the earliest American Consulates was opened in the city soon afterwards, and wonderfully authentic have been the names of its various consuls – Sparks, Flagg, Corrigan, Gerrity, Ferdinand L. Sarmento and John Q. Wood.) In the great days of the Republic appointment to an embassy in Venice was one of the most coveted of diplomatic promotions.

All these splendours died with the Republic. The decline of Venice had been protracted and painful. It began with Vasco da Gama's great voyage, which broke her eastern monopolies: but for three more centuries the Serenissima retained her independence, sinking, through infinite declensions of emasculation, from power to luxury, from luxury to flippancy, from flippancy to impotence. Her wide Mediterranean Empire was lost in bits and pieces – Negroponte, Rhodes, Cyprus, Crete, the Ionian islands, the Peloponnese, all to the rampant Turks. By the eighteenth century Venice was the most unwarlike State in Europe. 'The English use their powder for their cannon,' said a contemporary Italian observer, 'the French for their mortars. In Venice it is usually damp, and if it is dry they use it for fireworks.' Venetian soldiers were 'without honour, without discipline, without clothes – it is impossible to name one honourable action they have performed'. Addison described the purposes of Venetian domestic policy as being 'to encourage idleness and luxury in the nobility, to cherish ignorance and licentiousness in the clergy, to keep alive a continual faction in the common people, to connive at viciousness and debauchery in the convents'. Eighteenth-century Venice was a paradigm of degradation. Her population had declined from 170,000 in her great days to 96,000 in 1797 (though the Venetian Association of Hairdressers still had 852 members). Her trade had vanished, her aristocracy was hopelessly effete, and she depended for her existence upon the tenuous good faith of her neighbours.

No wonder Napoleon swept her aside. The Venetians, temporizing and vacillating, offered him no real resistance, and he ended their Republic with a brusque gesture of dismissal: *'Io non voglio più Inquisitori, non voglio più Senato; sarò un Attila per lo stato Veneto'* – 'I want no more Inquisitors, no more Senate: I will be an Attila for the Venetian State.' The last of the Doges, limply abdicating, handed his ducal hat to his servant with the febrile comment: 'Take it away, we shan't be needing it again.' (The servant did what he was told, and kept it as a souvenir.) The golden horses of the Basilica, the lion from his pedestal in the Piazzetta, many of the treasures of St Mark's, many of the pictures of the Doge's Palace, many precious books and documents – all were taken away to Paris, rather as so many of them had been stolen from Constantinople in the first place. Some diamonds from St Mark's Treasury were set in Josephine's crown, and a large statue of Napoleon was erected on Sansovino's library building, opposite the Doge's Palace. The last ships of the Venetian Navy were seized to take part in an invasion of Ireland: but when this was cancelled they were sent instead to be sunk by Nelson at Aboukir.

The Great Council itself ended the aristocratic Government of Venice, by a vote of 512 yeas to 30 nays and 5 blanks, and for the words *'Pax Tibi Marce'*, inscribed on the Venetian lion's open book, there was substituted the slogan 'Rights and Duties of Men and Citizens'. 'At last,' observed a gondolier in a phrase that has become proverbial – 'at last he's turned over a new leaf.' The dungeons of the Doge's Palace were thrown open: but according to Shelley only one old man was found inside them, and he was dumb. Even the poisons of the Council of Three had gone stale, and could hardly kill a fly.

*

It was the end of an era: for Venice, for Europe, for the world. There was, however, one final resurgence of national fire before Venice, united at last with the mainland, became just another Italian provincial capital. She was passed by the French to the Austrians; by the Austrians back to the French; after Waterloo, to the Austrians again: and in 1848, when half Europe rebelled against Vienna, the Venetians rose to arms too, proclaimed themselves a Republic again, expelled their Austrian occupiers, and defied the might of the Empire.

Times had drastically changed since 1797, and her leaders this time were men of the middle classes – professional men, lawyers, academics, soldiers. The difference in morale was astonishing. The president of the revolutionary republic was Daniele Manin, a half-Jewish lawyer who bore the same surname as the last of the Doges, and was determined to restore its honour. The Government he established was able, honest and popular. It was no mere nationalist protest body, but a fully organized administration, running Venice as a city-State. The revolutionaries published their own Official Gazette; opened correspondence with the British and French Governments, without getting any support from them; and printed their own paper money, which was widely accepted. The London *Times* said of them: 'Venice has again found within her walls men capable of governing, and people always worthy to be free.' The citizenry, in a last surge of the old spirit, made great personal sacrifices to sustain this brave campaign. One man gave a palace on the Grand Canal, another an estate on the mainland, a third a painting by Leonardo da Vinci. Some of the remaining treasure of St Mark's was sold to raise war funds, and more was melted down for bullion. Except for Venetian elements of the Austrian Navy, which had long since been demoralized, all sections of the population seem to have behaved, by and large, with honour: and at one period Manin himself was recognized, a bespectacled private in the Civic Guard, on sentry-go in the Piazza.

But the cause was hopeless. The revolution began in March 1848 – Via Marzo 22, the main western approach to the Piazza, is named for the day – and for a full year Venice was invested by the Austrians.

The lagoon was vigilantly blockaded. Austrian shells, lobbed from the mainland, fell in many parts of the city, and are still to be seen, stuck together like glutinous candies, decorating war memorials or embedded in the façades of churches. Provisions ran desperately short, cholera broke out. Without foreign help, the Venetians had hardly a chance, and in August 1849 the Austrian General Gorzkowsky accepted Manin's surrender and reoccupied the city. Manin was exiled, with thirty-nine of his colleagues, to Paris, where he survived for the rest of his days by giving Italian lessons to young ladies: only to return to the vast, dark, awful tomb that lies beneath the northern flank of St Mark's.

Venice subsided into sullen thraldom, boycotting everything Austrian, even the military band in the Piazza. Long after the triumph of the Risorgimento, when all the rest of Italy (bar Rome) was free, she remained subject to Vienna: until in 1866, after the Prusso-Austrian war, Bismarck rewarded the new Italy for her support by handing her the Serenissima. Venice became part of the Italian Kingdom, and was an entity no more.

Since then she has been a port, an art centre, something of a factory: but above all a showplace. In the First World War she was a base for the Italian operations against the Austrians: two-thirds of her people were removed elsewhere, and from the Campanile you could see the observation balloons above the front-line trenches. During Mussolini's régime she was an obediently Fascist city, her inhabitants soon discovering that jobs were easier to get and keep if you toed the party line. In the Second World War, though there was sporadic and sometimes heroic partisan activity in the city, the Venetians only offered serious resistance to the Germans in 1945, when the result was a foregone conclusion anyway. As for the British, when they took Venice in the last days before the Armistice, they found only two classes of opposition: one from gondoliers, who demanded a higher tariff; the other from motor-boat owners who, reluctant to see their pampered craft requisitioned yet again by the rough soldiery, did their best to smuggle them away to Como or Lake Garda.

The Venetians are no longer lordly. They were great a long time ago, and nobody expects them to be great again. No patriotic diehards writhe in impotence, to see their great Republic prostituted. The enormous Archives of the State have become no more than a scholar's curiosity. The Doge's Palace, the most splendid assembly hall on earth, is a museum. The Venetians have long since settled in their groove of resignation, and there remains only an old essence of power, a pomade of consequence, an echo of trumpet-calls (provided by the string orchestra at the Quadri, stringing away irrepressibly, its rigid smiles tinged with despair, at the rhythms of *Colonel Bogey*).

Gone are the great diplomats, the sealed crimson despatch-boxes, the secret liaisons, the Austrian Envoy in his box at the opera, His Excellency the Ambassador of The Most Christian Kingdom presenting his credentials to the Illustrious Signory of The Most Serene Republic. There are only Consulates in Venice nowadays. The Americans, the Argentinians, the Brazilians, the British, the French, the Greeks, the Panamanians and the Swiss all maintain 'career consuls': the rest are represented by Italians. The Americans own a house near San Gregorio. The British rent an apartment beside the Accademia (three-quarters of their work is concerned with the Commonwealth, rather than the United Kingdom). The Argentinians and the Danes live on the Grand Canal. The French live elegantly on the Zattere. The Panamanians have a villa on the Lido. The Monagesques occupy an uncharacteristically tumble-down house behind San Barnaba. The others are scattered here and there across the city, in back-alleys and culs-de-sac, or high on second floors.

Only three Consulates – the American, the British and the French – can afford to run their own motor boats, and when a number of Latin American consuls devised a scheme for sharing one, obvious difficulties of temperament and economy killed it. Only the Argentinians, the French and the Panamanians maintain Consuls-General in Venice, and the Russians maintain nobody at all, their old Embassy being converted into an unusually comfortable *pension*. Some of the consulates have wider responsibilities on the mainland: but there is an inescapably vacuous, faded flavour to the diplomatic corps of Venice today, and the consuls are largely occupied in comforting disconsolate tourists, pacifying the Italian authorities after sordid dock-side brawls, anxiously living it up with the socialites, or helping with cocktail invitations for visiting warships.

Just before Lent each year the city enjoys a brief season of Carnival. Recently this has become one of Europe's great sprees, drawing thousands of visitors and giving new life to hotels and restaurants at a formerly moribund time of the year. The jet-set loves it, its images get into all the fashionable magazines, and the making and selling of its masks appears to give the city a whole new industry and art form.

Not so long ago, though, what then seemed to be the last echoes of the legendary Venetian Carnival were full of pathos. Its chief celebrants in those days were the children of Venice, who bought their funny faces and moustaches from the chain stores and emerged to saunter through the city in fancy dress: here a devil, here a harlequin, a three-foot-three Red Indian, an infant Spanish dancer, matadors and Crusader ladies and gypsy girls, with real flowers in their baskets and vivid smudges of lipstick on their faces. Each exotic little figure walked alone with its family – the matador had no bull, the Spanish princess no serenader, the clown no tumbling partner; and they used to parade the Riva degli Schiavoni in prim and anxious demurity (for it would never do to crumple the feathers of a Venetian Sioux, or dirty a freshly laundered wimple).

On the final day of this celebration I was once walking home through the spider's web of little lanes and yards that surrounds the noble Franciscan church of the Frari; and as I turned a corner I saw before me, in a hurried glimpse, three small figures crossing a square from one lane to another. In the middle walked a thin little man, his overcoat rather too long for him and buttoned down the front, his gloves very neat, his hat very precise, his shoes very polished. Clutching his right hand was a tiny pierrot, his orange pom-pom waggling in the half-light. Clutching his left hand was a minuscule fairy, her legs wobbly in white cotton, her skirt infinitesimal, her wand warped a little with the excitement and labour of the day. Quickly, silently and carefully they crossed the square and disappeared from view: the fairy had to skip a bit to keep up, the pierrot cherished a sudden determination to walk only on the lines between the paving-stones, and the little man trod a precarious tight-rope between the indulgent and the conventional.

How small they looked, and respectable, I thought to myself! How carefully their mother had prepared them, all three, to survive the scrutiny of their neighbours! How dull a time they had spent on the quayside, walking self-consciously up and down! How thin a reflection they offered of Venice's rumbustious carnivals of old, her Doges and her masked patricians, her grand lovers, her tall warships and her princely artists! How touching the little Venetians, tight buttoned in their alley-ways!

But as I meditated in this patronizing way my eyes strayed upwards, above the tumbled walls of the courtyard, above the gimcrack company of chimneys, above the television aerials and the gobbling pigeons in their crannies, to where the great tower of the Frari, regal and assured, stood like a red-brick admiral against the blue.

THE CITY

11 Ex-Island

Venice stands, as she loves to tell you, on the frontiers of east and west, half-way between the setting and the rising sun. Goethe calls her 'the market-place of the Morning and the Evening lands'. Certainly no city on earth gives a more immediate impression of symmetry and unity, or seems more patently born to greatness. On the map Venice looks like a fish; or a lute, Evelyn thought; or perhaps a pair of serpents locked in death-struggle; or a kangaroo, head down for a leap. But to understand the modern topography of the place, you must throw the street plans away and go to the top of the great Campanile of St Mark, above the bustling Piazza. You can make the ascent by lift: but if you prefer to take a horse, like the Emperor Frederick III, there is a spiral ramp for your convenience.

From the bell-chamber of this great tower, once you have fought off the itinerant photographers and the picture-postcard sellers, you can see how curiously compact and undistracted is the shape of Venice. To the north stand the heavenly Alps, beyond the Treviso plain, sprinkled with snow and celestially silent; to the south is the Adriatic, a grim but handsome sea; around you stretches the Venetian lagoon, morose but fascinating, littered with islands. The horizons are wide, the air is crystalline, the wind blows gustily from the south; and in the very centre of it all, lapped in mud-banks, awash in history, lies the Serenissima.

By a paradox of perspective, there is not a canal to be seen from the bell-chamber, only a jumbled, higgledy-piggledy mass of red-tiled roofs, chimneys, towers, television aerials, delectable roof gardens, flapping washing, sculptured saints and elaborate weather-vanes: and the effect is not one of overwhelming grandeur, but of medieval intimacy, as though you are eavesdropping upon a fourteenth-century housewife, or prying into a thane's back yard. This is not a large city. You can see it all easily, from one end to the other. It is about two miles long by one mile deep, and you can walk from end to end of it, from the slaughter-house in the north-west to the Public Gardens in the south-east, in an hour and a half – less, if you don't mind shoving. The population of Venice is something over 360,000 but at least two-thirds of these people live in the new mainland suburbs – the big industrial quarter of Mestre and Porto Marghera whose shipyards and shining oil-tanks you can see away to the west.

The city proper shelters perhaps about the same number of inhabitants as Lincoln, say, or Watford. It is built, so they say, on an archipelago of 117 islets (though where an islet begins and a mud-bank ends, the geologists do not seem quite certain); and its canals and alley-ways follow the contours of the myriad rivulets which complicated these shallows before the arrival of the first Venetians. The sub-soil is soft to an average depth of 105 feet; the mean temperature is 56° Fahrenheit; and the altitude of Venice, so one guide book solemnly informs us, is seven feet above sea-level.

If you look beyond the Piazza you will observe a vague declivity among the buildings, as you may sometimes see, across the plains of the American West, the first distant indications of a canyon. This gulf sweeps in three abrupt but majestic curves clean through the city, dividing it into convenient halves. It is the Grand Canal, which follows the course of a river known to the ancients as *Rivo Alto* – the origin of the Rialto. Three bridges cross this tremendous waterway, forty-six side-canals enter it, 200 palaces line it, forty-eight alleys run down to it, ten churches stand upon its banks, the railway station stands gleaming at one end, St Mark's guards the other. It is at once the Seine and the New Jersey Turnpike of Venice, the mirror of her beauty and the highway by which the cargo barges, horns blaring and engines a-blast, chug towards her markets and hotels. The ordinary Venetian canal feels frankly man-made: but most people have to stifle an impulse, now and again, to call the Grand Canal a river.

Around its banks, and on the big neighbouring island of Giudecca, Venice is tightly packed, in six ancient segments. The city is a sequence of villages, a mosaic of old communities. Once each district was a separate island of the archipelago, but they have been jammed together down the centuries, and fused by common experience. Wherever you look from your eyrie you may discern one of these old local centres, with its fine church and its spacious square, its lively market, its homely shops, its banks, its taverns, its private tourist attractions. The very centre of Venice is said to be the pedestal in the middle of Campo San Luca, but the completeness of these various antique settlements means that the city is rich in depth: it has few barren quarters or sterile suburbs. No part of the city, wherever you look, lacks its great monuments or its pungency of character. To the east are the ramparts of the Arsenal, with its frowning tower-gates; to the north-west you may fancy, a blur among the tenements, the grey enclave of the Ghetto; to the south lies the long rib of Giudecca, where the boatmen live; and all around the perimeters of the place range the waterside promenades, lined with steamboats and fishing vessels and bobbing gondolas, a fine white liner at the Zattere, a timber boat from Istria beside the Fondamenta Nuove, where the lagoon sidles away mysteriously to the cemetery-island of San Michele. From the top of the campanile the whole Venetian story seems simple and self-explanatory, and you may let your eye wander directly from the brown sluggish mud-banks that represent the first beginnings of the city, to the golden ornaments and fret-work of St Mark's, memorials of its resplendent climax.

Away to the west, beyond the railway station, a noble double causeway strides across the water to the mainland. The prime fact about twentieth-century Venice is that the city is no longer an island. The causeway is a symbol, at once sad and high-vaulted, of Venice's lost supremacies. In her heyday Venetian communications were entirely maritime, and a highly organized system of boats linked the city with the mainland by four principal routes: through Fusina and the Brenta canal to Padua; through Mestre to Udine and Austria; through Pellestrina and Chioggia to the Po and Lombardy; through Treviso to Friuli. So long as Venice was a city-State, facing the ocean, her difficulties of landward communication were a positive advantage. In the fifteenth century, though, she established a mainland empire, setting up the winged lion in Padua, Ravenna, Verona, Treviso, Vicenza, Brescia, Bergamo, Belluno – half-way across Italy, to the approaches of Milan. Becoming at last a European Power, her outlook slowly changed: and by the final days of the Republic, when she was inextricably entangled in Italian affairs, the idea of a bridge to the mainland was being earnestly discussed. The Doge Foscarini carefully considered it, as a means of injecting some new commercial guts into the flaccid body politic, but decided instead to revive the languishing glass industry and merchant navy. Napoleon, so it is said, ordered his engineers to survey the ground for bridge-piles. A group of Italian business men, in the early 1840s, launched a company to finance a railway line to Venice. And the Austrians, in 1846, actually built a bridge. It linked Venice by rail with Vicenza, and it horrified the world's romantics (Ruskin likened it to 'a low and monotonous dockyard wall, with flat arches to let the tide through it').

It stands there today, 3,000 yards long, supported upon 222 arches, and provided with forty-eight explosive chambers, for easy demolition in emergencies. It brings about 100 passenger trains each day into Santa Lucia station, where the tourists, struggling out of their *wagons-lits*, are whisked bemused into gondolas and launched directly into the Grand Canal. There were once plans to have the trains puffing into the very heart of the city: they were to pass behind Giudecca on an elevated line, and end beside Palladio's church on the islet of San Giorgio Maggiore. Other nineteenth-century visionaries proposed a dual bridge, dividing at the entrance of the city, one part to run away across the lagoon to the Lido and Chioggia, the other to end at the island of Murano, to the north.

One bridge it remained, though, for nearly a century, until the railway line had become an essential part of the Venetian scene, and had extended into a meshwork of sidings beside the docks, and the city had long been accustomed to the wail of its sad steam-whistles in the night (now no longer to be heard, alas, above the hubbub of the motor-boat engines). A prolonged and bitter controversy preceded the building of the second causeway, the road bridge. On the one side stood the *pontisti*, the men of progress, who wanted ever closer links between Venice and the great modern world, with 'the heart of Italy beating against her own': on the other side were the traditionalists, the lovers of things old and honoured, who wished to keep their Venice as close to virginity as was physically possible, and who argued on a spectacular variety of premises, from the danger that a second bridge would stifle the flow of tides and kill the city by malaria, to the possibility that the rumble of cart-wheels would weaken the foundations of its buildings.

Thus they stood as exemplars of a perennial Venetian dispute: whether to modernize the Serenissima, or preserve her. Through any modern book on Venice this problem runs as a *leitmotiv*, tingeing every page with the thought that Venice, as we see her now, may not last much longer, and giving her future a microcosmic quality. The conflict between old and new, between the beautiful and the profitable, between progress and nostalgia, between the spirit and the crank-case, is one that involves us all: and in Venice you may sense it, if you are not too obsessed with the tourist sights, crystallized and in synthesis. It is not decided yet. Even Mussolini at first forbade the building of another bridge, and said that if he could have his way he would destroy the railway too: but in *Anno X* of his dictatorship, 1931, the *pontisti* won their particular campaign, and the motor causeway was completed. It has eight more arches than its companion, and swings away from it, as they enter the city side by side, to end with a bang at the Piazzale Roma in a cruelly expensive clutch of multi-storied car parks.

Consider, as you prop yourself against the wall of the Campanile (you cannot fall out, for there is a wire mesh to prevent suicides) how these two bridges have affected the character of Venice. First, they ended any pretence of insular Republican independence. Manin's forces, it is true, breached the railway bridge and defended it against all comers: but it is almost inconceivable that a city so intimately linked with the mainland could long have maintained its sovereignty, except as a kind of joke or fiscal fiddle. Secondly, the bridges weakened the isolation of the Venetian character. Many more mainland Italians followed the railway into the lagoon; many more Venetians visited the hinterland; the inbred, introspective complex of Venetian society was cracked. Thirdly, the causeways brought an influx of new life and vigour into the city, helping to account for the strange and sudden renaissance of 1848. They fostered trade, they encouraged tourism, and they did something to revive the languishing entrepôt activity of the port.

Finally, the bridges shattered a myth. They dispelled some of the gilded mystery of Venice, laid her open to the Cook's tour and the family motorist, forced her, willy-nilly, half-way into the modern world. She became, as she remains, an ex-island. Modern Venice begins, not at the distant entrances of the lagoon, where the sea shimmers beyond the lighthouses, but down there at the causeway, behind the petrol pumps and the station platforms. When you leave the bell-chamber, clutching your photographer's ticket ('*Reddy in Two Hours, Garanted Perfect*'), and pushing your way diffidently but firmly into the lift, mark the causeways black on your mind's map of Venice, and keep the rose-red for the canals.

12 'Streets Full of Water'

The life-stream of Venice arrives on wheels – her goods and her visitors, even the poor cattle for her municipal slaughter-house: but once at the station or the Piazzale Roma, all this mass of men and material, this daily army, must proceed by water or by foot. Thomas Coryat, before he visited Venice, met an English braggart who claimed to have 'ridden through Venice in post': this was, as Coryat indignantly discovered, 'as gross and palpable a fiction as ever was coyned'. Nobody ever rode through Venice in post, and there are still no proper roads in the city, only footpaths and canals. '*Streets Full of Water*', Robert Benchley cabled home when he first arrived there, '*Please Advise*'.

The only wheels in Venice proper are on porters' trollies, or perambulators, or children's toys, or on the antique bicycles used by a few taciturn knife-sharpeners as the motive force for their grind-stones. To grasp what this means, go down to the causeway in the small hours of the morning, and see the convoys of trucks and trailers that wait there in the half-light to be unloaded – scores of them every morning of the year, parked nose to tail, with their drivers sleepy at the wheel, and their bales and packing-cases bursting from the back. Some of this material will be loaded into ships and taken to sea: but most of it must be conveyed into Venice, on barges, rowing-boats, trollies, and even in huge conical baskets on the backs of men. The bridges of the lagoon have linked Venice irrevocably with the mainland: but she remains a wet-bob city still, in which Chateaubriand, who so rashly complained about her wateriness a century and a half ago, would feel no less irritated today.

The central artery of Venice is the Grand Canal, and from that incomparable highway the smaller canals spring like veins, through which the sustenance of the city is pumped daily, like insulin into the system of a diabetic. There are said to be 177 canals, with a total length of twenty-eight miles. They follow old natural water-courses, and meander unpredictably through the city, now wide, fine and splendid, now indescribably tortuous. The Grand Canal is two miles long; it is seventy-six yards wide at its grandest point, and never less than forty; it has a mean depth of about nine feet (thirteen feet at the Rialto bridge, according to the Admiralty Chart); and it is lively with incessant traffic. Other Venetian waterways are infinitely less imposing – they have an average width of twelve feet, and the average depth of a fair-sized family bath-tub. One canal goes clean under the church of Santo Stefano, and you can take a gondola along it if the tide is low; others are so narrow that only the smallest kind of boat can use them, or so short that there is only just room for their names on the map.

Their usefulness varies according to the tide, and the tide itself varies according to the time of year. The maximum spring tide is probably about seven feet, and the average rise and fall (at the Dogana entrance to the Grand Canal) is just over two feet. These fluctuations drastically alter both the appearance and the efficiency of the city. 'Like the tide – six hours up and six hours down', is how a Venetian saying describes the supposedly mercurial character of the citizenry. When the tide is low, the underpinnings of the Venetian houses are revealed in all their green and slimy secrecy. The bottoms of the canals are laid hideously bare, putrescent with rubbish and mud, and some of the smaller waterways almost dry up altogether, so that no boat with a propeller can use them. But when the swift scouring tide sweeps in from the Adriatic, clean, fresh and young, swelling down the Grand Canal and seeping through all its tributaries – then the whole place is richened and rejuvenated, the water surges into the palace doorways, the dead rats, broken dolls and cabbage-stalks are flushed away, and every canal is brimming and busy. Sometimes an exceptional spring tide topples over the edge, flooding the Piazza of St Mark, and people go to their favourite café in gondolas, or hilariously pole their boats about among the colonnades. And once every few centuries the canals freeze over, as you may see in an enchanting picture at the Ca' Rezzonico, and the Venetians build fires upon the ice, skate to the islands of the lagoon, and impertinently roast their oxen in the middle of the Grand Canal.

The canals have tempered the impact of the causeway. Venice is no longer an island, but her people are still islanders by temperament, for life in roadless Venice is still slow, erratic and sometimes infuriating, and totally unlike existence in any other city on the face of the earth. The Venetian business man can never summon his Alfa. The Venetian urchin cannot leap whistling upon his bicycle. The housewife has to take a boat to market, and the small boy has to walk each morning across a cavalcade of bridges, through a maze of alleyways, to be at school on time (the parents, if of nervous disposition, can often follow his progress half-way across the city, by mounting a powerful telescope on the terrace).

Trade and traffic churn their way heavily through the Venetian watereways, sometimes so busily and so uncomfortably that the whole place feels clogged and constipated with slow movement. The entire organization of one's private life is governed by the presence of the water. I was once leaning over the Grand Canal with a Venetian acquaintance when she suddenly breathed an extended and despondent sigh, surveyed the canal from one end to the other, and exclaimed: 'Water! Nothing but water! If only they'd fill the thing up, what a road it would make!'

The canals, some of which have ninth-century origins, have been successfully deepened to allow the passage of larger boats: but they also act as the drains of Venice, and are continually silting themselves up. Until the sixteenth century several rivers flowed through the middle of the lagoon, and they brought so much sediment with them that at one time the canals of Venice were almost choked, and you could walk from the mainland to the city without wetting your feet. The rivers were then diverted to the edges of the lagoon, and today the only mud that enters is sea-mud, to be swept out by the tide again each day. Every year, though, a mountain of excrement falls into the canals, and if you wander about Venice at low tide you will see, sometimes well above the water-line, the orifices by which, in the simplest possible process, most of the city's sewage leaves its houses. (Many houses nowadays have septic tanks, emptied periodically into barges: but here and there you may still see, jutting from the façades of old palaces, the little closets that used to act as the lavatories of Venice, emptying themselves directly into the water beneath, like the external privies that are attached to the hulls of Arab dhows.)

Tons of muck flows into the canals each day, and gives the crumbling back-quarters of Venice the peculiar stink – half drainage, half rotting stone – that so repels the queasy tourist, but gives the Venetian amateur a perverse and reluctant pleasure. Add to this the dust, vegetable peel, animal matter and ash that pours into every waterway, in defiance of the law, over the balconies and down the back-steps, and it is easy to conceive how thickly the canal-beds are coated with refuse. If you look down from a terrace when the tide is low, you can see an extraordinary variety of rubble and wreckage beneath the water, gleaming with spurious mystery through the green; and it is horrible to observe how squashily the poles go in, when a pile-driver begins its hammering in a canal.

The Venetians have never been much daunted by this substratum. In the fifteenth century they burnt joss-sticks, and ground scents and spices into the soil, to take away the smells: but not long ago even the most fashionable families used to bathe regularly in the Grand Canal, and I am told there was a notice near the Rialto sternly warning passers-by that it was 'Forbidden To Spit Upon The Swimmers.' As late as the 1980s ragamuffins and wild young blades of the place, in the sweltering summer evenings, were often to be seen taking wild dives into the murk from bridges and quay-sides, and you might sometimes observe fastidious boatmen, with expressions of

unshakeable hygiene, carefully washing out their mugs and basins in
the turgid fluid of a backwater.

The civic authorities, though, are necessarily obsessed with sanitation. Much of the foul refuse of Venice, like the mud, is washed
away by the tide, without which the city would be uninhabitable –
'the sea rises and falls there', as a fifteenth-century visitor said, 'and
cleans out the filth from the secret places'. The rest must be removed
by man. For centuries each canal was drained and scoured by hand
every twenty years or so (culs-de-sac more often, because the tide
does not wash through them): only the Grand Canal escaped – it has
only been emptied once, when a fourteenth-century earthquake
swallowed its waters in an instant and left it dry for two weeks. For
nearly thirty years the job has been neglected, so that many of the
canals are severely silted, and the effluences that flow into them are
obliged to ooze elsewhere. There was a scheme in the early 1990s to
dredge them all by mechanical means, but for myself I shall always
remember the old shovelling processes as one of the elemental
Venetian experiences.

It used to be an ominous sight for the householder, when a boat-
load of respectable men in overcoats appeared outside her back door,
painting numbers in red paint upon the walls: for it meant that her
canal was the next to be drained, exposing the bed in all its horror. A
vile miasma would then overcome the quarter. The inhabitants
shuttered their windows and hastened about with handkerchiefs
over their mouths, and far down in the gulley of the empty
waterway, beneath the ornate doorways and marble steps of the
palaces, you might see the labourers toiling in the sludge. They had
erected a little railway down there, and they stood knee-deep in black
glutinous filth, throwing it into tipper-trucks and wheeling it away to
waiting barges. Their bodies, their clothes, their faces were all
smeared with the stuff, and if you engaged them in conversation
their attitude was one of numbed but mordant resignation.

A wonderful variety of boats has been developed by the Venetians
over the generations, to make the best use of their unorthodox
highways. Their very first chronicler, visiting the wattle villages of

their original island settlements, remarked upon the boats tied up outside every house, for all the world as other people kept their horses. Today the ordinary Venetian is not generally a waterman, and looks at the canals with a mixture of pride and profound distrust; but sometimes you see a motor-boat driver, waiting for his patron, who does not bother to moor his craft, but stands on the quayside holding it with a loose rope, precisely as though it were a champing horse, and he a patient groom in a stable-yard. In the Natural History Museum there is a prehistoric canoe, dug up from a marsh in the lagoon, and now preserved in a fossilized condition. It looks almost as old as time itself, but in its blackened silhouette you can clearly recognize the first developing lines of the gondola.

If you take an aircraft over Venice, and fly low above her mottled attics, you will see her canals thick with an endless flow of craft, like little black corpuscles. Every kind of boat navigates the Venetian channels, for every kind of purpose, and many are unique to the place. There is the gondola, of course. There is the *sandolo*, a smaller but no less dapper boat, also rowed by one standing oarsman, facing forward. There is the *vaporetto*, which is the water-bus. There is the *motoscafo*, which is the motor launch. There is the *topo*, and the *trabaccolo*, and the *cavallina*, and the *vipera*, and the *bissona*, not to speak of semi-mythical rigs like the *barcobestia*, or ceremonial barges like the *bucintoro*, or skiffs from the two old Venetian rowing clubs (the Querini and the Bucintoro), or frisky outboards, or sleek speedboats,or dustbin barges, or parcel-post boats, or excursion launches, or car ferries, or canoes paddled by visiting German students, or inflatables with outboard engines, or yachts, or schooners from Yugoslavia, or naval picket boats, or the smelter's barge with a billowing furnace on it, or ambulance boats, or hearses, or milk-boats, or even the immaculate humming cruise-ships that sail into the wide canal of Giudecca from Athens, the Levant or the Black Sea.

For a cross-section of this vivacious armada, I like to stand on my corner balcony and watch the boats pass down the Grand Canal. Here (for instance) comes the chugging *vaporetto*, loaded deep and foaming at the prow: a trim and purposeful little ship, painted green and black. Here is a squat fruit barge, loud with oranges and great banana bunches, a haughty black dog at its prow, a languid leathery brown-skinned man steering with a single bare foot on the tiller. An elderly couple, he in a woollen flapped cap, she in a threadbare khaki jacket, laboriously propel a skiff full of vegetables towards some minor city market. Eight students in a heavy hired motor boat stagger nervously towards the Rialto, singing an unconvincing roundelay. Out of a side-canal there lumbers, with a deafening blare of its horn, a gigantic barge-load of cement; its crew are white with dust, wear hats made of newspaper (like the Walrus's Carpenter) and periodically pass around the deck the single stump of a cigarette – a puff for each, and two for the steersman. A Coca-Cola barge potters cheerfully by, bottles clinking: its helmsman wears the standard Coca-Cola uniform, as you may see it on delivery trucks from Seattle to Calcutta, and on his Venetian face there has been transplanted, by the alchemy of capitalism, the authentic Middle American smile.

Backwards and forwards across the Grand Canal the ferry gondolas dart daintily, like water-insects, with a neat swirl and decoration at the end of each trip, as they curve skilfully into the landing-stage. The Prefect rides by in his polished launch, all flags and dignity. From the cabin of a taxi there reaches me an agreeable mixture of Havana and Diorissima, as a visiting plutocrat sweeps by towards the Danieli, with his pigskin suitcases piled beside the driver, and his blasé befurred wife in the stern. Outside the Accademia art gallery they are loading an enormous canvas, an orgasm of angels and fleshy limbs, into a sturdy snub-nosed lighter. A couple of executive-style Milanese scud by in a *sandolo*, rowing earnestly in the Venetian manner – for the rich part-time Venetian, traditional rowing is a substitute for jogging, just as some of the old Venetian boat-types make fashionable yachts. Beyond San Trovaso, splendid between the houses, a liner pulses to its moorings, and behind the dome of the Salute I can see, like the twigs of some exotic conifer, a warship's intricate radar.

And always somewhere on the Grand Canal, drifting pleasantly with the tide, struggling loftily into the lagoon, tossing at a post or protruding its aristocratic beak between a pair of palaces, there stands a high-prowed, lop-sided, black-painted, brass-embellished gondola, the very soul and symbol of Venice.

The water transport of Venice is easygoing but generally efficient, after fifteen centuries of practice. Traffic regulations are not stringent, and are often genially ignored. The speed limit for boats in the city is nine kilometres an hour – say 5 m.p.h. – but everybody expects you to go a little faster if you can. You should pass a powered boat on its port side, a rowing-boat on its starboard: but in the wide Grand Canal nobody much cares, and anyway the gondola is surrounded by so powerful a mystique, is so obviously the queen of the canals, that when you see her tall sensitive silhouette gliding towards you, why, you merely curtsy and stand aside. Surprisingly few collisions occur, and only rarely will you hear a violent splutter of expletives, trailing away into muttered imprecations, as one barge scrapes another outside your window. The watermen of Venice are robust but tolerant, and do not make difficulties for one another.

The prime passenger carrier of Venice is the water-bus. The first steamboat appeared on the Grand Canal in 1881. She belonged to a French company that had won a municipal concession, and with seven tall-funnelled sister ships she had sailed from the Seine all around the toe of Italy, to begin the first mechanical transport service Venice had ever known. Till then, passengers had either travelled grandly in a gondola, or had taken passage up the canal in a long communal boat, not unlike a Viking long-ship, which two men rowed from the station to St Mark's (you may see a surviving example in the naval museum at the Arsenal, and a direct descendant is still used by the Giudecca ferry-men). The advent of the *Società Vaporetti Omnibus di Venezia* plunged the gondoliers into alarm, and they instantly went on strike: but they survived, and on Giudecca, off the Rio della Croce, you may see an *ex voto*, erected by the ferry-men of that island, thanking the Holy Mother for her kindness in ensuring that they were not *entirely* ruined by the steamboats.

The steamboat line flourished too, and presently (in the way of successful foreign concessions) it was nationalized, and eventually metamorphosed into the *Azienda del Consorzio Trasporti Veneziano* –

ACTV for short. It now has more than 100 boats – since 1952 all propelled by diesel or motor engines, though everybody still calls them *vaporetti*. Except for the very latest vessels, the whole fleet has been successively modified, redesigned, rebuilt, re-engined, so that each craft, like a great cathedral, is the product of generations of loving hands and skills – a steam-cock from one period, a funnel from another, a wheel-house from a third, all embellished and enhanced by some very fine early twentieth-century life-belts. The line has its own shipyards, near the Arsenal: and like the mason's yard at Chartres, they are always busy.

ACTV runs at a loss, because in the dim Venetian winter only a third of its seats are occupied, and because its fares are artificially low. This is no index of the efficiency of the line, which is impressive (though in the high tourist season Venetians often complain that they cannot get even standing room on their own public transport system). Its services are frequent, fast and reasonably comfortable, and it is only rarely that you see a *vaporetto* ignominiously towed towards the shipyard by the stripped and gaunt old steamboat that serves as a tug. The crews are sometimes surly, but generally cordial. At each station there is a gauge-mark, a metre high, for the measurement of children and the calculation of half-fares: but it is touching how often the official on duty, with a slight downward pressure of his hand and the distant suspicion of a wink, manages to usher your children beneath it. There is even a beauty to the *vaporetti*, if you are not inalienably attached to the picturesque; for a fine rollicking spirit compels these little ships, when they plunge into the lagoon on a bright windy morning, wallowing deep and threshing hard, with the spray surging about their stems and the helmsman earnest in his little glass cabin.

And threading a snooty way among these plebs, one step down in the maritime scale but two or three up in price, are the Venetian motor launches. About 100 are private, owned by firms or families – and sometimes, perhaps, taxation being what it is, by both at the same time. Some 150 others are taxis, organized in companies of resounding title – the San Marco, the Serenissima, the Salute. They are fine wooden boats of a design unique to Venice: built in the boatyards of the city (many of them at the eastern end of Giudecca) and often powered by British or American engines. Their tariffs are high. Their décor is ornate, going in for tasselled curtains, embroidered seats, white roof-covers, flags and occasional tables. The newest have an almost racy air to them, while the oldest look like floating Rolls-Royces.

Their drivers, warped by 40 horse-power and the awful vulnerability of their polished mahogany, are often cross and sometimes oddly incompetent. There hangs around them, whether they are taxis or private vehicles, an air of snobbishness and conceit very far from the horny *bonhomie* of the bargees and the fishermen: and sometimes, when their wash spills arrogantly over the bulwarks of some poor person's boat (in particular, mine) they remind me of heedless nobles in a doomed and backward kingdom, riding their cruel black horses across a peasant crop.

Different indeed is the character of the gondola, a boat so intimately adapted to the nature of this city that it is difficult to imagine Venice without it. The origin of the craft is said to be Turkish, and certainly there is something about its grace and lofty pose that smacks of the Golden Horn, seraglios and odalisques and scented pashas. It is also clearly related to the boats of Malta: not long ago you could sometimes compare them, for when ships of the British Mediterranean Fleet visited Venice, they usually brought with them a Maltese boatman, to provide cheap transport for the crews, and you might see his bright butterfly-craft bobbing provocatively among the black Venetian boats. What the word 'gondola' means nobody quite knows. Some scholars suggest it comes from the Greek κόνδυ, a cup; others derive it from κύμβη, the name the Greeks gave to Charon's ferry; and a few dauntless anti-romantics plump for a modern Greek word that means, of all things, a mussel. I think it odd that in the modern world the word has had only four applications: to a kind of American railway wagon; to the under-slung cabin of an airship; to the cabin of a ski-lift; to the town carriage of the Venetians.

The gondola is built only in the boatyards of Venice, squeezed away in smoke and litter in the back-canals of the city (some of them will also make you, if you pay them well, exquisite and exact miniatures of the craft). It is constructed of several different woods – oak, walnut, cherry, elm or pine – and is cut to a pernickety design, perfected at last through innumerable modifications. The first gondola was a much less spirited craft, if we can go by the old wood-cuts, its form governed by the clumsy practice of boarding it over the bows: the present model has been so exactly adapted to the needs of the city that there are said to be only two places, even at the lowest tide, where a gondola cannot pass – one near the Fenice Theatre, the other near the church of San Stae.

The gondola is immensely strong. An adventurous eccentric once sailed in one to Trieste, rowed by a crew of eight. I have seen a gondola with its bows chopped clean off in a collision, still confidently afloat; I have seen one, salvaged after months under water, restored to gleaming perfection in a few days; and if ever you have your gondola towed by a motor boat, and race across the lagoon with its prow hoisted high and the salt foam racing by you, the violent but harmless slapping of the water on the boat's belly will tell you how soundly it is built, like an old Victorian railway engine, or a grandfather clock.

The gondola can also be fast. I once found it extremely difficult, in my outboard motor boat, to keep up with a gondola practising for a regatta beyond San Giorgio. Two gondoliers will effortlessly take a pair of passengers from Venice to Burano, a good six miles, in less than two hours. With a load of four talkative tourists, and an unhurried gondolier, the gondola easily keeps up with a man walking along a canal bank in the city. (All the same, when the Republic presented a gondola to Charles II of England as a wedding present in 1662, and sent a couple of gondoliers to man it, Evelyn reported that it was 'not comparable for swiftnesse to our common wherries'.)

The modern gondola never has the *felze*, the little black cabin that used, in poetical eyes anyway, so to intensify its air of suggestive gloom: but it is still thickly carpeted, and fitted with brass sea-horses, cushioned seats, coloured oars and a heavy layer of shiny black varnish – gondolas have been black since the sixteenth century, when the sumptuary laws ordained it, though you may sometimes see one painted a bright blue or a screaming yellow for a regatta. All gondolas are the same, except some rather bigger versions for the fixed ferry runs, and a small toy-like model for racing. Their measurements are standard – length 36 feet, beam 5 feet. They are deliberately lop-sided, to counter the weight of the one-oared rower at the stern, so that if you draw an imaginary line down the centre of the boat, one half is bigger than the other. They have no keel, and they weigh about 1,300 lb apiece.

At the prow is the *ferro*, a steel device, often made in the hill-towns of Cadore, with six prongs facing forwards, one prong astern and a trumpet-like blade above. Most people find this emblem infinitely romantic, but Shelley likened it to 'a nondescript beak of shining steel', and Coryat described it confusedly as 'a crooked thing made in the forme of a Dolphin's tayle, with the fins very artificially repre-sented, and it seemeth to be tinned over'. Nobody really knows what it represents. Some say it is descended from the prows of Roman galleons. Some say it is a judicial axe. Others believe it to reproduce the symbol of a key that appeared on Egyptian funerary boats. The gondoliers themselves have homelier theories. They seem generally agreed that the six forward prongs represent the six districts of Venice, but disagree wildly about the rest. The top is a Doge's hat/ a Venetian halberd/a lily/the sea/the Rialto bridge. The rear prong is the Piazza/Giudecca/the Doge's Palace/Cyprus. The strip of metal running down the stem of the boat is sometimes interpreted as the Grand Canal and sometimes as the History of Venice. Now and then, too, in the Venetian manner, a *ferro* has only five forward prongs instead of six, and this necessitates an agonizing reassessment of the whole problem: and if you ever do settle the symbolism of the thing, you still have to decide its purpose – whether it is for gauging the heights of bridges, whether it balances the boat, or whether it is merely ornamental. All in all, the *ferro* of a gondola is a controversial emblem: but few sights in Venice, to my mind, are more strangely suggestive than seven or eight of these ancient talismans, curved, rampant and gleaming, riding side by side through the lamplight of the Grand Canal.

A gondola is very expensive to build, and every three weeks or so in summer it must go back to the yards to be scraped of weeds and tarred again. Since the gondoliers are largely unemployed in the winter months, fares are necessarily high, and every now and then the Gondoliers' Co-operative announces, in a spate of emotional posters, the impending disappearance of the very last gondola from the canals of Venice, unless the municipality agrees to raise the tariff again. In the sixteenth century there were 10,000 gondolas in Venice. Today there are less than 400; but since a ride in one is a prime experience of any Venetian visit, and since they form in themselves one of the great tourist spectacles, they are unlikely to disappear altogether. Even on severely practical grounds, the gondola is still useful to Venetians, for there are several gondola ferries across the Grand Canal, three of them working all night (they have gay little shelters, often charmingly decorated with greeneries and Chinese lanterns, in which off-duty gondoliers picturesquely sprawl the hours away, sometimes engaging in desultory argument, or playing with a communal cat). The gondolier is essential to the spirit and self-esteem of Venice. 'The gondolier', says a municipal handbook, 'cannot demand, even as a tip, a higher fare than is indicated on the notice that must be affixed to his gondola'; but it is wonderful what circumventions he can devise to augment his income, and how expensive his diverse pleasantries somehow prove to be, his odd droppings of curious knowledge, his mastery of saints' days and Old Customs, his improbable historical anecdotes and his blue persuasive eyes, when at length you reach the railway station.

For myself, I am willing to pay a little extra for the delight of watching his dexterity. At first the gondola may strike you as wasp-like and faintly sinister: but soon you will be converted to its style, and recognize it as the most beautiful instrument of transport on earth, except perhaps the jet aircraft. Each example, they say, has a distinct personality of its own, fostered by minute variations of woodwork or fitting, and the gondolier plays upon this delicate soundbox like a virtuoso. Some of his attitudes are very handsome – especially when Carpaccio portrays him, poised in striped tights on a gilded poop, in the days before the sumptuary laws. In particular there is a soft gliding motion, to convey the boat around sharp corners, that reminds me irresistibly of a ski-turn: the feet are placed in a ballet-like position, toes well out; the oar is raised to waist level; the body is twisted lithely in the opposite direction to the turn; and round the gondola spins, with a swing and a swish, always crooked but never ungainly, the gondolier proud and calm upon its stern.

He utters a series of warning cries when he makes a manoeuvre of this sort, throaty and distraught, like the call of an elderly and world-weary sea-bird. These cries so affected Wagner, during his stay in Venice, that they may have suggested to him (so he himself thought) the wail of the shepherd's pipe at the opening of the third act of *Tristan*: and they are so truly the *cri de coeur* of Venice that during the black-outs of the two world wars, pedestrians adopted them too, and sang them out as warnings at awkward street corners. The basic words of the admonition are *premi* and *stali* – 'left' and 'right': but it is difficult to discover precisely how they are used. Ruskin, for example, observes obscurely that 'if two gondoliers meet under any circumstances which render it a matter of question on which side they should pass each other, the gondolier who has at the moment least power over his boat cries to the other "*Premi!*" if he wishes the boats to pass with their right-hand sides to each other, and "*Stali!*" if with their left.' Other writers are more easily satisfied, and believe that when a gondolier is going left he cries '*Premi!*' and when he is going right he cries '*Stali!*' Baedeker, frankly defeated by the whole system, merely records the unpronounceable exclamation '*A-Oel!*' – which means, he says bathetically, 'Look out!' The poet Monkton Milne, in some verses on the problem, says of the gondoliers' cries:

> *Oh! they faint on the ear as the lamp on the view,*
> *'I am passing – premi! – but I stay not for you!'*

Nowadays the gondoliers seem to vary their cry. I have often heard the old calls, but generally, it seems to me, the modern gondolier merely shouts '*Oi!*' (for which Herr Baedeker's translation remains adequate) and I know one modernist, who, swinging off the Grand Canal into the Rio San Trovaso, habitually raises his fingers to his teeth for a raucous but effective whistle.

It is not at all easy to row a gondola. The reverse stroke of the oar is almost as laborious as the forward stroke, because the blade must be kept below water to keep the bows straight; and skilful manipulation, especially in emergencies, depends upon instant movement of the oar in and out of the complicated row-lock (which looks like a forked stump from a petrified forest). To see this skill at its most advanced, spend ten minutes at one of the Grand Canal *traghetto* stations, and watch the ferry-men at work. They move in a marvellous unity, two to a gondola, disciplined by some extra-sensory bond, and they bring their boats to the landing-stage with a fine flamboyant flourish, whipping their oars neatly out of the row-locks to act as brakes, and coming alongside with a surge of water and an endearing showmen's glance towards the audience on the bank.

Boats, boatmanship and boatlore are half the fascination of Venice. Do not suppose, though, that the Venetians never set eyes on a car. You can see them any day, of course, at the Piazzale Roma, or on the resort-island of the Lido, but they sometimes get far nearer St Mark's. At the Maritime docks, near the Zattere, you may often see cars running about behind the barricades, and sometimes observe a great diesel lorry that has hauled its trailer direct from Munich to the inner fringe of the sea-city. When there is an especially important celebration, the authorities land television and loudspeaker trucks in the Piazza itself, where they sit around in corners, skulking beneath the colonnades and looking distinctly embarrassed. The British took amphibious vehicles to the Riva degli Schiavoni, when they arrived in Venice at the end of the Second World War. Cargoes of cars (and railway wagons, too) often chug across the inner lagoon on ferry-boats. And I once looked out of my window to see a big removal truck outside my neighbour's front door, on the Grand Canal itself: it had been floated there on barges, and its driver was sitting at the steering-wheel, eating a sandwich.

13 Stones of Venice

There are many houses in Venice that do not stand upon canals, and are inaccessible by boat: but there is nowhere in the city that you cannot reach on foot, if you have a good map, a stout pair of shoes and a cheerful disposition. The canals govern the shape and pattern of Venice. The streets fill the gaps, like a filigree. Venice is a maze of alleys, secluded courtyards, bridges, archways, tortuous passages, dead ends, quaysides, dark overhung back streets and sudden sunlit squares. It is a cramped, crowded, cluttered place, and if its waterways are often sparkling, and its views across the lagoon brilliantly spacious, its streets often remind me of corridors in some antique mouldy prison, florid but unreformed. It is a very stony city. A few weeks in Venice, and you begin to long for mountains or meadows or open sea (though it is extraordinary, when once you have tied your sheets together and jumped over the wall, how soon you pine for the gaol again).

There are several different grades of street and square in Venice. The *fondamenta* is a quayside, usually wide and airy. The *calle* is a lane. The *salizzada* is a paved alley, once so rare as to be worth distinguishing. The *ruga* is a street lined with shops. The *riva* is a water-side promenade. The *rio terra* is a filled-in canal, and the *piscina* a former pond. Then there is something called a *crosera*, and something called a *ramo*, and a *sotto-portico*, and a *corte*, and a *campo*, and a *campiello*, and a *campazzo*. There is a Piazzale in Venice (the Piazzale Roma, by the car park). There are two Piazzettas (one on each side of the Basilica). But there is only one Piazza, the stupendous central square of the city, which Napoleon called the finest drawing-room in Europe.

Each section of the city, as we saw from the Campanile, clusters about its own square, usually called a *campo* because it used to be, in the virginal days of Venice, a soggy kind of field. The most interesting *campi* in Venice are those of San Polo, Santa Maria Formosa, San Giacomo dell' Orio, Santo Stefano, and Santa Margherita – the first rather dashing, the second rather buxom, the third rather rough, the fourth rather elegant, the fifth pleasantly easy-going. In such a *campo* there is usually no glimpse of water, the canals being hidden away behind the houses, and all feels hard, old and urban. It is, as the guides would say, 'very characteristical'.

In the middle of Campo Santa Margherita (for example) there stands an inconsequential little square building, rather like an old English town hall, which was once the Guild of the Fur-Makers, and it is the local office of a political party. At one end of the square is an antique tower, once a church, now a cinema, and at the other is the tall red campanile of the Carmini church, with an illuminated Madonna on its summit. Between these three landmarks all the spiced activities of Venice flourish, making the *campo* a little city of its own, within whose narrow confines you can find almost any-thing you need for sensible living. There is a bank, in a fine old timbered house; and three or four cafés, their radios stridently blaring; and a swarthy wineshop, frequented by tough old ladies and dominated by a an enormous television set; and a second-hand clothes dealer; and a dairy, and a couple of well-stocked groceries, and a delightful old-school pharmacy, all pink bottles and panel-ling. At the brightly coloured newspaper kiosk the proprietor peers at his customers through a small cavity among the film stars, as though he has nibbled a way between the magazines, like a dormouse. The draper's shop is warm with woollies and thick stockings; the tobacconist sells everything from safety-pins to post-age stamps; and each morning they set up a market in the square, beneath gay awnings, squirming with fish and burgeoning with vegetables.

Like many another Venetian *campo*, Santa Margherita is an un-sophisticated place. No elegant socialites sit at its cafés. No actresses cross their legs revealingly on the steps of its war memorial. The passing tourists hurry by anxiously consulting their street plans, on their way to grander places. But there is no better way to taste the temper of Venice than to sit for an hour or two in such a setting, drinking a cheap white wine from the Veneto, and watching this particular small world go by.

*

Extending from the squares, like tenuous roots, run the alleyways of Venice, of which there are said to be more than 3,000. Their total length is more than ninety miles, but some are so small as to be almost impassable. Browning was delighted to find one so narrow that he could not open his umbrella. The narrowest of all is said to be the Ramo Salizzada Zusto, near San Giacomo dell' Orio, which is 2½ feet wide, and can only be traversed by the portly if they are not ashamed to try sideways. The lanes of Venice often have lovely names – the Alley of the Curly-Headed Woman; the Alley of the Love of Friends Or of the Gypsies; the Filled-In Canal of Thoughts; the Broad Alley of the Proverbs; the First Burnt Alley and the Second Burnt Alley, both commemorating seventeenth-century fires; the Street of the Monkey Or of The Swords; the Alley of the Blind. Not long ago, before peoples' skins grew thinner, there was even a Calle Sporca – Dirty Lane.

The lanes are often beguilingly unpredictable, ending abruptly in dark deep canals, plunging into arcades, or emerging without warning upon some breathtaking vista. They can also be misleading, for you will frequently find that the palace looming at the end of an alley-way is separated from you by a wide waterway, and can only be reached by an immense detour. This means that though Venetian houses may be close to one another, they are not necessarily neighbours, and it has led to the evolution of a complicated sign language, enabling housemaids to converse with each other at long range, or conduct gentle flirtations across the chasm: I once saw a young man in the very act of blowing a kiss to a girl across such a canal when his window-pane fell down with a busybody thump, fatally weakening his aplomb. The mystery, secrecy and romance of the lanes is always a fascination, especially if you learn, as the Venetians do, to *andare per le fodere* – 'move among the linings', or poke your way through the little subsidiary passages that creep padded and muffled among the houses, like the runs of city weasels.

They used to have running-races in the crook-back, zigzag streets of Venice, and you can make good speed along them if you develop the right techniques of side-step and assault. The best way to move about Venice, through, is by a combination of methods, based upon

careful analysis. You can walk from the Rialto to the church of
Ognissanti in half an hour: but if you know the place, you will catch
the express *vaporetto* to San Samuele – take the *traghetto* across to the
Ca' Rezzonico – follow the linings through the Calle Traghetto, the
Calle Lunga San Barnaba, the Calle delle Turchette, the Fondamenta
di Borgo, the Fondamenta delle Eremite, the Calle dei Frari, the Rio
Terra degli Ognissanti – and in a dazed minute or two, emerging
panting upon the Campo Ognissanti, you are there.

'Turn up on your right hand,' said Launcelot to Gobbo, when that
old gentleman was looking for Shylock's house – 'turn up on your
right hand at the next turning, but at the next turning of all, on your
left: marry, at the very next turning, turn of no hand, but turn down
indirectly to the Jew's house.'

'By God's sonties,' the old boy replied, "twill be a hard way to find'
– and O Heavens! he was right.

Long centuries ago the Venetians, looking around them at these
peculiar circumstances, and examining the best Greek, Roman and
Byzantine models, devised their own kind of house. Many an
ephemeral taste has embellished their architecture since then, and
many fluctuations of fortune have affected their style, so that today
Venice is a gallimaufry of domestic architecture, so tightly packed
and heavily loaded with buildings that sometimes it feels like one
massive jagged stone hillock, projecting irregularly from the waters
of the lagoon.

The classic Venetian house remains the palace of the old aristocracy. It is found all over the city, in innumerable back-alleys and
little-frequented courtyards – in the best modern guide to Venice 334
such houses are thought worthy of mention. Many a modest old
doorway masks a lovely house, and often a butcher's shop or a
grocer's has been built into the side of an exquisite small fifteenth-
century mansion. You can see the greater houses at their best and
grandest, though, along the banks of the Grand Canal, where their
architecture springs from three distinct periods – the Byzantine, the
Gothic, the Renaissance – which are instantly recognizable to writers
of guide books, but often indistinguishable to me. Some of these

houses are appealingly decrepit. Some have been ruthlessly restored. Some are charming, some (to my mind) perfectly hideous. Some are simple and demure, some massively ostentatious, with immense heavy doorways and ugly obelisks on their cornices. They are, at least those of the Gothic pattern, unique to Venice: but when Mr Tiffany and his associates wanted to erect a jeweller's mansion on Fifth Avenue, and when the committee of the Army and Navy Club were planning their new premises in Pall Mall, all those gentlemen cast their eyes admiringly towards the Grand Canal, and built their own Venetian palaces at home.

Their basic design is lofty but practical, and clearly derived from Rome and Byzantium. A typical house is roughly rectangular, but with its façade (on the canal) rather broader than its back (on an alley). It has four, five or six stories. The front door opens spaciously upon the water, where the boats are moored at huge painted posts – unless there is a boathouse at the side, like a garage. The back door opens discreetly into a lane, or into a high-walled and often disregarded garden. If the house is venerable enough, there may be a flagged courtyard with a well-head, from which a wide staircase marches upwards, as in the houses of Damascus and Baghdad.

The ground floor of the palace is the entrance hall and boatyard, where the family gondola used to be laid up, high, dry and mysterious, in the winter months, and where the old merchant aristocrats stored their bales of silk, their bundles of ivory, their tapestries, their perfumes and even their shivering apes – 'from Tripolis, from Mexico, and England', as Shakespeare once imaginatively put it, 'From Lisbon, Barbary and India'. The first floor is the *mezzanino*, the business quarter of the house, where the merchants did their accounts, concluded their agreements and dismissed their dishonest servants. The second is the *piano nobile*, the most elegant of the apartments, designed for the pleasure of his honour the proprietor. It has a long, dark, imposing central room, often running the whole length of the house, with a large balcony over the canal, and an alcove each side with windows over the water. From this central *sala* bedrooms lead off on either side, trailing away in a warren of bathrooms, dressing-rooms and miscellaneous offices.

Above the *piano nobile* the house loses some of its grandeur, each floor becoming successively pokier until at last, above the ultimate attic, you emerge upon the higgledy-piggledy roof, and find there the wooden platform, called the *altana*, which was originally designed to allow Venetian ladies privacy while they bleached their hair in the sun, but which nowadays generally flutters with washing. The house may once have been covered with frescoes and vivid ornamentation, sometimes vaguely visible to this day, when the sun is right: now it is probably reddish, brownish, or stone-coloured, and enlivened chiefly by its gay mooring-posts, like barbers' poles, its striped awnings, and the delectable flower-boxes, bird-cages and odd domestic foliage with which elderly Venetian ladies like to freshen their windows.

Plastered and stuccoed on the façades of these houses are the mementoes of progress: bits and pieces of decoration left behind by successive restorers, like sea-shells in a grotto. Angels, cherubs, scrolls and lions abound on every window-sill, and sometimes there are huge pyramidal spikes on the roof, like the rock-temples of Petra. The side façade of a Venetian palace, in particular, can be immensely complicated by these accretions. I once examined the side elevation of a house near mine, and found that beneath its domed tower and its copper weather-vane it was embellished with four chimney-pots, of three different designs; fifty-three windows, of eight different shapes and sizes, two of them blocked and three grilled; the casement of a spiral staircase; twelve iron staples; eight inlaid pieces of white masonry; a defaced memorial slab; a carved rectangular ornament of obscure significance; four buttresses; five external chimney flues; scattered examples of bare brick, cement, piping, stonework and embedded arches; various bits of isolated tiling; a heavy concrete reinforcement at the water's edge; a carpet hung out to air; a quizzical housemaid at a third-floor window; and an inscription recording the fact that a celebrated French actress had lived there.

The greatest of these strange houses, though much smaller than the country palaces of the English patricians, are very large indeed. (Their owners often had mansions on the mainland, too: the Pisani family had fifty such villas, and at one house in the Veneto 150 guests could be entertained at a go, together with their servants – it contained two chapels, five organs, a concert hall, a printing press and a couple of theatres.) In the early days of Venice, the citizens all lived in virtually identical houses, 'to show their unity and equality in all things': later the palaces became symbolic of wealth and success, the most gloriously ostentatious way of keeping up with the Contarinis.

Many stories testify to the pride of the old Venetian householders, as they erected these grandiose homes. One tells of the aristocrat Nicolo Balbi, who was so anxious to move into the new Palazzo Balbi that he lived for some months in a boat opposite the building site: alas, he caught cold, and before he could take up residence in the mansion, poor old Balbi died. Another concerns a determined suitor who, refused a lady's hand because he did not possess a palace on the Grand Canal, promptly built one so large that, as he pointed out, any one of its principal windows was bigger than his father-in-law's main portal: the young man's house is the Palazzo Grimani, now the Court of Appeal, and the old man's the Coccina-Tiepolo, almost opposite. A third story says that the truncated Palazzo Flangini, near San Geremia, was once twice its present size, but that when two brothers jointly inherited it, one of them demolished his half in a fit of jealous dudgeon. The Palazzo Venier dei Leoni remains unfinished, so it is said, because the owner of the immense Palazzo Corner, directly opposite, objected so strongly to the impertinence of its completion: it was certainly going to be enormous, as you may see from a model in the Correr Museum. The palace of the Duke of Sforza, near the Accademia, was apparently intended by that ambitious *condottiere* to be more of a fortress than a mere house, and that is why it remains at half-cock, with a princely set of stairs but a modest elevation.

The Grand Canal, as Gautier once said, was the register of the Venetian nobility – 'every family has inscribed its own name on one of these monumental façades'. The Palazzo Vendramin, where Wagner died, was built by the Loredan clan, and passed in aristo-cratic succession to the Duke of Brunswick, the Duke of Mantua, the Calerghi family, the Grimani family, the Vendramin family, the

Duchesse de Berri (mother of Henri V) and the Duca della Grazia. Countless and often fabulous were the festivities mounted in such houses, in the days of the Venetian decline. They used to have bull-baitings in the courtyard of the Ca' Foscari, and sometimes people erected floating platforms on the canal outside their front doors, and had dances on them.

Only a few years ago a ball of legendary luxury and splendour was held in the Palazzo Labia, beside San Geremia, and the grandest parties of the Grand Canal are still among the greatest events of the international season. Few of the larger palaces, though, are still private houses, and if they are, their proprietors are not usually Venetians. One or two patrician families maintain their old homes, usually keeping well out of the social limelight: but their palaces are likely to be divided among different members of the family, floor by floor, with a chaperone or housekeeper to give a respectable unity to the *ménage*.

Many other palaces are now institutions – the Municipality, which occupies two, the Museum of Modern Art, the winter casino, the Franchetti Museum, the Ca' Rezzonico Museum, the International Centre of Art and Costume, the headquarters of the Biennale, the Museum of Natural History, the Prefecture, the municipal pawn-shop. Some of the finest are hotels. Some are offices, some are antique shops, one is a mosaic workshop, two are showrooms of Venetian glass. Many more are apartments, mostly expensive (especially at the southern end of the Grand Canal), some magnifi-cent. The ownership of these structures can be involved, for they are often divided by floors, so that one landlord owns the top of the house, and quite another the middle, and a third the garden and the water-gate, and a fourth the path that leads you into the common land of the back-alley. Sometimes ownership extends to part of the pavement outside. Near the Rialto there is a house whose garden gate juts abruptly into the passing lane. Across the angle thus made with the wall of the alley a stone has been set in the pavement, enclosing an area of about two square feet between the gateway and the wall, and upon it is engraved the inscription: '*Private Property*'. I once put my foot across this mystic barrier, into the forbidden inches beyond: and sure enough, such is the strength of Venetian tradition, a queer tingle ran up my leg, like a psychic admonition.

Do not judge the prosperity of a Venetian house by the opulence of its doorway, especially if it stands well away from the Grand Canal. There are, of course, many poor houses in Venice, drab uniform tenements, dreary cottages, even the remnants of rock-bottom slums. The apparent squalor of many homes, though, is merely a veneer. Downstairs the house may be dank, messy, derelict or even sinister: but once you are inside, and past the musty obscurity of the hall, and up the rickety stairs, and through the big black door of the principal apartment, and along a gloomy echoing corridor or two, and up a few shaky staircases – then suddenly, passing through a heavy curtain, you may find yourself in the brightest and most elegant of rooms, locked away in that dark exterior like a pearl in a knobbly oyster. (Venetians have always liked to live out of doors, anyway, as you may see from the countless cheerful citizens who take their knitting and their newspapers each summer evening to the cafés of the Riva or the quaysides and trattorias near the docks.)

Do not think, either, that Venice has no gardens. In the winter, when all this maze of buildings is cold, shuttered and depressed, it can feel the most barren of cities, starved of green, sap and juices. This is misleading. Hundreds of gardens lie hidden among the stones of Venice, protected by iron gates and old brick ramparts, so that you only catch a quick passing glimpse of wistaria, or a transient breath of honeysuckle. The Venetians love flowers. Florists abound, and there are shops where you can buy edible essence of rose-petal, or bunches of orange marrow-blossom to fry in flour. There are trees in Venice, too – hundreds of pines, regimentally paraded, in Napoleon's Public Gardens; handsome plane trees in several squares: myrtles, laurels, oleanders, pomegranates, tamarisks and palms in many a private garden. There is even, a learned man once assured me, 'a genuine lodogno tree,' in the Campo San Zaccaria – information I could only accept in respectful silence.

There is a beguiling secrecy and seclusion to these green places of Venice, and they are often littered with quaint statues and carvings, and haunted by cats, and dignified by old overgrown well-heads. On

Giudecca, once the garden-island of Venice, there are still one or two rich flower gardens running down to the lagoon, their heavy fragrance hanging like a cloud above the water; and even in the very centre of the city, where you should take nothing for granted, solemn forbidding buildings often secrete small bowers of delights. Behind the old convent of the Servites, enclosed by high walls, there is a vegetable garden (tended by nuns in cowls and gum-boots), so wide and richly cultivated that it feels like a transplanted patch of Tuscany, snatched from the farmlands: and above the low roof of the Palazzo Venier you may see the tall luxuriant trees of its garden, a place of deep evocative melancholy, like a plantation garden in the American South.

Such places are not often public. Most of the Venetian gardens are jealously locked, and impenetrable to strangers. On the entire southern shore of Giudecca there is now only one spot where ordinary people may wander down to the water. To see the gum-booted nuns at work you must persuade some friendly local house-wife to give you access to her roof, and look at them over the wall. Few benches stand among the Venetian greeneries as encouragements to dalliance, and the ones in the big Public Gardens, at the end of the Riva, are nearly always occupied.

Venetians, indeed, do not always have much feeling for gardens. Many a private paradise is cruelly neglected, while others are laid out with crude display. Some neighbours of mine, in a spasm of enthusiasm, recently engaged a landscape gardener to rearrange their entire garden, hitherto a tangled wilderness. They ordered it all by the book, complete with a lawn, a garden path, a flower-border, a handful of small trees and a garden gate with brass insignia. The gardeners worked hard and skilfully, and within a month they had created a spanking new garden, as neat, correct and orderly as a ledger: and some time later, when the flowers came out, I observed the mistress of the house wandering among the roses with a catalogue in her hand, making sure she had got what she ordered.

Where an alley meets a water-way, there you have a Venetian bridge. The bridges, as Evelyn observed, 'tack the city together'. There are more to the square mile in Venice than anywhere else on earth – more that 450 of them, ranging from the gigantic twin spans of the causeway to the dainty little private bridge on Giudecca which, if you open its wicket gate and cross its planks, deposits you prudently in the garden of the Queen of Greece. There is the Bridge of Fists and the Bridge of Straw and the Bridge of the Honest Woman and the Bridge of Courtesy and the Bridge of Humility and the Little Bridge and the Long Bridge and the Bridge of Paradise and the Bridge of the Angel and the Bridge of Sighs, where Byron stood, lost in sentimental but misinformed reverie.

The arched bridge turned the canals into highways: but to this day many of the Venetian bridges are so low, so dark and so narrow that the gondolier has to crouch low on his poop to get through them, while his passengers clutch their new straw hats and laugh at their own echoes (and if it is one of those bridges whose undersides are flecked with moving water-reflections, going beneath it is like gliding behind a silent waterfall). The ubiquity of bridges has given the Venetians their peculiar clipped gait, and contributes heavily to the swollen ankles and unsteady heels with which unaccustomed visitors, swearing inexpressible enjoyment, stagger back to a restorative bath after an afternoon of sightseeing.

The early Venetian bridges were used by horses and mules as well as humans, and therefore had ramps instead of steps. They had no parapets, and were made of tarred wood, as you can see from Carpaccio's famous *Miracle of the True Cross at the Rialto*. Today the ramps have all disappeared, but there is still one example of a bridge without parapets, on the Rio San Felice near the Misericordia. Most of the minor bridges nowadays are single-spanned, high-arched, and built of stone. There are still a few flat wooden bridges, approached by steps from the pavement, like an English railway bridge. There is a three-arched bridge over the canal called Cannaregio. There is an eccentric junction of bridges near the Piazzale Roma, where five separate structures meet in a baffling confrontation of steps and directions. There are some private bridges, ending abruptly and haughtily at the great wooden doors of palaces. There are a few iron bridges, some of English genesis. At certain times of the year there are even pontoon bridges, erected by Italian Army engineers from

the Po Valley garrisons. In November one is thrown across the Grand
Canal to the Salute. In July they build one across the wide Giudecca
Canal to the church of the Redentore, for the commemoration of
another plague delivery (for thirty hours no ship can enter or leave
the inner port of Venice). They used also to build one, on All Soul's
Day, to the cemetery of San Michele: but today a water-bus will take
you to the graveside anyway, in a matter of mournful moments. For
the rest, the little bridges of Venice are so numerous, and so
unobtrusive, and so alike, that you may cross ten or twenty in the
course of half an hour's stroll, and hardly even notice them.

Three bigger bridges span the Grand Canal. Until the last century
there was only one, the Rialto – which all Venetians meticulously call
Ponte di Rialto, the Rialto being, in their long memories, not a bridge
but a district. There have been several bridges on this site. The first
was a bridge of boats. The second was broken during the Tiepolo
revolution in 1310, when the rebels fled across the canal. The third
collapsed in 1444 during the Marchioness of Ferrara's wedding
procession. The fifth, portrayed in Carpaccio's picture, had a drawbridge in the middle. It was temporarily removed in 1452 to let the
King of Hungary pass by in suitable state with the Duke of Austria;
and it became so rickety over the years that one chronicler described
it as 'all gnawed, and suspended in the air as if by a miracle'.

The sixth was the subject of a famous sixteenth-century architectural competition. Sansovino, Palladio, Scamozzi, Fra Giocondo and
even Michelangelo all submitted designs (you may see Michelangelo's, I am told, at the Casa Buonarotti in Florence). Most of the
competitors suggested multi-arched bridges, but one, Antonio da
Ponte, boldly proposed a single high arch, based upon 12,000 stakes,
with a span of more than 90 feet, a height of 24, and a width of 72.
This was a daring gesture. Da Ponte was official architect to the
Republic, and the Signory was hardly lenient with employees' errors
– Sansovino himself was presently to be imprisoned when his new
library building unfortunately fell down. Nevertheless, da Ponte's
design was accepted, and the bridge was built in two years. It has
been a subject of controversy ever since. Many Venetians disliked it
at the time, or mocked it as an unreliable white elephant; many others

objected when its clean arch was loaded with the present picturesque superstructure of shops; and it has been, until recently, fashionable to decry it as lumpish and unworthy (though several great painters have fondly pictured it, including Turner in a lost canvas).

Structurally, it was a complete success – during rioting in 1797 they even fired cannon from its steps, to dispel the mobs: and for myself, I would not change a stone of it. I love the quaint old figures of St Mark and St Theodore, on the station side of the bridge. I love the Annunciation on the other side, angel at one end, Virgin at the other, Holy Ghost serenely aloft in the middle. I love the queer whale-back of the bridge, humped above the markets, and its cramped little shops, facing resolutely inwards. I think one of the great moments of the Grand Canal occurs when you swing around the bend beside the fish market and see the Rialto there before you, precisely as you have imagined it all your life, one of the household images of the world, and one of the few Venetian monuments to possess the quality of geniality.

For another three centuries it remained the only bridge over the Grand Canal. As late as 1848 the Austrian soldiers could prevent subversive foot passage across the city simply by closing the Rialto bridge. Then two iron structures were thrown across the water-way – one by the railway station, one near the Accademia gallery. They were flat, heavy and very ugly, and the Accademia bridge was sometimes known, in mixed irony and affection, as *Ponte Inglese*. Both lasted until the 1930s, when they had to be replaced because of the increased size of the *vaporetti*. The new station bridge was a handsome stone structure, far higher than the Rialto. The new Accademia bridge was of precisely the same proportions, but because money was short it was built (just for the time being, so they cheerfully said) of tarred wood – a return to the original materials of Venetian bridge-building.

And here is an extraordinary thing. There are only these two modern bridges across the Grand Canal, the world's most resplendent water-way; but one day not long ago I took a *vaporetto* to Santa Maria del Giglio, and walked across to the Fenice Theatre, and crossed Campo San Fantin, and took the first turning on the left, and the third on the right, and followed the alley to the left again, and knocked on the door of third house on the right, and when the face of a jolly housekeeper had inspected me from an upstairs floor, and the door had clicked open, I found myself shaking hands with the architect who designed and built them both – one of the most remarkable monuments any man of our time has erected to himself.

14 City Services

Into their hugger-mugger city the Venetians have had to insert all the paraphernalia of modern urban life. Industry has generally been kept at arm's length, on the perimeters or on the mainland, but within the city proper a couple of hundred thousand people live, vote and pay their dues – and it is disconcerting how often the Venetian tax-collector seems to come around, shuffling with his receipt book among the buttressed alleys. Venice must be policed, lit, watered, cleaned, like any other city, adapting all the techniques to fit its strange and antique setting.

The old Venetians used to drink rain-water, supplemented by water from the Brenta river. It was channelled into elaborate cisterns and purified through sand-filters: the carved well-heads that you see in Venetian squares are often only the outlets of great underground storage tanks, sometimes almost filling the area of the *campo*. (The cisterns are sometimes still full of water, and sustain the struggling green foliage that persistently presses through the paving-stones.) Since 1884 drinking water has come by pipe from artesian wells at Trebaseleghe, on the mainland. It is stored in reservoirs near Sant' Andrea, and is so good that even Baedeker was prepared to commend it. During the First World War the aqueduct burst some-where underground, and only swift engineering action, kept secret from the people, prevented a calamity: today the supply is plentiful even in drought, and some of the public drinking fountains splash away merrily all day.

Electric power marches across the lagoon on pylons from its mountain sources. Petrol comes in barges, ships and tanker-trucks –

there are several petrol stations in Venice, including one near St Mark's and one on the Grand Canal. The city gasometer is tucked discreetly away near the northern church of San Francesco della Vigna, far from railing purists. The municipal slaughter-house is near the station: the cattle are driven there from the railway track, two mornings a week, by way of the Square of the Pork Butcher and the Alley of Butchers, and the waters around the building are stained with their blood. The radio station shares with the Municipal Casino the great Palazzo Vendramin, giving rise to a piquant juxtaposition of sound-proof walls, florid fireplaces, gaming tables, marble pillars, ermine and jazz.

The telephone department occupies a beautiful cloister near San Salvatore. The prison stands bleakly, guarded by lions of St Mark, in the shambled warehouse area near the car park, and if you pass by on visiting day you may look between its open doors and see the poor inmates talking gravely with their women-folk through the grilles. The lunatic asylum, isolation hospital, old people's home and consumptive sanatorium are all on islands in the lagoon. The fire brigade stands, its old red motor boats warily shining, beneath a shady arcade near Ca' Foscari, just off the Grand Canal: when they are summoned to a fire the engines are launched with such fierce momentum that one boat, recently misjudging a manoeuvre in the heat of its enthusiasm, struck the side of a palace and knocked its entire corner askew. The milk comes by truck from the mainland and is distributed by barge, with a tinny clanking of bottles in the half-light – though sixty years ago there were, besides the English herd, cows in sheds at Campo Angelo Raffaele and Santa Margherita. The Conservatoire of Music lives in a vast Renaissance palace near the Accademia bridge, from where the strains of its not very elfin horns emanate relentlessly across the waters. The tax department works in the cloister of Santo Stefano: always a place of controversy, for here Pordenone, commissioned to paint a series of Biblical frescoes, is said to have worn his sword and buckler on the job, in case his ferocious rival Titian came storming through the archway.

Several different kinds of policemen keep Venice safe and on the move. There are the extravagantly accoutred *Carabinieri*, whose

faces, between their cocked hats and their gleaming sword-hilts, are
often disconcertingly young and vacuous. There are the State police,
drab in workaday grey, who cope with crime. There are the civic
police, handsomely dressed in blue, who are responsible for traffic
control, and are often to be seen vigilantly patrolling the Grand Canal
in tiny speedboats, like toys. You do not need a driving licence in
Venice, but your engine must be registered and taxed, if it generates
more than three horse-power, and you must have permission to
drive mooring stakes into the canal beside your door; so that the city
police spend a great deal of time examining credentials and distributing documents, and generally leave the traffic to look after itself. The
stringent regulations announced before every ceremonial begin
strictly enough, but always peter away as the hours pass, until in the
end the policemen, succumbing to the invariable geniality of the
occasion, take very little notice at all, and allow the festival boats to
swirl about in delightful but sometimes inextricable confusion.

There are a few traffic notices in Venice, reminding boatmen of the
speed limit. There is one familiar intersection sign, marking the
crossing of two canals. There are many one-way signs. There are
even two sets of traffic lights, very popular amongst tourist guides.
The novice boatman, like a suburban housewife up for the day's
shopping, must learn where he can park his craft with impunity –
difficult at St Mark's, dangerous on the Riva (because of the swell),
impossible on the Grand Canal, simple in the poor, friendly, good-
natured districts that stretch away beyond Rialto to the Fondamenta
Nuove. Mostly, though, the Venetian policemen will not bother him,
and I am told they are much sought after as sons-in-law.

Much less full of circumstance are the garbage men, who supple-
ment the natural emetic of the sea-tides with a fleet of some twenty
grey motor barges. Under the Republic the refuse men formed an
influential guild, and a plaque in their honour was mounted above
the church door of Sant' Andrea, behind the car park. They were
so grand, indeed, that once they had established family monopolies
of the business, they employed other people to do the work for
them, and lived comfortably at home on the profits. Today they
are not usually proud of their calling, and do not much like to be

photographed at work: but very efficient and impressive they are, all the same, as their barges swirl in convoy into the Grand Canal, cluttered with obscure equipment, blasting their horns and roaring their engines, like warships of advanced and experimental design.

The fleet is run by private enterprise, under municipal contract. A small army of uniformed men, pushing neat metal trolleys, collects the plastic bags each morning from the houses of Venice, and hurries them through the alley-ways towards a rendezvous with their barges. The engines whirr; the rubbish is stacked automatically deep in the hold; and away the barge chugs, no dirtier than a vegetable boat, or smellier than a fish-cart. Ruskin caustically described Venice as a City In The Mud, but she is also a City Upon The Garbage: for they take that rubbish to the islet of Sacca Fisola, at the western tip of Giudecca, and eventually, mixing it hideously with sand, silt and seaweed, use it as the basis of new artificial islands.

The municipal hospital of Venice is a vast and rambling structure near the church of San Zanipolo, occupying the cloister of the church as well as the former building of the Scuola di San Marco. Going into hospital is thus a queer experience, for the way to the wards passes through one of the quaintest façades in Venice, a marvellous *trompe-l'oeil* creation of the fifteenth century, replete with lions, grotesqueries, tricks of craftsmanship and superimpositions. The reception hall is a tall dark chamber of pillars, and the offices, operating theatres and wards run away like a warren to the distant melancholy quayside of the Fondamenta Nuove, looking directly across to the cemetery. If you happen to take a wrong turning, on your way to the dispensary, you may find yourself in the fabulous chapter room of the Great School of St Mark, now a medical library, with the most magnificently opulent ceiling I have ever seen. If you should chance to die, they will wheel you at once into the old church of San Lazzaro dei Mendicanti, which now forms part of the hospital, and is only opened for funerals: it is remarkable partly for its manner of ingrained despair, and partly for a monument to a seventeenth-century worthy so hugely domineering that it faces two ways, one supervising the entire chancel of the church, the other demanding instant obeisance from anyone entering the vestibule. And in an arched boatyard beneath the hospital stand the duty ambulances, powerful blue motor boats which, summoned to an emergency, race off through the canals with a scream of sirens and a fine humanitarian disregard of the traffic rules.

Other city services cannot be wholly mechanized, and retain rituals and conventions passed down from the Middle Ages. The water scavengers, for example, do their work in the old way, scooping up floating scum in baskets, or pottering grimly about in boats with nets and buckets: the man who cleans our side-canal also carries a bottle of wine among his tackle – in case, he once cheerfully told me, his zest should momentarily fail him. The postal service, too, has changed slowly down the centuries. The central post office occupies the enormous Fondaco dei Tedeschi near the Rialto bridge, once the headquarters of the German mercantile community – it contained their offices, their warehouses, their chapel, and even hotel accommodation for visiting traders. This building was once decorated with frescoes by Titian and Giorgione, after those two young geniuses had prudently helped to extinguish a fire there. Today the place is gloomy and echoing, and from it nearly 100 postpersons go out each day in their smart blue uniforms, slung with satchels. They take the *vaporetto* to their allotted quarters, and then walk swiftly from house to house, popping the mail into baskets lowered from upstairs floors on long strings, and sometimes singing out a name in a rich and vibrant baritone.

Since the twelfth century the city has been divided into six *sestieri* or wards: to the north and east of the Grand Canal, the *sestieri* of Cannaregio, San Marco and Castello; to the south and west, San Polo, Santa Croce and Dorsoduro (which includes Giudecca and the island of San Giorgio Maggiore). Within each of these sections the houses are numbered consecutively from beginning to end, regardless of corners, cross-roads or culs-de-sac. The *sestiere* of San Marco, for example, begins at No. 1 (the Doge's Palace) and ends at No. 5562 (beside the Rialto bridge). There are 29,254 house numbers in the city of Venice, and within the limits of each sector their numbering is inexorable. Through all the quivering crannies of the place, the endless blind alleys and cramped courtyards, the bridges and arches and shuttered squares – through them all, coldly and dispassionately, the house numbers march with awful logic. The postman's task thus retains a Gothic simplicity and severity. He begins at No. 1, and goes on till he finishes.

Away down the Grand Canal stands the superb Palazzo Corner della Regina. This now houses the archives of the Biennale, Venice's international art festival, but not so long ago it was the Monte di Pietà, the municipal pawnshop. Nothing could have been more tactfully organized than this institution was. On the ground floor, to be sure, there was a sale room of a certain ragbag ebullience, haunted by fierce-eyed bargain hunters and eager dealers: but upstairs, where you deposited your treasures and drew your cash, all was propriety. The atmosphere was hushed. The counters were discreet and sombre, as in an old-fashioned bank. The attendants were courteous. There was none of the flavour of old clothes, rusty trinkets and embarrassment that pervades an English pawnbroker's. The Monte di Pietà used to suggest to me a modest but eminent Wall Street finance house, or perhaps a College of Heraldry.

A pawnshop is a pawnshop, though, however kindly disguised; and if you hung around the lane beside that great building you would often encounter the sad people of the hock-shop world, broken old men with sacks of junk, or wispy ladies, hopefully hurrying bent-backed with their mattresses and disjointed sewing-tables.

Everybody dies in Venice. The Venetians die in the normal course of events, and the visitors die as a matter of convention. In the Middle Ages the population was periodically decimated by the plague, which was often brought to Venice by way of the Levantine trade routes, and was only checked, on repeated occasions, by lavish votive offerings and prayers. Immense doses of Teriaca failed to keep the plague at bay. A single fifteenth-century epidemic reduced the population by two-thirds: nearly 50,000 people died in the city, it is said, and another 94,000 in the lagoon settlements. So concerned were the old Venetians with these perennial horrors that they even stole, from Montpellier in France, the body of St Roch, then considered the most effective champion against bacterial demons,

and they built five churches in thanksgiving for the ends of plagues –
the Salute, the Redentore, San Rocco, San Sebastiano and San Giobe
(Job was locally canonized, in the plague areas of the Adriatic shores,
because of his affinity with sufferers).

Many a precious fresco has been lost because the Venetians
whitewashed a wall to stifle the plague germs; and the whole floor of
the church of San Simeone Grande was once laboriously rebuilt and
elevated, owing to the presence of plague corpses beneath its
flagstones. When Titian died of the plague, in 1576, only he among
the 70,000 victims of that particular epidemic was allowed burial in a
church. Nor is this all very ancient history. A silver lamp in the Salute
was placed there as recently as 1836, to mark the end of a cholera
plague: and there were ghastly scenes of suffering – corpses lowered
from windows into barges, mass burials in the lagoon – when cholera
attacked Venice during the 1848 revolution.

Malaria, too, has killed or debilitated thousands of Venetians down
the centuries, and is only now checked by the new chemicals
(mosquitoes are still pestilential in the late summer); and the harsh
Venetian winters, with their rasping winds and interminable rains,
have been fatal to innumerable sickly pensioners. For all its glorious
spring idylls, the climate is treacherous – if balanced nowadays by the
relative peacefulness of a city without cars. Often the days feel
mysteriously depressing and enervating, as though the sadness of
Venice has impregnated its air; and it is said that Eleanora Duse
suffered all her life from the moods induced by these moments of
climatic hopelessness.

The experts say, indeed, that Venice is unusually healthy. 'The
barometric pressure', says one official pamphlet in its best bed-side
manner, 'is maintained at a uniform level because of the evenness of
its oscillations.' 'Bacterioscopical laboratory tests', says another,
'have proved that the water of the lagoon possesses auto-purifying
powers.' It is odd, all the same, how often foreign consuls and
ministers have died in Venice in the course of their duties, to leave
their high-flown honorifics mouldering on island tombstones: and
many a visiting lion has roared his last in Venice. Wagner died in the
palace that is now the winter casino. Browning died in the Ca'

Rezzonico, on which the municipality has inscribed his famous couplet of gratitude to Italy. Diaghilev died here, and Baron Corvo, and so did Shelley's little daughter Clara, after a journey from the Euganean Hills complicated by the fact that Shelley had left their passports behind.

A fourteenth-century Duke of Norfolk, banished from England after a quarrel with the future Henry IV, was buried in the Basilica, until he was exhumed and taken home by his descendants – he had retired himself to Italy, so Shakespeare wrote of him,

> *And there, at Venice, gave*
> *His body to that pleasant country's earth,*
> *And his pure soul until his captain, Christ.*

In San Zanipolo you may still see the grandiose tomb of 'Odoardo Windsor, Barone Inglese', who died in 1574. The Scotsman John Law, perpetrator of the Mississippi Bubble, died in Venice in poverty, and is buried in San Moise. Even Dante died of a fever contracted during a journey to Venice. The angry Venetian modernists like to say that this has become a city 'where people come to expire'. The gentle last-ditchers, inspired by so many distinguished predecessors, only wait for the day.

There is nothing more characteristically Venetian than one of the funeral cortèges that plough with such startling frequency down the Grand Canal, on their way to the island cemetery of San Michele (to which Napoleon decreed that all the city's dead should be carried). Today there is only one model of hearse, a plain blue motor launch with an open cockpit for the coffin and the undertaker's men, a curtained cabin for the mourners. Not so long ago a saturnine variety of craft offered far more opportunities for *grand guignol*. The most expensive was a straight-prowed, old-school motor boat, heavily draped in brown, black and gold, and steered by an unshakeably lugubrious chauffeur. The next was a kind of lighter, huge, forbidding and encrusted with gold, like a floating four-poster. Then came an elaborately gilded barge, rowed by three or four elderly boatmen in black tam-o'-shanters, at the bows a lion crying into a handkerchief, at the stern that prodigy of paradise, a bearded angel. And

cheapest of all was a mere gondola in disguise, a little blacker and
heavier than usual, mournfully draped, and rowed by two men in
threadbare but unmistakably funereal livery. Photographs of the
various vehicles used to be displayed in the undertakers' windows:
and once I overheard a small boy, looking at these pictures with his
sister, remarking in a phrase that I found hauntingly ambiguous:
'There! That's Daddy's boat!'

Marvellously evocative is a winter funeral in Venice. A kind of
trolley, like a hospital carriage, brings the coffin to the quayside, the
priest shivering in his wind-ruffled surplice, the bereaved relatives
desperately muffled; and presently the death-boat chugs away
through the mist down the Grand Canal, with a glimpse of flowers
and a little train of mourning gondolas. They keep close to the bank,
in the shade of the tall tottering palaces (themselves like grey symbols
of the grave), and thus disappear slowly into the distance, across the
last canal.

The procession is not always so decorous when it arrives at San
Michele, for this cemetery still serves the whole of Venice, and often
there are two or three such cortèges arriving at the landing-stage
simultaneously. Then there is a frightful conglomeration of brass
impediments, a tangle of plumes, motor boats backing and roaring,
gondoliers writhing at their row-locks, hookers straining on the
quay, mourners embarrassingly intermingled. It is a funeral jam. I
once saw such a *mélange*, one bright summer morning, into which a
funeral gondola of racy instincts was projected forcibly by an
accomplice motor boat, slipping the tow neatly as it passed the San
Michele landing-stage: never were mourners more mute with aston-
ishment than when this flower-decked bier came rocketing past their
gondolas, to sweep beside the quay with a jovial flourish.

Once ashore, though, and there will be no such contretemps, for
San Michele is run with professional efficiency, and the director
stands as proudly in his great graveyard as any masterful cruiser
captain, god-like on his bridge. The church at the corner of the island
is beautifully cool, austere and pallid, and is tended by soft-footed
Franciscans: Paolo Sarpi is buried at its entrance, and the Austrians
used its convent as a political prison. The cemetery itself is wide and

calm, a series of huge gardens, studded with cypress trees and awful monuments. Until quite recently it consisted of two separate islands, San Michele and San Cristoforo, but now they have been artificially joined, and the whole area is cluttered with hundreds of thousands of tombs – some lavishly monumental, with domes and sculptures and wrought-iron gates, some stacked in high modern terraces, like filing systems. There is a pathetic little row of children's graves, and around the cloister at the entrance many an old Venetian worthy is buried, with elaborate inscriptions on big stone plaques (many of which have been unaccountably defaced, by scribbled signatures and lewdities).

The cult of death is still powerful among the Venetians, and a constant flow of visitors moves silently among the graves, or meditates among the pleasant flower-beds of the place. Many of the grander tombs, already inscribed and shuttered, are not yet occupied, but await a death in the family. Others are so spacious, well built and frequented that they are more like nightmare summer-houses than tombs, and remind me of the hospitable mausoleums in Cairo's City of the Dead. Inside others again there hang, in the Italian manner, portraits of the departed, giving them rather the feeling of well-polished marble board-rooms, awaiting a quorum. There is an annual pilgrimage of ballet-lovers to the modest tomb of Diaghilev; and an increasing trickle of visitors finds its way to the obscure burial-place, high in a tomb-terrace, of Frederick William Serafino Austin Lewis Mary Rolfe, 'Baron Corvo'. He died, according to British Consulate records, in October 1913, in the Palazzo Marcello, at the age of 53: his life in Venice had sunk from eccentricity to outrage to depravity, but he refused ever to leave the city, wrote some incomparable descriptions of it, died in poverty and obloquy, and was buried (characteristically) at his brother's expense. Silently this multitude of shades lies there beneath the dark trees of San Michele; and at night-time, I am told, a galaxy of little votive lamps flutters and twinkles on ten thousand tombstones, like so many small spirits.

At the eastern corner of San Michele is an old Protestant graveyard of very different temper. It is like a Carolina churchyard, lush, untended and overgrown, shaded by rich gnarled trees, with grassy walks and generations of dead leaves. Most of its graves are obscured by weeds, earth and foliage, and it is instructive to wander through all this seductive desolation, clearing a gravestone here and there, or peering through the thickets at a worn inscription. There are many Swiss and Germans in these graves; and many British seamen who died on their ships in the port of Venice. There is an English lady, with her daughter, who perished in a ferry disaster off the Lido in the early 1900s; and several Americans with names such as Horace, Lucy or Harriet; and one or two diplomats, among whose flowery but almost illegible epitaphs you may discern a plethora of adjectives like 'noble-minded', 'lofty', 'much-respected', 'eminent'. There is a long-forgotten English novelist, G. P. R. James, whose merits as a writer, we are ironically assured, 'are known wherever the English language is spoken'; and there is an unfortunate Mr Frank Stanier, of Stafford-shire, whose mourners wrote of him in a phrase that might be kindlier put, that he 'Left Us In Peace, Febry 2nd, 1910'.

The marble-workers who erect the fancy mausoleums of San Michele are understandably cynical about the expenses of death in Venice, and say that only the rich lie easy in their graves. Certainly the Venetians have sometimes paid heavily for immortality. One sixteenth-century patrician directed in his will that his body should be washed in aromatic vinegar by three celebrated physicians, wrapped in linens soaked in essence of aloes, and placed in a lead coffin enclosed in cypress wood: upon the surrounding monument the virtues of the deceased were to be engraved in Latin hexameters, in letters large enough to be easily read at a distance of twenty-five feet, and the history of the family was to be added in a series of 800 verses, specially commissioned from some expensive poet. Seven commemorative psalms were also to be composed, and twenty monks were to chant them beside the tomb on the first Sunday in every month for ever. (But if you want to see how Pietro Bernardo's executors honoured this will, go and look at the bourgeois memorial they in fact erected to him in the Frari, and ask how often the monks sing those psalms these days.)

Humbler Venetians, too, have always hankered after a comfortable oblivion in the tomb. 'Here we poor Venetians become landowners at last,' said a Venetian woman to W. D. Howells, as they approached the cemetery just a century ago: but it is not strictly true. For twelve years they lie at peace in their graves: but then, unless their relatives are prepared to pay a substantial retaining fee, their bones are briskly exhumed and dumped in a common grave, and their pitiful little headstones, inscriptions and memorial photographs are left cracked and mouldering on a rubbish dump. Until a few years ago their bones were shipped away to a distant island of the lagoon. Nowadays they remain upon San Michele, and extra land is being reclaimed on the eastern side of the island, to make room for more.

This anonymous destiny has long coloured the Venetian's attitude to death. Nothing is more wryly comical to him than the whole paraphernalia of San Michele. Nothing excites his cynical instincts more bitterly than the cost of serenity after death. 'Here we all stop in the end', says the gondolier in a Venetian epigram, as he passes San Michele, 'rich and poor alike' – but his employer's reply is typically astringent. 'Perfectly true', he says. 'We all stop here in the end – but in the meantime, my friend, keep rowing.' To understand how strongly the Venetians feel about graves, coffins and urn-burials, try suggesting the advantages of burial at sea. 'In the water!' the Venetians will exclaim, those old sea-wanderers, 'where all the fishes and crabs will nibble your corpse!' And they throw up their hands in disbelieving horror, as though you had suggested being buried alive, or roasted, like many of the city's favourite martyrs.

Death and Venice go together, as Thomas Mann demonstrated: but it is a curious truth that while nearly everybody remembers a Venetian funeral, and fits it easily into the mould of the city's life, Venetian weddings go unnoticed. This was not always so. In the fifteenth and sixteenth centuries Venetian brides were celebrated throughout Europe for the magnificence of their clothes and the display of their weddings. They wore their hair long to the altar, cascading down their backs interwoven with threads of gold. On their heads were exquisite jewelled coronets. Their shoulders were bare, and their gorgeous full-skirted dresses were made of silk damask and gold brocade (unless they happened to be widows, who had to be veiled and dressed in unrelieved black, and must be married on the stroke of midnight).

Sometimes even today, if a princess marries in Venice, or a millionaire's daughter, there are spectacular celebrations, and frothy pictures in the illustrated magazines: but generally the wedding, unlike the honeymoon, is not regarded as a Venetian institution, and seldom graces the folk-lore of the guide books. This is not at heart a blithe city. A gondola wedding can be a charming function, though, with the bride's lace veil streaming over her velvet cushions, the gondoliers in yellow or red or blush-pink, the flowers hermetically sealed in cellophane, the bridegroom indescribably formal in his morning suit, and the wedding guests chugging along in their motor boats behind.

I saw one such wedding party emerging, on a crisp spring day, from the church of Santa Maria Formosa. The bride was very pretty; the husband was elegant; the guests were grand; the boats were immaculate; the priest, advancing paternally from the church, looked at once gay and godly; the bystanders, loitering with their shopping-bags upon the bridge, were properly pleased. But moored directly behind the bridal gondola was a lumpish grey dustbin boat, and its captain stood there four-square among his garbage, arms akimbo. The expression on his face, as the lily-perfume reached him, was a salty mixture of the caustic and the benign, and when the bridal party glided away down the canal, in a flutter of satin and pink ribbon, he started his engines with an oily rumble, and merrily set off towards the reception.

15 Age

The buildings of Venice are mostly very old, and sometimes very decrepit, and for centuries it has been a popular supposition that Venice will one day disappear altogether beneath the waters of her lagoon. She sprang from the sea fifteen centuries ago, and to round her story off aesthetically, so many a writer and artist has felt, she only needs to sink into the salt again, with a gurgle and a moan.

Tintoretto, in a famous painting, portrayed the city finally over-whelmed by a tidal wave. Rose Macaulay, when she died, was planning a novel about the last submergence of the place. 'Noiseless and watchful', is how Dickens saw the water of Venice, 'coiled round and round . . . in many folds like an old serpent: waiting for the time when people should look down into its depths for any stone of the old city that had claimed to be its mistress.'

Certainly the disappearance of Venice would give her history a wonderful symmetry of form – born out of the water, and returned at last into the womb; and you have only to take a trip in a gondola, observe the crumbled façades about you and watch the thickened lapping of the canals, to realize how precariously aged Venice is. Many a palace seems to bulge and totter, like an arthritic duke in threadbare ermine, and many a tower looks disconcertingly aslant. The old prison building on the Riva stands noticeably out of true, and sometimes I think, in the pink of a summer sunset, that the Doge's Palace itself is subsiding at its south-western corner. Venice depends for her longevity upon the long line of islands, artificially buttressed, which separate the lagoon from the Adriatic, and keep the sea-storms away from her delicate fabrics. She lives like a proud parchment dowager, guarded by the servants at the door.

She is built upon soggy mud-banks (though the Doge's Palace, as it happens, stands upon clay, on the stiffest portion of the Venetian under-soil). She rests upon an inverted forest of stakes – 1,156,672, so they say, support the Salute – so nobody can wonder if she wobbles a bit now and then. Over the centuries her wooden supports have been repeatedly weakened, partly by natural corrosion, partly by the wash of powered boats, partly by the deepening of canals, which has taken their waters to a depth unforeseen by the old engineers. Every now and then some ancient structure, tired of the fight against age, wind and corrosion, dies on its feet and disintegrates into rubble. The Venetian chroniclers are full of such collapses, and old historians often record, with enviable sang-froid, the spontaneous disinte-gration of a church or a celebrated bridge.

In particular the Venetian campaniles have a long tradition of subsidence, and several of them look doomed today. Santo Stefano,

San Giorgio dei Greci, San Pietro di Castello – they all lean violently, and if you stand at their feet with an imaginative ear you may almost hear them creaking. Even the tower of San Giorgio Maggiore, which was completed only in 1790, is no longer upright, as you can see if you take a boat into the lagoon and line it up against the campanile of St Mark. The campaniles were among the first Venetian structures, serving originally as look-outs as well as bell-towers, and sometimes as lighthouses too. Since fashions in towers change sluggishly, they often survived when their accompanying churches were rebuilt, and thus remained as memorials to earlier styles of architecture. In the sixteenth century there were more than 200 of them – old prints of Venice sometimes depict the city as one immense forest of bell-towers. Today there are about 170; the rest have fallen down.

When the tower of the Church of La Carità, now part of the Accademia, fell into the Grand Canal in the eighteenth century it caused such a wave that a fleet of gondolas was left high and dry in a neighbouring square. When the old tower of San Giorgio Maggiore collapsed in 1774 it killed a monk and left, as one observer recorded, 'a dismal vacancy among the marvels'. The campanile of Sant' Angelo fell three times before they finally demolished it. The campanile of Santa Ternita survived its demolished church and was used for half a century as a house; but it collapsed in 1882, temporarily burying its tenant in the ruins. The tower of San Giorgio dei Greci leaned from the moment it was built, and has been causing intense anxiety at least since 1816, when an urgent plan was prepared for its restoration. The campanile of Santo Stefano was so unsafe after an earthquake in 1902 that they built a small subsidiary bell-tower, still to be seen above the rooftops of Campo Santo Stefano. When the campanile of the Carmini was shaken by lightning in 1756, the monks were actually ringing its bells, but abandoned their peal in such haste that one man ran his head against a wall and was killed. At least seven campaniles have, at one time or another, been demolished just in time, as they staggered towards their fall. Outside the church of Santa Maria Zobenigo you may see a rectangular brick travel agency that is the stump of an unfinished campanile, intended to replace an unsafe predecessor, but stifled at an early age owing to a dissipation of funds. Earthquakes, lightnings and violent winds have all humiliated Venetian campaniles; muddy ground, vegetation among the masonry, subterranean water, inadequate foundations, inferior bricks all threaten their assurance. This is dangerous country for bell-towers.

When the most famous of them all fell down, the whole world mourned. There is a *traghetto* station on the Grand Canal, near San Marcuola, whose members have long had the fancy of recording events in large irregular writing upon the wall. Changes of fare are written there, and hours of service, and among several almost illegible inscriptions one stands out boldly. '*14 Luglio 1902*' (it says, in the dialect) '*Ore 9.55 Cadeva La Torre di S. Marco*' – 'On 14 July 1902, at five to ten in the morning, the tower of St Mark fell down.' Nothing in the whole of their history seems to have affected the Venetians more deeply, and you will still hear as much about the eclipse of the old Campanile, the prime symbol and landmark of Venice, as you will about the fall of the Republic.

The building was begun, so we are told, on St Mark's Day, 25 April 912. Its summit was once sheathed in brass, to act as a perpetual day-time beacon, and its flashing could be seen twenty-five miles away. Warning cressets were also lit in its bell-chamber, and during the wars against the Genoese five cannon were mounted up there. Countless great expeditions were welcomed home by the bells of the Campanile. Scores of criminals died to the slow beat of the *Maleficio*, the bell of evil omen. In the belfry Galileo demonstrated to the Doge his latest invention, the telescope, and from the platform below it Goethe caught his first sight of the sea. Since the seventeenth century the revolving gilded angel on the summit had been the master weather-vane of Venice.

Nothing on earth seemed stronger and stabler than the Campanile of St Mark's. It had, so one eighteenth-century guide book observed, 'never given the slightest sign of leaning, shaking or giving way'. It was so much a part of Venice, had supervised so many years of changing fortune, that it seemed eternal, and the people regarded it with an almost patronizing affection, and called it 'the Landlord'. According to popular rumour, the foundations of the tower ran deep beneath the pavement of the Piazza, extending star-wise in all directions; and every visitor to Venice made the ascent of the Campanile, whether he was an emperor inspecting the lagoon defences, or a renegade priest from the mainland, hung from the belfry in his wooden cage. All through the years, though, like a game but rocky old uncle, the Campanile was secretly weakening. It had been repeatedly struck by lightning, its gilded summit positively inviting calamity – as early as 1793 it was fitted with a lightning conductor, one of the earliest in Europe. It had been injudiciously restored and enlarged, and some rash structural alterations had been made inside the tower. Its bricks had been half-pulverized by centuries of salt wind and air. Its foundations, though strong, were not nearly as invulnerable as legend made them: though the tower was 320 feet high, the piles that supported it were driven less than sixty feet deep.

Thus, early that July morning, this famous tower gave a gentle shudder, shook itself, and slowly, gently, almost silently collapsed. The catastrophe had been foreseen a few days before: the firing of the midday cannon had been cancelled, in case it shook the structure, and even the bands in the Piazza were forbidden to play. Soon after dawn on the 14th the Piazza had been closed, and the anxious Venetians gathered around the perimeter of the square, waiting for the end. When it came, 'Il Campanile', it was said, 'se stato galantuomo' – 'the Campanile has shown himself a gentleman'. Not a soul was hurt. A hillock of rubble filled the corner of the Piazza, and a cloud of dust rose high above the city, like a pillar of guidance, or a shroud: but the only casualty was a tabby cat, said to have been called Mélampyge after Casanova's dog, which had been removed to safety from the custodian's lodge, but imprudently returned to finish its victuals. The weather-vane angel, pitched into the Piazza, landed at the door of the Basilica, and this was regarded as a miraculous token that the great church would not be damaged: nor was it, much of the debris being kept from its fabric by the stumpy pillar in the south Piazzetta from which the laws of the Republic used to be proclaimed. When the dust had cleared, and the loose masonry had subsided, there was seen to be lying unbroken on the debris the Marangona, the senior bell of Venice, which had called the people to their duties for six centuries. Even half a dozen shirts, which the custodian's wife had been ironing the day before, were found as good as new under the wreckage.

In a matter of moments it was all over, and only a pyramid of bricks and broken stones was left like an eruption in the square. (The remains were later taken away in barges and dumped, with a mourning wreath of laurel, in the Adriatic.) I once met a man who was present at this melancholy occasion, and who still seemed a little numbed by the shock of it. 'Weren't you astonished that such a thing could happen?' I asked him. 'Well,' he replied heavily, 'yes, it *was* a surprise. I had known the Campanile all my life, like a friend, and I never really expected it to fall down.'

The news of this old great-heart's death rang sadly around the world. The silhouette of Venice, one of the most universally familiar scenes on earth, was dramatically altered, and the skyline was left looking oddly flat and featureless, like a ship without masts. The city council met the same evening under the chairmanship of an old Venetian patrician, Count Grimani, who was mayor of the city for more than thirty years: and grandly aristocratic was its decision. There were some Venetians who thought the rebuilding of the tower would cost more than it was worth. There were many others who thought the Piazza looked better without it. The council, however, did not agree. The Campanile would be rebuilt, they decided, 'as it was and where it was', and the phrase has become famous in Venetian lore – *'Com' era, dov' era'*.

Money poured in from many countries; the greatest experts came from Rome; in nine years the Campanile was built again, modernized in structural design, 600 tons lighter, but looking almost identical. The shattered bells were recast at a foundry on the island of Sant' Elena, and paid for by the Pope himself – that same Pius X whom we saw returning so triumphantly to Venice half a century later. The foundations were reinforced with 1,000 extra piles. The broken little loggia at the foot of the tower was put together again, piece by piece, and so were the lions and figures at the top. The angel's cracked wings were splinted. On 25 April 1912, a millennium to the day after the foundation of the old Campanile, the new one was inaugurated. Thousands of pigeons were released to carry the news to every city in Italy: and at the celebratory banquet six of the guests wore those rescued shirts, whose ironing had been so abruptly interrupted nine years before.

For all these sad precedents, Venice is not going to collapse altogether from sheer senility. Her palaces were stoutly built in the first place, by engineers of great vision, her foundations in the mud at least have the advantage of a certain elasticity, and it is said that her sub-aqueous pilings are petrified by the saltiness of the water (the salinity of the Adriatic here is the highest in Europe). It is extraordinary how few of her antique buildings are uninhabitable, and how successfully the old place can be patched and buttressed, as a wrinkled beauty is repeatedly rejuvenated by surgery, cosmetics and the alchemy of love.

The engineers have no exact precedents to follow: in this respect, as in many others, Venice is all on her own. Her methods have always been bold and sometimes startling. As long ago as 1688 an ingenious engineer succeeded in straightening the toppling tower of the Carmini church. He did it by boring holes into the brickwork on three sides of the tower, driving wedges of wood into them, and dissolving the wood with a powerful acid. The tower settled into the cavities thus created, and the engineer is gratefully buried inside the building, underneath a seat. Even earlier, in 1445, a Bolognese named Aristotle guaranteed to straighten the tower of Sant' Angelo by a method secret to himself (it entailed excavating ground beneath the base of the campanile). The work was elaborate, the tower was in fact straightened, but the very next day after the removal of the scaffolding the building collapsed altogether, and Aristotle fled ignominiously to Moscow, where he built part of the Kremlin. In the nineteenth century the Doge's Palace itself was restored in a brilliant engineering work, in the course of which some of the vital columns of the arcade were removed altogether and replaced with stronger pillars.

Today many a campanile is supported with hidden stanchions and supports, and some buildings (like the former church of San Vitale) are visibly held together with strips of iron. The palaces of Venice, when they need support, are strengthened by the injection of concrete into their foundations, as a dentist squeezes a filling into a rotting but still useful tooth. The Basilica is constantly attended by its own private consultant, the resident engineer, successor to a long line of Architects to St Mark's. This learned and devoted man knows every inch of his church, and spends his life devising ways of strengthening it without spoiling its antique irregularities. He has a staff of nearly forty men working all the year round, and a mosaic workshop manned by twelve skilled craftsmen. He is always experimenting, and has in particular perfected a means of replacing broken chips of mosaic in the ceiling by cutting through the masonry above, and inserting the precious fragments from behind. No Venetian experience is more satisfying than to wander round the dark Basilica with Professor Forlati, and absorb the meticulous but daring care with which he keeps that almost mythical building from falling apart. The engineers of Venice, like most of her professional men, are impressive people: and we need not doubt that they will at least keep the city on its feet for many a long century to come.

It is less certain that they can keep its toes dry. Though the process is much less spectacular than the jeremiads imply, it is more or less true that Venice is slowly sinking into the lagoon. At high tide, as you can see from the Campanile, the lagoon is mostly water, but at low tide it is mostly mud – Goethe climbed the bell-tower twice, to see the difference. Within its wide enclave two geological evolutions are occurring: the water is going up, the mud is going down. The sub-soil of Venice is alternately hard and soft. To a depth of more than 100 feet it is usually soft mud; then there is a slab about ten feet thick of good firm clay; and below that there are layers of spongy peat, sandy clay and watery sand. It is apparently the gradual compression of the stiff clay, the basis of Venetian stability, that causes the subsidence: and the water is being forced upwards, here as everywhere, by the slow melting of ice in the Arctic. The water level is rising, so they say, at an average of nearly an inch every five years – which means, so I calculated on a rainy afternoon, that in just 1,806 years the potted

azalea on the balustrade of my apartment will be watered directly by
the Grand Canal, or more pertinently that most of the Venetian
streets will be awash within a century or so.

This is an old story. There are many places in Venice where
columns and doorways, once at ground level, are now well below it –
the entrance to the Basilica, for example, which was originally flat
with the Piazza, but is now down a couple of steps. When they
remove the paving-stones for a drain or a water-pipe, they often find
the remains of another street about a yard below, built in the Middle
Ages when the lagoon was lower. You could no longer store your
damasks in the ground floor of a Grand Canal palace – the damp
would ruin them in a week. The Piazza floods are a modern
excitement, caused by the rise of the water: in February 1340 the
waters 'rose three cubits higher than had ever been known in Venice'
– but the Piazza remained dry. The pillars of the Doge's Palace have
often been criticized as 'gouty' and 'dumpy', but they were much
more elegant, and a good deal taller, before the level of the Piazza
had to be raised around them – five older pavements lie beneath the
present one. All over the city you may see such evidence of the rising
water – pillars that have been successively heightened, stone lions
whose whiskers are washed by the tides, damp rot on a hundred
palace walls. Venice has often hitched up her skirts to keep clear of
the wet, but the water is always gaining on her.

It is mainly a natural phenomenon, but is partly humanly induced.
The dredging of deep-water entrances into the lagoon has increased
the flow of the tides and affected the natural balance of the waters. So
has the deepening of canals inside the city, and the constant scouring
of the water-ways. The diversion of the rivers that used to pass
through the lagoon has apparently raised the level of the water rather
than lowered it. Earthquakes have contributed to the subsidence of
the mud-flats, but so have various industrial activities on the
mainland, and drilling for methane gas and fresh water under the
lagoon floor.

Since the great flood of 1966, the worst in living memory, the whole
western world has concerned itself with saving Venice from
extinction, and the first thing that now enters most people's minds,

when they hear the name of Venice, is the prospect of her submergence. Restorers and engineers from a dozen countries have offered their solutions to the municipal problems. From Naples to Vancouver charity balls, esoteric auctions and excruciatingly fashionable fêtes have raised funds to patch the crumbled noses of Venetian statuary, touch up the faded colours of Titian and Tintoretto and cure those leprous palaces. An international conclave of hydrologists has decided that Venice can be saved from future flooding by the building of lock gates at the lagoon entrances. Teams of visiting restorers have set to work upon the city churches – Frenchmen at the Salute, Britons at Madonna del Orto, Germans at Santa Maria dei Miracoli, Americans almost everywhere else – citizens of Los Angeles, for instance, unexpectedly assuming responsibility for the hitherto almost totally ignored San Pietro di Castello. The Italian Government has voted a large subsidy for the city, and UNESCO has produced its customary folio of answers to everything. Nobody could call Venice neglected today. Art and ecstasy may enter her presence more warily than of old, but ecology has made her all its own.

I write sourly, for disliking artificially conserved communites I have tended to see the salvation as more distressing than the threat: but in my more rational moments I do recognize that letting Venice sink, my own solution for her anxieties, is a counsel of perfection that cannot be pursued. She will be saved, never fear: it is only in selfish moments of fancy that I see her still obeying her obvious destiny, enfolded at last by the waters she espoused, her gilded domes and columns dimly shining in the green, and at very low tides, perhaps, the angel on the summit of the Campanile to be seen raising his golden forefinger (for he stands in an exhortatory, almost an ecological pose) above the mud-banks.

16 The Bestiary

Somebody once won a handsome prize from the Republic for suggesting in a laborious sonnet that Venice was divinely founded. I am myself often reminded in this city (though nobody is going to reward me for it) of the old tag about those whom the gods destroy. Venice went half-mad in the decades before her fall, reeling through her endless carnival with such abandon that one disapproving observer said of her that 'the men are women, the women men, and all are monkeys'. The mass lunacy of it all reached such a pitch that you sometimes saw a mother giving her baby suck, both wearing dominoes. Today Venice is relatively sober, except for the ostentatious aliens who sweep in during carnival and the high months of summer: but I sometimes fancy among its buildings – the megalomaniac palaces of the Grand Canal, the dark elaborate churches, the contorted back streets – some seeds or droppings of insanity.

Take, in particular, the myriad carved animals that decorate this city, and contribute powerfully to its grotesquerie. Often these figures conform to old animal symbolisms – the hare for lust, the fox for cunning, the pelican for loyalty, the lamb for meekness, the crane for vigilance, the spider for patience. Sometimes they represent family emblems – *riccio* the porcupine, for instance, for the house of Rizzo. Others, though, seem to portray degeneracies, cruelties, horrors and freaks with a perverse and peculiar relish. There is no zoo in Venice, but a mad-cap menagerie is carved upon its walls, for wherever you go these unhinged creatures peer at you from the masonry: dogs, crocodiles, birds, cockatrices, crabs, snakes, camels, monsters of diverse and horrifying species. There are innumerable eagles that seem to be made out of pineapples. There are some very queer dromedaries (the Venetian artists never could do camels, and the two on the façade of San Moisè seem to have the heads of turtles). There is a misshapen porcupine on a well-head in Goldoni's house, and a skew-eyed ox in the church of Sant' Aponal, and a long-necked imaginary bird peers myopically over the Rialto end of the Merceria.

Most of this monstrous bestiary seems to be malignant, from the contorted dragons on the church-cinema of Santa Margherita, who are grappled in a dreadful death-struggle, to the arrogant cocks on the floor of San Donato, in Murano, who are carrying a fox upside down on a pole, as you might take a hapless grizzly back to camp. An entire column-head in the arcade of the Doge's Palace is devoted to animals gorging their prey – a lion with a stag's haunch, a wolf with a mangled bird, a fox with a cock, a gryphon with a rat, a bear with a honeycomb. The stone animals of Venice all seem to be gnawing, or tearing, or wrestling, or biting, or writhing, or embroiled in a mesh of limbs, teeth, hair, ears and saliva. If you look at the mosaic of Christ's baptism in the Baptistery of the Basilica, you will discover that even the sacred Jordan is infested with swordfish. Nothing could be sweeter than the little animals of Venetian painting, from Carpaccio's curly dog to the ironical donkey in Tintoretto's *Crucifixion*, sadly chewing withered palm leaves behind the Cross: but the Venetian sculptors infused their animal life with a streak of paranoia, progressively declining in delicacy and originality until they reached their nadir in the hideous head, half-human, half-beast, that stands on the wall of Santa Maria Formosa, its eyes bulging and its tongue a-lick.

An altogether different, gentler kind of derangement informs the sculptured lions of Venice, which stand grandly apart from all these degradations. The lion became the patron beast of Venice when St Mark became the patron saint, and for a thousand years the lion and the Serenissima were inseparable, like China and the dragon. Pope wrote contemptuously of Venice in her degeneracy as a place where

> . . . *Cupids ride the lion of the deeps;*
> *Where, eased of fleets, the Adriatic main*
> *Wafts the smooth eunuch and enamoured swain.*

In earlier times the lion had more honourable roles to play. He rode rampant upon the beaks of the Venetian war-galleons, and fluttered on the banner of St Mark. His friendship for St Jerome automatically elevated that old scholar high in the Venetian hagiarchy. He stood guard beside thrones and palaces, frowned upon prisoners, gave authenticity to the State documents of the Republic. His expression varied according to his function. In one Croatian town, after a rebellion against Venetian rule, a very disapproving lion was erected: the usual words on his open book, *Pax Tibi, Marce*, were replaced with the inscription *Let God Arise, and Let His Enemies Be Scattered*. In Zara, which revolted seven times against Venice, and withstood thirty-two Venetian sieges, a lion was erected, so the chroniclers tell

us, 'with a gruff expression, his book closed and his tail contorted like
an angry snake'. In a seventeenth-century map of Greece the lion is
shown striding into action against the Turk, his wings outstretched, a
sword in his paw, and the Doge's hat on his head. The Venetians
respected him so much that some of the patricians even used to keep
live lions in their gardens. A fourteenth-century writer reported
excitedly that the pair in the zoological gardens beside the Basin of St
Mark's had given birth to a couple of thriving cubs: they were fed,
like the pelicans of St James's Park, at the expense of the State.

I cannot help thinking that the old Venetians went a little queer
about lions, for the profusion of stone specimens in Venice is almost
unbelievable. The city crawls with lions, winged lions and ordinary
lions, great lions and petty lions, lions on doorways, lions supporting
windows, lions on corbels, self-satisfied lions in gardens, lions
rampant, lions soporific, amiable lions, ferocious lions, rickety lions,
vivacious lions, dead lions, rotting lions, lions on chimneys, on
flower-pots, on garden gates, on crests, on medallions, lurking
among foliage, blatant on pillars, lions on flags, lions on tombs, lions
in pictures, lions at the feet of statues, lions realistic, lions symbolic,
lions heraldic, lions archaic, mutilated lions, chimerical lions, semi-
lions, super-lions, lions with elongated tails, feathered lions, lions
with jewelled eyes, marble lions, porphyry lions, and one real lion,
drawn from the life, as the artist proudly says, by the indefatigable
Longhi, and hung among the rest of his *genre* pictures in the Querini-
Stampalia gallery. There are Greek lions, Gothic lions, Byzantine
lions, even Hittite lions. There are seventy-five lions on the Porta
della Carta, the main entrance to the Doge's Palace. There is a winged
lion on every iron insurance plate. There is even a sorrowing lion at
the foot of the Cross itself, in a picture in the Scuola di San Marco.

The most imperial lion in Venice is the winged beast painted by
Carpaccio in the Doge's Palace, with a moon-lily beside his front
paw, and a tail four or five feet long. The ugliest pair of lions lie at the
feet of a French Ambassador's tomb in the church of San Giobbe, and
were carved, with crowns on their heads and tongues slightly
protruding, by the French sculptor Perreau. The silliest lion stands in
the Public Gardens, removed there from the façade of the Accademia:

Minerva is riding this footling beast side-saddle, and on her helmet is perched another anatomical curiosity – an owl with knees. The eeriest lion is the so-called crab-lion, which you may find in a dark archway near the church of Sant' Aponal, and which looks less like a crab than a kind of feathered ghoul. The most unassuming stands on a pillar outside San Nicolo dei Mendicoli; he holds the book of St Mark in his paws, but has never presumed to apply for the wings. The most froward stands on a bridge near Santa Chiara, behind the car park, where a flight of steps runs fustily down to the canal like a Dickensian staircase in the shadows of London Bridge, and this unlikeable beast glowers at you like Mrs Grundy.

The most pathetic lion is an elderly animal that stands on the palisade of the Palazzo Franchetti, beside the Accademia bridge, bearing listlessly in his mouth a label inscribed *Labore*. The most undernourished is a long lion on the south façade of the Basilica, three or four of whose ribs protrude cruelly through his hide. The most glamorous is the winged lion on his column in the Piazzetta, whose eyes are made of agate, whose legs were damaged when Napoleon removed him to Paris, and whose Holy Book was inserted neatly under his paws when he was first brought to Venice from the pagan East, converted from a savage basilisk to a saint's companion.

The most indecisive lion is the creature at the foot of the Manin statue, in the Campo Manin, whose creator was evidently uncertain whether such carnivores had hair under their wings, or feathers (as Ruskin said of another pug-like example, which has fur wings, 'in several other points the manner of his sculpture is not uninterest-ing'). The most senile lions are the ones on the Dogana, which are losing their teeth pitifully, and look badly in need of a pension. The most long-suffering are the porphyry lions in the Piazzetta dei Leoncini, north of the Basilica, which have been used by generations of little Venetians as substitutes for rocking horses. The frankest lions, the ones most likely to succeed, are the pair that crouch, one dauntless but in chains, the other free and awfully noble, beneath the fine equestrian statue of Victor Emmanuel on the Riva degli Schiavoni.

The most enigmatical is the floridly maned lion, outside the gates of the Arsenal, whose rump is carved with nordic runes. The most confident is the new lion that stands outside the naval school at Sant' Elena, forbidding entry to all without special permission from the commandant. The most athletic looks sinuously past the Doge Foscari on the Porta della Carta. The most threatening crouches on the façade of the Scuola di San Marco, his paws protruding, ready to leap through the surrounding marble. The most reproachful looks down from the Clock Tower in the Piazza, more in sorrow than in anger, as though he has just seen you do something not altogether creditable beneath the arcade. The jolliest – but there, none of the lions of Venice are really very unpleasant, and comparisons are invidious.

They provide an essential element in the Venetian atmosphere, an element of cracked but affectionate obsession. It is no accident that in the very centre of Tintoretto's vast Paradise, in the Doge's Palace, the lion of St Mark sits in unobtrusive comfort, nestling beside his master amid the surrounding frenzy, and disputing with that saintly scribe, so Mark Twain thought, the correct spelling of an adjective.

Bestial, too, were the men of Venice, when the madness of politics or revenge caught hold of them. If you have a taste for Grand Guignol, Venice has much to offer you: for here, to this day, the spirit of melodrama lives on in shrouded triumph, if you care to rap the tables and seek it out. To the early Victorians Venice was synonymous with tyranny and terror. The hushed and sudden methods of the Venetian security agencies, controlled by the Council of Ten and the Council of Three, cast a chill across all Europe, and have left behind them (now that we are quite safe from the strangler's cord) an enjoyable aftermath of shudder.

They worked in a ghastly secrecy, but it was part of their technique to surround themselves with an aura of unspeakable horror, so that the French essayist Montesquieu, jokingly told one day that he was 'being watched by the Three', packed his bags that very morning and fled helter-skelter home to Paris. 'The Ten send you to the torture chamber,' so the Venetians used to whisper, 'the Three to your grave' – and they would cross themselves, as a pious but not always infallible insurance. Even foreign embassies were not immune: every diplomatic household contained at least two State spies among its servants, and the agents of the Three examined each envoy's house for secret passages or hidden chambers.

Enemies of the State were precipitately strangled, beheaded between the two pillars of the Piazzetta, or hanged between the upper columns of the Doge's Palace (two of them still stained, so tradition wrongly says, with the blood of traitors). Sometimes malefactors were publicly quartered, and the several parts of their bodies were exposed on the shrines of the lagoon: as late as 1781 this happened to Stefano Fantoni, who had helped his mistress to kill her husband, chop him in bits, and distribute him among the canals and wells of the city. Sometimes it was all done without explanation, and early morning passers-by would merely observe, on their way to work, that a couple of fresh corpses were hanging by one leg apiece from a rope suspended between the Piazzetta columns. If a wanted man ran away from Venice, hired assassins of dreadful efficiency were almost sure to find him. If he stayed, he invited the attentions of the terrible Venetian torturers, the most advanced and scientific of their day.

The dungeons of the *Piombi* (the Leads, or attics) and the *Pozzi* (the Wells) were horribly celebrated in their time, and even more so after Casanova's escape from them – engineered, so some people think, because he was really a secret agent of the Three. 'I see, sir' (said the gaoler to the great adventurer, in the most famous chapter of his memoirs), 'that you want to know the use of that little instrument. When their Excellencies order someone to be strangled, he is seated at a stool, his back against the wall, that collar around his neck; a silken cord goes through the holes at the two ends, and passes over a wheel; the executioner turns a crank, and the condemned man yields up his soul to God!'

Most ingenious, Casanova thought it; and a sense of hooded contrivance still hangs murkily over the prisons of the Doge's Palace, assiduously though the tourists chew their gum, as they peer through the peep-holes of the dungeons. ('Your tickets also entitle you to visit the *Dungeons*,' says Mr Grant Allen in his *Historical Guide*,

1898. 'I am not aware of any sufficient reason why you should desire to avail yourself of this permission.') Horror runs in the blood of Venice: not just because the Venetian gaolers were crueller than the French or the English, or because the *Pozzi* were more dreadful than the cells of the Tower, the rats more noisome or the strangling machines more meticulous – but because Venice was so small a place, her symbolisms were so compact, and all the apparatus of medieval autocracy, gorgeously gilden and embellished, was established within a few hundred yards of the Doge's Palace.

Modern Venetians, conditioned by this grisly heritage, often have a taste for the macabre. They like it to be authentic, though, and have little time for idle superstitions, however gruesome. It is true that Alfred de Musset, when he paid a catastrophic visit to Venice with George Sand, who promptly ran off with a handsome young doctor – it is quite true that de Musset occupied Room 13 at the Hotel Danieli ('Alfred was a sad flirt', said Swinburne, 'and George was no gentleman'): but in Venice nobody much cares about spilling salt or walking under ladders – which indeed, propped across the narrow alley-ways of the place, often give you no choice. There are few Venetian ghost stories. The Palazzo Contarini delle Figure, near Byron's palace on the Grand Canal, is said to be haunted. In the fifteenth century it belonged to an irrepressible squanderer, who married a beautiful heiress and successively gambled away first her lands, then her palace, and finally the heiress herself: today, so it is said, it is plagued by queer knockings and opening of doors, as of phantom brokers' men. Another story is attached to the church of San Marcuola, whose vicar, having foolishly announced from the pulpit his utter disbelief in ghosts, was promptly taken in hand by the corpses of his own churchyard, who dragged him from his bed and soundly beat him.

The most famous such tale used to concern a house known as the Casino degli Spiriti, which stands beside a rectangular inlet of water in the northern part of the city, and was until recently a lonely and desolate place. This house has had a chequered past. It was once owned, so they say, by a *bon viveur* of intellectual tastes, who made it a centre of artistic and literary society, and gave gay parties in its gardens: but it stands on the route of the funeral processions to San Michele, and is said to have been used also as a theatre for autopsies – corpses lay the night there before passing to their graves in the morning. Other rumours say that it was once a mart for contraband, and that the smugglers deliberately surrounded it with ominous legends, to keep the curious away. Whatever the truth of its history, it has a creepy reputation, and its ghost story, a long and rather tedious one, concerns a love-triangle, a dead coquette and a possessive phantom.

Even today, though no longer isolated, the Casino degli Spiriti can still feel spooky. Some people claim to hear disconcerting echoes there. Others say the very look of it, alone on its promontory, slightly curdles the blood. The legend of the ghosts has faded, and only the name survives: but a few years ago two evil gondoliers, perhaps still languishing in prison, robbed a woman of her money, murdered her, dismembered her body, bundled it into a sack, and dropped it into the water only a few yards from the terrace of this weird and ill-omened house.

Venice scarcely needs fables to strengthen her strain of the ghastly. There is macabre enough for most tastes in the pictures and sculptures of the city – the vivid torture-scenes of its holy paintings, the corpses, severed ligaments, shrivelled limbs and metallic death-masks of its countless relics, the lolling head of Goliath in the church of San Rocco, the writhing ghosts of Tintoretto's *Last Judgement* in Madonna dell' Orto ('rattling and adhering', as Ruskin saw it with relish, 'into half-kneaded anatomies, that crawl, and startle, and struggle up among the putrid weeds'). There is the Palazzo Erizzo, near the Maddalena church, which was decorated by a conscientious member of the Erizzo family with pictures showing one of his illustrious ancestors being sawn in half, while still alive, by the Turks. There is the stark and curdling figure of the Crucifixion that suddenly confronts you in a little glass cabinet, if you climb the winding staircase inside the church of the Gesuiti. There are the blackened, mutilated statues that stand in the burnt chapel of the Rosary, in San Zanipolo.

The streets of Venice, too, are alive with ancient horrors. In the streets around San Zaccaria three Doges have been, at one time or another, assassinated – Pietro Tradonico in 864, Vitale Michiele I in 1102, Vitale Michiele II in 1172. In the Campo San Polo Lorenzino de' Medici, himself a practised murderer, was fallen upon by two hired ruffians as he came out of the church: they cut his head in half with one sword-blow. Near the church of Santa Fosca, Paolo Sarpi was stabbed by hired assassins of the Pope (one of whom is said to have been a Scot). He was left for dead with a dagger embedded in his cheek-bone, but recovered miraculously and hung the dagger as an *ex voto* in his monastery church, after his doctors had tried it on a dog and a chicken, to make sure it was not poisoned. There was once a murder in the Palazzo Vendramin, the Municipal Casino. During the Revolution of 1848 a mob chased an Austrian naval officer up and up the spiral staircase of one of the Arsenal towers, driving him ever higher until, trapped at the top, he was killed with an iron bar and allowed to tumble bloodily down the stone steps again. In the church of the Misericordia a seventeenth-century Venetian author was murdered by a priest who poisoned the Host. The innumerable wayside shrines of the city, usually in obscure street corners, were originally set up at places notoriously haunted by footpads – partly because their candles would illuminate the place at night, partly as a call to the criminal conscience. In the twelfth century false beards were prohibited in Venice, because so many assassins wore them in disguise. There is even a Calle degli Assassini, near Santo Stefano – a church which was consecrated on six separate occasions, because of repeated bloodshed within its walls.

There are many Venetian burial-places of morbid and sinister import. Resting on iron brackets in the Frari, high on a wall beside the right transept, you will see a wooden coffin of the crudest kind. This was intended, so it is said, for the unfortunate *condottiere* Carmagnola, who led a Venetian army to defeat in 1431, was enticed back to Venice, accused of treason, tortured and beheaded: but his body now lies in Milan, and this grim box, so high among the dust and shadows, contains, as a mordant but still inadequate substitute, the ashes of a murdered Venetian nobleman. Somewhere in Santo Stefano is buried another enemy of Venice, Novello Carrara of Padua, who was captured in battle in 1406 and secretly murdered with his two sons in the Doge's Palace: he was buried in the church with hypocritical pomp, the very day after his strangulation, but nobody now knows the position of his grave – though for centuries people thought that the initials carved on the tomb of a harmless merchant called Paolo Nicolò Tinti really stood for *Pro Norma Tyrannorum*, and showed where the old grandee lay.

On San Michele is buried the French painter Léopold Robert, who killed himself in 1835, ten years to the day after his brother had done the same thing: his epitaph was written by Lamartine, and observes loftily, describing the suicide as *'un accès de défaillance'*, that 'whereas Michelangelo would have vanquished it, Léopold Robert succumbed'. In the church of San Francesco della Vigna there is a tomb of the Barbaro family, surmounted by the ancestral device of a red circle on a field argent: this emblem was granted to the Barbaros in gratitude to Admiral Marco Barbaro, who cut off the hand of a Moor during a twelfth-century battle, whipped the turban from the poor infidel's head, traced a triumphant red circle upon it with the bleeding stump of his arm, and flew it from his mast-head as an ensign of triumph.

Among a series of sarcophagi on the portico of the Museum of Natural History, in the Fondaco dei Turchi, there is one without decoration or inscription. This once belonged to the Faliero family, one of the greatest Venetian houses. In 1355 Marin Faliero, then the Doge of Venice, was convicted of treason and decapitated on the steps of his palace ('You are condemned', so the court messenger brusquely informed him, 'to have your head cut off within the hour'). His body, with its head between its feet, was displayed to the public for twenty-four hours, and then taken quietly by boat to San Zanipolo, where the Faliero sarcophagus then lay. The centuries passed, and in 1812 the vault was opened, disclosing the body of the disgraced Doge, with its skull still between its leg-bones. The sarcophagus was emptied, removed from the church, and used for years as a reservoir by the apothecary of the civic hospital, around the corner. Then it was taken into the country and used as a cattle trough. Now it stands, vast and brooding, all disregarded beside the water-steps of the museum, *sans* skulls, *sans* crest, *sans* inscription, but instinct with sad memory: and what has happened to the poor Doge's skeleton, nobody seems to know.

Most horrific of all in its associations is the memorial to the Venetian admiral Marcantonio Bragadino that stands in the right-hand aisle of San Zanipolo. Bragadino was a distinguished Venetian commander who defended Famagusta during the sixteenth-century wars against the Turks. His resistance was brave and competent,but after many months of siege he was forced to surrender. The Turkish commander offered him honourable terms, and Bragadino left the fortress to sign the surrender, dressed in the purple robes of his office, attended by the officers of his staff, and shaded from the sun by a red ceremonial umbrella. The Pasha at first received him courteously: but suddenly, in the course of the ceremony, the Turk sprang from his seat, accused Bragadino of atrocities against his prisoners, and ordered the officers of the Venetian staff to be instantly hacked into pieces.

Bragadino's fate was worse. Three times he was just about to be beheaded when, as a refinement of suspense, the executioner was told to stop. His nose and ears were cut off, his body was mutilated, and every morning for ten days he was loaded with baskets of earth and driven to the Turkish fortifications, pausing before the Pasha's pavilion to kiss the ground before it. He was hoisted to the yardarm of a ship and left for hours to dangle there. He was subjected to all kinds of degrading and sadistic mockery. Finally he was taken to the main square of the city, stripped, chained to a stake, and slowly skinned alive in the presence of the Pasha. His skin was stuffed with straw and paraded through the streets on a cow, its red umbrella held above it in irony: and when at last the Pasha sailed home in triumph to the Golden Horn, this grim trophy swayed from the bowsprit of his flagship.

The skin was placed, a memento of victory, in the Turkish arsenal at Constantinople: but years later the Venetians acquired it, some say by purchase, some by theft. It was, so we are told, still as soft as silk, and it was cleaned, blessed, and placed inside an urn. Today a bust of Bragadino (after whom a *vaporetto* is named, if nothing else) gazes serenely from his great monument in San Zanipolo. Above him is a detailed fresco of his flaying, mercifully obscured by age and shadow. Beside him two lions stare numbly into the nave. And directly above his head, if you look closely, you will see the small stone urn in which his yellowing scarred skin lies peacefully folded, like a pocket handkerchief in a linen drawer.

17 Arabesques

In the Strada Nuova, on the way to the station, there stands a small outdoor market in which I sometimes like to pause, and close my eyes, and lean against a pillar. There is a sweet market smell there, tinged with fish, pepper and a suggestion of cloves; there is a clatter of wooden-soled shoes and a hubbub of high-pitched voices; there is a swish of dresses, a clashing of pans, a clamour of pedlars and stallholders, a creaking of old wood, a flapping of canvas awnings; and sometimes a dog barks, and sometimes a harridan screams. As I lean bemused against my pillar in this place, and let my mind wander, I find that Venice fades around me, west turns to east, Christian to Muslim, Italian to Arabic, and I am back in some dust-ridden, fly-blown, golden market of the Middle East, the tumble-down *suk* at Amman, or the bazaars beside the Great Mosque of the Ummayads, in the distant sunshine of Damascus. I can all but hear the soft suck of a hubble-bubble in the café next door, and if I half-open my eyes and look at the tower of the Apostoli, along the street, I swear I can see the muezzin up there in the belfry, taking a deep dogmatic breath before summoning us to prayer.

In Venice, as any gilded cockatrice will tell you, the East begins. When Marco Polo returned with his father and uncle from his travels, so we are told, he went straight to his house near the Rialto and knocked upon the door. Nobody recognized him (he had been away for nearly twenty years, and had grown a bushy beard) and nobody believed the wild tales he told of Chinese splendour – tales so

interspersed with superlatives and rodomontades that they nick-
named him *Il Milione*. He soon convinced them, though, by a sudden
display of fabulous wealth, sacks of rubies, emeralds and carbuncles,
velvet cloaks and damask robes such as no man in Europe had seen
before: and from that day to this the Venetians have been hopelessly
enthralled by the spell of the East. They love to think of their city as a
bridge between Occident and Orient, and periodically have noble
dreams of mediation between the colours and religions and aspir-
ations of East and West.

Colour, intrigue, formality, pageantry, ritual – all these eastern
enthusiasms have long been reflected in the daily life of Venice, just
as her buildings are cluttered with Oriental treasures, and her
legends reek of frankincense. Her history has been inextricably
interwoven with the East, since the first Venetians entered into an
ambivalent communion with the Byzantine emperors. The wealth
and strength of Venice was built upon the eastern trade, and she
obtained a monopoly of commerce with the legendary lands that lay
beyond the Levant. Booty of diverse kinds poured into Venice from
the Orient, to be piled in shining heaps upon the Riva, and
sometimes these stolen valuables suffered curious sea changes –
pagan basilisk into Venetian lion, or wicked emperor into Doge. The
Pala d'Oro in the Basilica, which epitomizes the riches brought to
Venice from Constantinople, contained (until its partial despoliation
under Napoleon) 1,300 large pearls, 400 garnets, 90 amethysts, 300
sapphires, 300 emeralds, 15 rubies, 75 balas rubies, 4 topazes, 2
cameos, and unmeasured glitters of gold, silver, gilt and precious
enamel. The jewels were polished but only cut *en cabochon*, and
the screen was divided into 86 layers and sections, all equally
astonishing.

Many Oriental ideas, too, have helped Venice, from geographical
theories to the system of ventilation which cools some of her
hotels, and is directly related to the wind-towers of the Persian Gulf.
Even the Oriental peoples themselves were familiar to the city. In
1402 an embassy arrived in Venice from Prester John, the legendary
Emperor of Ethiopia, whose robes were woven by salamanders and
laundered only in fire, who was attended by 7 kings, 60 dukes, 360

viscounts, 30 archbishops and 20 bishops, who was descended from Melchior, Caspar and Balthazar, and around whose hospitable table 30,000 guests could eat at a sitting. Few visitors have been more honoured than the Japanese Christian envoys who arrived in 1585, and were fêted gorgeously as possible allies against the pretensions of the Papacy. One of the most popular figures of eighteenth-century Venice was a dear old Moorish eccentric who used to wander the streets in turban and sandals, ringing a big bell and calling upon everybody to be happy; and as late as the 1820s the Piazza was full of Arabs, Turks, Greeks and Armenians, drinking sherbet, nibbling ices, or plunged in opium dreams.

All this you will still feel in Venice, for there is a mandarin quality to the city's spirit. The wooden Accademia bridge, for example, curves gracefully across the Grand Canal in a distinct willow-pattern, and sometimes a column of bobbing umbrellas trails across it in the rain, precisely as in a Hokusai print. The boatmen of the lagoon, standing in the poops of their dragonfly craft, often seem to be rowing across a sea of rice-paper: and when, one magic spring morning, you see the distant white line of the Alps from the Fondamenta Nuove, you almost expect to find Fujiyama itself reflected among its pine-trees in the water. Real Japanese fishing-boats sometimes arrive in Venice, from their grounds in the Atlantic, and their small black-eyed sailors, in well-worn blue denims, fit easily enough into the texture of the city. I sometimes encounter a Chinese man-servant in the lanes behind San Stae: I have never discovered where he works, but he always seems to be carrying a dish with a white coverlet, deliciously steaming – Peking Duck, no doubt, or roast pheasant with chestnuts.

More often, though, the allusions of Venice are arabesque, for once they had discovered China, the Venetians dealt chiefly with the peoples of the Middle East. The great trade routes which kept the Serenissima rich and powerful converged, out of Turkestan and Persia, Afghanistan and Arabia, upon the seaports of the Levant, where the Venetians maintained their own great *khans* and warehouses (you can still see one of the most important, among the bazaars of Aleppo); and the wars in which she was almost incessantly engaged took her fighting men repeatedly to Muslim seas and shores, whether they were cynically supporting a Crusade, defending Europe single-handed against the Turks, or suppressing, in the last Republican exploit of all, the eighteenth-century Barbary pirates of North Africa – those pestilent Moors who took their ships as far as the Bristol Channel, and whose reputation was so black among the English that even poor Welshmen were called Morris after them.

Arab ways and thoughts strongly influenced the Venetians. The great Bishop's throne in San Pietro di Castello, traditionally used by St Peter at Antioch, has a quotation from the Koran carved upon it, and you can see Arabic letters, if you look very hard, on a column on the façade of the Basilica itself. A few Venetian dialect words have Arabic derivations, and some Arabic words have come through the Venetian entrepôt to us: *dar es sinaa* (house of art) = *arzena* = *arsenale* = arsenal: *sikka* (a die) = *zecca* (a mint) = *zecchino* (a coin) = sequin. The Venetians learnt much from the Arabs in the art of navigation, and their architects shared with the great Islamic builders a common heritage of Byzantium, so that St Mark's and the Dome of the Rock are, if not precisely brothers, at least distant cousins, estranged by circumstance.

For all these affinities, when the Venetians spoke of pagans they usually meant Muslims: and most strange foreigners were characterized as Moors, dark, heathen, muscular people, to be exploited as slaves or victimized as villains. Nobody knows the identity of the four little porphyry knights who stand, affectionately embracing each other, outside the main entrance to the Doge's Palace: but Venetian popular legend long ago determined them to represent a band of despicable Moors caught trying to ransack the Treasury of St Mark's. Four enchantingly enigmatical figures in a *campo* near Madonna dell' Orto have been known as Moors for so long that the square itself is named for them (though the one on the corner with the iron nose is Signor Antonio Rioba, once a sinister, later a comical figure, and it used to be a great joke to direct ignorant errand boys with messages to that gentleman).

Two marvellous Moors, twenty feet high and glistening with sweat, support the monument of the Doge Giovanni Pesaro in the

Frari, their white eyes bulging and their backs bent double with toil. Two others strike the hours, with surprising delicacy, on the top of the clock-tower in the Piazza: it is true they once inadvertently hit a workman, precipitating him into the square and breaking his neck, but after all their centuries of hammering they have made only a modest indentation in the surface of the bell. The quaintest of sculptured Moors, twisted and one-legged, urges a reluctant camel on the wall of the Palazzo Mastelli. It used to be the custom, if a small child was destined to be a gondolier, for his godfather to screw into his ear an amethyst carved in the shape of a Moor's head, and to this day half the grander front doors of Venice seem to have thick-lipped Negroes as door-knobs. The classic Venetian souvenir, in the heyday of the Grand Tour, was one of those little black wooden pages, sashed and turbaned, which you sometimes see beside the doors of the more self-conscious English antique shops, like Indians outside American tobacconists: these were reminders of the days when the Venetians had live black slaves at their disposal, only replacing them with wooden substitutes when the slave-traffic petered out.

The Venetians always seem a little offended at Shakespeare's conception of Othello, and like to suggest that it was all a misunderstanding, and that the prince was not a Moor at all, but a Venetian gentleman named Moro who originated from the Morea – and whose effigy still stands, they add, in shining and very Christian armour, on the corner of his palace in the Campo dei Carmini. But despite a few imperial prejudices, there is no colour bar among the Venetians. The Turks, when they were allowed to establish their national warehouse on the Grand Canal (the Fondaco dei Turchi), were so severely circumscribed that no woman or child was allowed to enter the building at all: but even in the fifteenth century a youth of noblest birth was thrown into the *Pozzi* for a year for violating the honour of a black slave-girl.

Many and delectable are the suggestions of Islam in Venice – though sometimes, to be sure, they are older than Islam itself, and came direct from old Constantinople in the days before the Arab armies had burst out of their deserts. There are the old iron window-grilles and the cool shaded courtyards of the city; and the Arab schooners you sometimes see, slim and romantic, in the boat-yards of Giudecca; the cobblers, their spectacles on the tips of their noses, and the brawny bare-armed coppersmiths among their lions and sea-horses; the dark little workroom near San Polo where the girls sit cross-legged darning eiderdowns; the small sockets in the walls of houses that act as refrigerated larders; the Bedouin-like mats, all gay stripes, that hang in the windows of the poorer drapers; the little tenement houses of Giudecca, like seaside cottages in Beirut, and the big modern blocks of Sant' Elena that might be in Heliopolis; the fountains and sudden gardens of the place, like ravishing glimpses of Syria; the images of camels, turbaned merchants, forgotten eastern emperors, that stand sentinel in many a disregarded courtyard; the nasal murmured songs of the girls, such as sometimes emerge from behind the black veils of Arab women; the ladies who peer, like wives in purdah, from the closed windows of lofty palaces; the languid sense of *dolce far niente* that pervades the Venetian summer; the carved studded doors of Venice, and the coffee-trays that stand upon its official tables, and the jasmine-scented evenings of Giudecca, and the burnous-like cloaks of the policemen. The white fringes of the gondola covers are like camel-trappings, and the star-speckled blue of the Clock Tower is like a tomb at Karnak, and the great Basilica itself, which Mark Twain saw as a 'vast warty bug taking a meditative walk', strikes most people as an eastern treasure-house, a Saracen war-tent or a tasselled Shah's pavilion.

In Venice you can enjoy the pleasures of the Orient without suffering its torments. Flies are few, mosquitoes are decreasing, beggars are unpersistent, water is wholesome, nationalism is restrained, nobody is going to knife you, or talk about Zionism, or blame you for Kashmir, or make you drink brick tea and eat sheep's eyes. But in Venice, as in the Arab countries, you have the comforting feeling that if you let things drift, and treat life undemandingly, your objectives will eventually be achieved. Do not be alarmed, if you lose sight of your friend on a disappearing steamboat: hang about the Piazza for a while, and she will turn up, miraculously, without surprise or reproach. Do not be despondent if the hull of your boat is splintered by a passing barge: it may look irreparable, but somehow or other, if you do not make a fuss, the boatyard will be able to mend it, and the money will arrive unexpectedly from New York, and you will find the craft more elegant and seaworthy than ever.

Nothing is more reminiscent of the Middle East than one of the gondoliers' quarrels that have given so much picturesque pleasure to visitors down the centuries. They start in some niggling disagreement about a mooring or a rope, and they proceed in a series of abrupt crescendoes and deflations, as the protagonists flex their muscles. Sometimes, when their rancour has flared to one of its successive apexes, one gondolier suddenly walks off into the Piazza, turning his back on the whole affair, as if he is suddenly wearied of it all; but after a few moments of utter silence, such as precedes a thunderstorm or a caterwaul, he swivels violently around again and advances upon his rival with a fresh torrent of abuse. The quarrel thus proceeds sporadically, in fits and starts, gradually increasing in warmth and invective, getting louder and shriller and more sustained and more ferocious, the eyes flashing, the voices trembling, the feet stamping, until at last the ultimate exchange seems upon us, the flow of insult is almost uninterrupted, the outbreak of actual physical assault seems inescapable – and suddenly all evaporates, the gondoliers are inexplicably reconciled, the expectant crowd laughingly disperses, and the disagreement trails away in a murmur of mingled self-justification and understanding. I have seen the same process a hundred times in the streets of Egypt, when one man has often been on the very point of cutting his opponent's throat, and then lost interest.

All these things – buildings, memories, manners – bind Venice to the East, and make the exotic seem common-place. In the 1920s there returned to Venice a grandee who had been governor of an Italian colony in East Africa. He brought with him a stalwart African servant, and dressing him flamboyantly, as his forebears had dressed their slaves, in a red turban and a green sash, taught him to drive the family motor boat. The Venetians, I am assured, scarcely looked twice at this spectacular figure, so immemorial have been their associations with the East, just as they hardly seemed to notice the *grande dame* whose handsome Indian leopard habitually occupied the front seat of her gondola.

The noises of Venice are often Oriental, too, not least the blaring radios and television sets that hurl their melodies after you down the back-streets, and the din of porters, whistles and importunate guides that greets you at the railway station. Many long years ago the city lost its silver reputation for silence. The steamboats did not entirely shatter it, for they used to ease their way down the Grand Canal with the gentle chugging, thumping and hissing that went with polished brass and oiled pistons: but once the petrol engine arrived in Venice, the peace of the city was doomed.

Today Venice is at least as noisy as any mainland city. The throbbing of engines, the blowing of horns, the thudding of steam-hammers, the shouting of irate boatmen, the girl next door laboriously practising her Chopin, the warning cries of the gondoliers, the communal singing of students, the inanities of louts, the jollities of drunks – all are hideously magnified and distorted by the surface of the water and the high walls that surround it, and reverberate around the houses as from a taut drum-skin. (It is disconcerting to hear a snatch of your own conversation, as you meander home from a midnight party, and realize in a moment of clarity how far and how loudly it carries down the canals.) I used to be woken every morning by a terrible racket of engines, klaxons and voices outside my window – as an infatuated Victorian poet put it, 'From the calm transparent waters Float some thrilling sounds of Amphionic music'. You might have thought, from the babel of it all, that the Goths were in the lagoon at last: but in fact it was only the dustbin convoy streaming into the city, foam at the prow, helmsmen high and threatening in the stern.

There are other, more evocative noises. The streets of Venice have their own sound, the quick tap of heels upon stone flagstones. From a thousand houses comes the chirping of a myriad canaries. At the backs of trattorias skittle balls clatter against wood. The postman's call rings richly through the streets, and sometimes a bargee announces his eruption into the Grand Canal with a magnificent bellow from the pit of his stomach. The rattle of shutters is a familiar sound, for this is a resolutely closeted city, and is always opening and closing its windows.

The boom of a ship's siren is a Venetian noise, and the trumpeting of tugs; and in the foggy winter nights, when the city is blanketed in gloom and damp, you can hear the far-away tinkling of the bell-buoys out in the lagoon, and the distant rumble of the Adriatic beyond. The great Piazza of St Mark, on a high summer day, is a rich medley of sounds: the chatter of innumerable tourists, the laughter of children, the deep bass-notes of the Basilica organ, the thin strains of the café orchestras, the clink of coffee cups, the rattling of maize in paper bags by the sellers of bird food, the shouts of newspapermen, bells, clocks, pigeons, and all the sounds of the sea that seep into the square from the quayside around the corner. It is a heady, Alexandrian mixture. Fielding's blind man said that he had always imagined the colour red as being 'much like a sound of a trumpet': and if you want a visual equivalent for the symphony of the Piazza, think of a sheet of vermilion, shot with gold and dyed at the edges with sea-green.

Venice is no longer the supreme city of music, as she was in the eighteenth century, when four celebrated conservatoires flourished there, when her choirs and instrumentalists were unrivalled, and when the abbé Vivaldi, suddenly inspired with a melody in the middle of celebrating Mass, instantly rushed off to the Sacristy to scribble it down. Music, nevertheless, often sounds in the city. The strains of great symphonies rise, in the summer season, from breathless floodlit courtyards; twelve-tone scales and electronic cadences ring from the International Festival of Contemporary Music, which frequently brought Stravinsky himself to conduct his own works in the Fenice; the noble choir of St Mark's, once trained by Monteverdi, sings seraphically from its eyrie among the high mosaics of the Basilica. The gondoliers no longer quote Tasso to one another, or sing old Venetian love songs (most of the popular tunes nowadays are from Naples, London or New York): but sometimes an ebullient young man will open his heart and his lungs together, and float down the canal on the wings of a throaty aria.

To hear the bells of Venice it is best to come at Christmas, when the air is mist-muffled, and the noises of the city are deepened and richened, like plum-duff. A marvellous clash of bells rings in Christmas morning, noble bells and frenzied bells, spinsterish bells and pompous bells, cracked bells and genial bells and cross reproving bells. The bells of San Trovaso sound exactly like Alpine cowbells. The bells of the Carmini sing the first few notes of the Lourdes hymn. The bells of Santa Maria Zobenigo are rung 'with such persistency', so one Victorian visitor recorded, 'that the whole neighbourhood must be driven almost to distraction'. The bells of the Oratory of the Virgin, near San Giobbe, so annoyed the monks of the neighbouring convent that in 1515 they went out one night and razed its little campanile to the ground: they had to rebuild it at their own expense.

The great Marangona bell, rescued from the ruins of the old Campanile of St Mark, no longer sounds, but hangs there in the belfry looking frail and venerable: but the big new bell of St Mark's is alone permitted to sound at midnight, and also rings, to an erratic timetable, at odd intervals during the day. There is a little bell that strikes the hours on the north-western corner of the Basilica, beneath a small stone canopy; and this seems to act as a kind of trigger or stimulus to the two old Moors on the Clock Tower, who promptly raise their hammers for the strike. All these bells, and a hundred others, welcome Christmas with a midnight flourish, and for long echoing minutes after the hour you can hear them ringing down again, softer and softer across the lagoon, like talkative old gentlemen subsiding into sleep.

And there is one more sound that evokes the old Venice, defying the motor boats and the cacophony of radios. Sometimes, early in the morning, as you lie in bed in the half-light, you may hear the soft fastidious splash of oars outside, the swish of a light boat moving fast, the ripple of the waves against the bulwarks of the canal, and the swift breathing of the oarsman, easy and assured.

A sense of Islamic denial seems to govern the Venetian attitude to pleasure. This is no longer a city of boisterous and extrovert enjoyment, and the Venetians have long lost the harum-scarum gaiety that characterized the place during the last decade of its decline. The modern Venetian is a deliberate kind of man, bred to scepticism. He looks an indulgence firmly in the eye, and examines the world's delights analytically, as a hungry entomologist might dissect a rare but potentially edible spider. Venice is still a fine place for dawdling or frivolity: but like the cities of the Muslim world, it is not ideal for orgies.

It is not, for example, a gourmet's city. Once upon a time the *cucina Veneziana* was considered the finest in the world, specializing in wild boar, peacock, venison, elaborate salads and architectural pastries. Even then, though, some perfectionists thought it was spoiled by an excessive use of Oriental spices: Aretino, the poet-wastrel, used to say that the Venetians 'did not know how to eat or drink', and another commentator reported caustically that the pride of Venetian cookery was the hard biscuit, which was particularly resistant to the nibblings of weevils (some left in Crete in 1669 were still edible in 1821). Certainly by now the victuals of Venice have lost any traces of antique glory, and generally conform tamely enough to the Italian cuisine.

There is no drink that feels organic to Venice, as beer seems to spring from the fields of Germany, and *arak* from the very sap of the Baghdad date trees. The wines of the Venetian hinterland are mostly ordinary, and limited indeed are the foreign varieties stocked by the vintners. Most Venetian restaurants merely offer you red or white (if it is one of the simpler trattorias, they call it *nero* and *bianco*.) The most famous bar of the city is excellent, but always feels contrived: Harry's Bar is Venetian-owned and Venetian-staffed, and loves to talk about its visiting celebrities – Hemingway, spectacularly slung with bandoliers and dead birds, striding in from Torcello; Orson Welles propped beside the toasted sandwiches; duchesses (with and without dukes); presidents (in and out of office); film stars (contracted, resting, or in predatory attendance at the Film Festival); a bishop or two, Truman Capote, a few Nobel prizewinners, and Winston Churchill himself, the last of the nabobs, hugging a paint-box.

Here the Italian aristocracy, heavily made up about the eyes, loves to sit in smoky silence, looking terribly distinguished or fearfully scandalous, and here the barman will offer you a Bellini or a Tiziano, two of his cocktail specialities. At Harry's Bar the jet set assembles in summer, and Venetians speak of it with a certain pride, for since its foundation in the 1920s it has been a fairy-tale success: but it feels harshly at odds with the mouldering spirit of Venice, her lofty monuments and her reflective soul.

The pleasures of sex, of chance, of intrigue, of display – all are drawn largely in the Venetian chronicles, and reflected in the voluptuous canvases of the Venetian artists: but the pleasures of wine seldom appear, and it has been said that Carnival itself was a means of escaping into unreality without getting drunk. Everyday hospitality in Venice has always been abstemious – a glass of Marsala, a sickly nip from a ready-mixed cocktail bottle, a box of biscuits, and everyone is satisfied. If the old palaces of Venice could drink today, they would probably stick to the most expensive kind of coffee, especially imported from the western shores of Arabia, and served in chipped gold cups at the card-table.

And they would eat with lofty frugality. One restaurant in the city advertises its merits in an appealing jingle:

> From north to south of Italy
> Runs Nane Mora's fame.
> His precious cooking is the queen
> Of every Gent and Dame.
>
> And the almond cake, oh wonder!
> It's a glory of its kind.
> Have a try, your griefs will sunder
> When you taste its crispy rind!

Not every Gent or Dame, though, will relish the meals of Venice. Even the Venetians have their doubts. I once saw a party of Venetian restaurateurs assembling at the Patriarchate for a convention: most of them looked sallow and pimply, and some seemed actually under-nourished. You can eat expensively and quite well at two or three of the grander hotels, but a cruel monotony informs the menus of the average restaurant. In the first years of this century E. V. Lucas spent a month eating in every Venetian restaurant in turn, and decided that there was only one he wanted to visit a second time. I have tried about thirty, and shall not feel intolerably misused if denied re-entry to any of them (though I shall cherish an affectionate nostalgia for the innumerable modest eating-houses which put up your dinner in a bag for you and send you steaming homewards through the streets, reeking of prawns and lasagna).

The service in Venetian restuarants is usually rough and ready, sometimes off-hand, and occasionally downright rude, and the food, after the first dozen meals, begins to acquire a soporific sameness. The meat revolves sluggishly around a gristly core of veal. The salads are unimaginative, and are redeemed chiefly, if you insist, by the liberal use of fennel. It is only when you come to the fish, the native food of the Venetians, that you may feel a spark of enthusiasm. Venetian *scampi* are magnificent. There is a dish called *mista mare*, a fried pot-pourri of sea-foods, that can be delicious, at least for the first twenty or thirty times. Various kinds of eel are splendid, and so are innumerable small shellfish and minor molluscs. If the season is right, and the restaurant not too pretentious, you may be given some delicious soft-shelled crabs, which are a great delicacy in America, but considered coarse fare in Venice.

Indeed to my mind the lower you slither in the hierarchy of the Venetian kitchen, the more you are likely to enjoy yourself, until at last, turning your back on the *crêpe suzette* of the hotels and the avaricious gentility of the big restaurants, you find yourself in some water-front trattoria eating a fine but nameless fish from the lagoon, garnished with small crabs, washed down with a flagon of rasping white wine, and fortified by a glistening slab of *polenta*, the warm maize bread of the Venetians, which, eaten in tandem with an eel, a trout or a haunch of tunny, is food fit for Doges.

To live in Venice is one of the supreme pleasures that this world can offer. But though I have often been indescribably happy there, and often dazed with admiration, and often surfeited with the interest and enchantment and variety of it all, yet I have never felt in the least Bacchanalian. The Levantine attitudes of the Venetians are catching. More than once, watching a gay party of visitors float down the Grand Canal, singing to an accordion, exchanging holiday badinage, and toasting each other's fortunes in beakers of red wine, I have examined my reactions meticulously, and caught myself estimating how much they would get back on the bottles.

18 The Seasons

Venice is a seasonal city, dependent more than most upon weather and temperature. She lives for the summer, when her great tourist industry leaps into action, and though each year nowadays the season grows longer, and visitors pour in throughout the calendar, still on a winter day she can be a curiously simple, homely place, instinct with melancholy, her Piazza deserted, her canals choppy and dismal. The winter climate of Venice is notorious. A harsh, raw, damp miasma overcomes the city for weeks at a time, only occasionally dispersed by days of cold sunny brilliance. The rain teems down with a particular wetness, like unto like, stirring the mud in the bottom of the Grand Canal, and streaming magnificently off the marbles of the Basilica. The fog marches in frowardly from the sea, so thick that you cannot see across the Piazza, and the *vaporetto* labours towards the Rialto with an anxious look-out in the bows. Sometimes a layer of snow covers the city, giving it a certain sense of improper whimsy, as if you were to dress a duchess in pink ruffles. Sometimes the fringe of a *bora* sweeps the water in fierce waves up the narrower canals, and throws the moored boats viciously against the quays. The nights are vaporous and tomb-like, and the days dawn monotonously grey.

So Venice sits huddled over her inadequate stoves, or huggermugger in her cafés. The palaces of the Grand Canal are heavily clamped and boarded, with only a handful of dim lights burning from ugly tinkling chandeliers through fusty dark brown curtains. The boatmen crouch at their tillers, shrouded in sacks and old overcoats, and sometimes clutching umbrellas. The alley-cats squat emaciated behind their grilles, and the pigeons cluster dejectedly in sheltered crannies of the Piazza. All Venice snivels with influenza, colds in the nose and throat infections (when the Republic secretly did away with three of its political enemies in the fifteenth century, the cause of death was blandly announced as catarrh, and everyone was satisfied). Not a fiddle plays in the Piazza. Not a tout hangs around the arcades. Scarcely a tourist complains about the price of hot chocolate. It is a very private city.

Its celebrations have a club-like feeling, free of prying outsiders. A Venetian Christmas is a staunchly family festival. The trains are full of returning migrants, waiters and labourers from Paris, mothers' helps from the Home Counties, and there is a great deal of hand-shaking in the streets, and many a delighted reunion at the steam-boat station. Suddenly everyone in Venice seems to know everyone else. An endless stream of shoppers, dressed in their elegant best, pushes so thickly through the narrow Merceria that sometimes the policemen, stationing themselves at intersections, impose a system of one-way traffic. The windows burgeon with Christmas trees. Every passing barge seems full of bottles, or parcels, or little firs from the mountains, and every child in Venice seems to trail a red balloon.

In the plushy cafés of St Mark's (Regency stripes and spindly chairs) spruce infants listen with deference to the interminable reminiscences of immaculate uncles: and in the cafés on Christmas Eve 20,000 families giggle before the television sets, drinking Cinzano and eating sticky cakes, while the favourite melody of the day is passed from shop to shop, from square to square, down one dark alley to another, like a cheerful watchword in the night. The Christmas services are warm, bright and glistening; the cribs are crude but touching; the choirs sing lustily; and Venice feels less like a grand duchess than a buxom landlady, enjoying a glass of stout when the customers have gone (except for the mysterious permu-tations of clergy, gold and crimson and misty with incense, that you may glimpse passing and repassing the open doors of the Basilica).

To see the Serenissima without her make-up on, try getting up at three in the morning one foggy February day, and watch the old lady reluctantly awakening. As you stand on your terrace above the canal, it is as though you are deposited plumb in the middle of an almost disused nowhere, so deathly silent is the place, so gagged and pinioned with mist. There are sombre pools of lamplight on the shrouded Grand Canal, and the only person in sight is a solitary eccentric in a fur hat, reading the Rules and Regulations at the steamboat pontoon with a cold and unnatural intensity. And when you have plastered your sweaters on, and crept down the scrubbed echoing staircase of your palace (past the sleeping advocate on the second floor, the Slav Baronessa on the first, the one-eyed ginger tom in his niche, the mighty padlocked coal-cellar doors, the pigeon-streaked bust of an unknown hero by the entrance, the little neglected Madonna on the wood shed, the arid tangle of a lawn and the stiff squeaking iron gates) – when you are out at last, you will find the whole great city damp and padded in sleep. In London or New York the night is never absolute: in Venice, at three on a foggy winter morning, it feels as though the day will never come.

All is dank, swirling, desolate. If you stand still for a sudden moment, allowing the echo of your steps to retreat around a corner, you will hear only the sad slapping of the water on a tethered boat, the distant clanging of a fog bell, or the deep boom of a steamer at sea. Perhaps there will be, far away across the rooftops, a distant sporadic splutter of men's voices. Perhaps a pale faithful light will flicker before a tinsel *ex voto*. The white cat who lives beneath the seat of a gondola in the Rio della Toletta may spring like a demon from his lair; or there may even scurry by, wrapped in worn wool, with a scarf over her nose and mouth and a string shopping-bag in her hand, some solitary poor conscientious soul off to clean a heartless office or buy the first cabbage of the dawn. For the rest, it is wet, dismal, mist-muffled silence. Water pours miserably from an antique pump. Lamplight shines sullenly among the alleys, and sometimes picks out, with a gleam of wet masonry, half a sculptured saintly nose, the tail end of a carved peacock, a crown, a crest, or a crab in a medallion.

In winter Venice wakes up at her edges. Down beyond the empty car park life begins early. Outside the church of Santa Chiara, where a burly watchman walks heavy-shouldered up and down the quay, light shines from the hatches of a dozen barges, throwing the huge moving shadows of their engineers on the wall across the water. At the end of the causeway the daily parade of trucks and trailers waits to be unloaded, hung about with diesel fumes. Harsh voices and the banging of crates emerge from the big warehouses by the docks, and there is a smell of eels, apples, onions and cheap tobacco. There are lights about, and policemen, a few bright steamy coffee shops, a chatter and clutter of life beside the wharves.

Slowly, hesitantly, as you range the streets, this animation of morning spreads across Venice. The fringes of the city curl, and colour, and burst into wintry flame. When you walk back across Dorsoduro, shafts of light from opening doors punctuate the fog. The myriad cafés are raising their shutters, and their bottles, coffee-machines and sugar containers stand sleepily shining in the mist. In San Polo a butcher and his assistant are laboriously heaving a carcass into their window. By the Bridge of Fists, around the corner from the Alley of Haste, a fruit-seller, yawning and grunting, climbs blearily from the hold of his barge. A boat-load of wild fishermen from the lagoon is sluicing itself in water under a bridge. Beneath the high arch of the Accademia two hulking cement barges labour up the Grand Canal, their crews shouting to one another, grand, slow and heavy in the gloom, like ancient galleys. Outside the church of San Maurizio two pale novice-nuns are scrubbing the marble steps. Inside Santa Maria Zobenigo the twisted baroque angels of the altar look down compassionately upon an early Mass (a priest, an acolyte, three nuns, and a sad-faced woman in grey). By Harry's Bar a sailor steps off the *vaporetto* carrying his rifle wrapped up in newspaper, and along the intersecting alley-ways platoons of litter-men swish their brushes energetically in the cold.

So the day comes up again, pinkish and subdued, a Turnerish, vaporous, moist, sea-birds' day. 'Nasty morning', you say to the waiter, as you order your café breakfast: but he only shrugs his shoulders and smiles a separate, melancholy smile, as a Doge might smile at an importunate emperor, or a great sea-captain patronize a Turk.

And then one morning the spring arrives. Not any old morning, but specifically 15 May, for the Venetians believe in the infallibility of the calendar, and regard the beginning of each season as a strictly immovable feast. Eccentric indeed is the foreigner who bathes before 1 June, when the bathing season opens, and it really does seem to be true that on 25 July each year (St James's Day) the swallows vanish from the city, and leave the field clear for the mosquitoes.

In spring the swallows are still arriving, and bring a new element of delicate frenzy to the place – *'There goes a swallow to Venice, the stout seafarer! Seeing those birds fly, makes one wish for wings.'* Generally Venice is not a dancing city, like New York on a frosty morning, or London in early summer, when every man feels like Fred Astaire, and every girl like Cleopatra. Here the whistle is inclined to fade from your lips, as the pensive Venetian faces go by, or a mob of raggle-taggle tourists advances upon you with grimaces, mistaking you for the man who is going to show them round the glass factory. In spring, though, the city has it moments of brilliant exhilaration, when you can happily echo the parodist's verses:

> With due respect to old R.B.
> My own especial spring-time prayer
> Is 'Oh to be in Italy,
> In Venice, now the spring is there!'

These are the halcyon days of the Venetian year. The city is not too crowded, the sun is not too hot, the fogs have gone, there is a sense of discomforts survived and prosperity to come. The coal man knocks on your door with an eager smile, to say that he is perfectly willing to buy back your unused stocks of anthracite (at a slightly reduced price, of course). The vegetable man plucks a carnation from the vase behind him and offers it to you with a truly Neapolitan flourish. Streaks and flecks of green appear in the city at last, softening its urban stoniness. The female cats, one and all, fatten with kittens: the toms disappear into the shrubbery. As the days brighten, and the warm winds blow up from the south, the very pavements of the city seem to be cherished and revived, not to speak of its dank and frigid drawing-rooms. Spring floods into Venice like a tingling elixir or a dry Martini, or perhaps a dose of Teriaca.

Now the massive tourist machine of Venice greases its cogs and paints its upper works for the summer. Wherever you go in the city, bits and pieces of gondolas hang fresh-painted on its walls, totems of May – shiny seats, velvet cushions, a brass sea-horse dangling from a window-knob, a black walnut panel propped against a door. The boat-yards are full of holiday craft, having the weed scraped from their bottoms. The Grand Canal, which spent the winter as a plain market highway, a bus route, a business street, now becomes the supply route of tourism, as all the curtains, paint pots, upholsteries, cutlery, bedspreads, furniture and chromium fittings of the new season flood towards St Mark's. The first cruise ship of the year anchors tantalizingly in the lagoon, bright with awnings, with a scent of the Aegean to her funnel vapours, or a thin flicker of rust from the Hudson river. The first spring tourists parade the Piazza, wearing tarbooshes, Maltese slippers, Spanish skirts or burnouses, according to their earlier itinerary. The first visiting warship moors at the Dogana, and its officers of the watch strut on deck in red sashes and swords. The first British seaman of the season retires to the municipal hospital after a jolly brawl on the Riva degli Schiavoni.

Now the hotels and the *pensions* and the restaurants spring into full life again. Their brass-work is polished, their landing-stages are bright with blue and gold. If you want to book a room the receptionist no longer greets you with cheerful informality, as he did a month ago, but cocks a sophisticated seasonal eyebrow, turns a supercilious page, and informs you kindly that luckily, owing to a late cancellation from Venezuela, he *is* able to let you have one small but pleasant room, not unfortunately over the Grand Canal, but overlooking the very characteristic, if a trifle noisy, alley-way at the back – without bathroom, alas, though there is one at the end of the corridor, beyond the maids' pantry – on the sixth floor, but with lift service, of course, to the fourth – and all this, he nearly forgets to add, at a special price which, expressed in Italian lire, seems very little more than you would pay for the royal suite at the Ritz. With a distant smile he adds your name to the register: for it is spring, and the Venetian instincts are reviving.

Up and down the waterways, too, the ponderous mansions are burgeoning with flower-pots, canary-cages and varnish. There is a stir of impending arrival among the servants of the peripatetic rich. In many a winter-shuttered apartment the maids and house-men are at work, in a cloud of dust and a flash of aprons, and not a few astute householders are packing their own bags in expectation of lucrative summer tenants. 'On their first evening', a Venetian nobleman once told me, 'my American tenants will find everything prepared for them, from butler to candlesticks – within an hour of their arrival they will be able to entertain a dozen guests to a succulent dinner: but if this high standard of service falls off a little during their occupancy of my apartment, well, it is a difficult world, is it not, and heavy with disillusionment?'

And sometimes, in the Venetian spring, you awake to a Canaletto day, when the whole city is alive with sparkle and sunshine, and the sky is an ineffable baby-blue. An air of flags and freedom pervades Venice on such a morning, and all feels light, spacious, carefree, crystalline, as though the decorators of the city had mixed their paints in champagne, and the masons laced their mortar with lavender.

With a thud, a babble of voices and a crinkle of travellers' cheques, summer falls upon Venice. The pleasure factory works at full blast, and the city's ingrained sadness is swamped in an effulgence of money-making. This is not quite so unpleasant as it sounds. Venice in her hey-day has been described as 'one vast joint-stock company for the exploitation of the east'. Today her money is in tourism. Her chief function in the world is to be a kind of residential museum, a Tintoretto holiday camp, just as Coventry makes cars and Cedar Rapids corn flakes: and though the city in summer can be hideously crowded and sweaty, and the mobs of tourists unsightly, and the Venetians disagreeably predatory, nevertheless there is a functional feeling to it all, as of an instrument accurately recording revolutions per minute, or a water-pump efficiently irrigating.

There is nothing new in this. 'The word *Venetia*', wrote one old chronicler, 'is interpreted by some to mean *Veni Etiam*, which is to say, "Come again and again".' The Venetians have always exploited the holiday assets of their city. Even in the fourteenth century it was a city of hotels – the Hat, the Wild Savage, the Little Horse, the

Lobster, the Cock, the Duck, the Melon and the Queen of Hungary. (It was a city of rapacious monopolists, too – one man owned nine of these hostelries.) One inn, on the site of the modern prison, was kept by an Englishman, and was much patronized by English tourists because of its excellent stables. Another, which still exists, was temporarily closed in 1397 when its landlord was condemned for giving short measure. As early as the thirteenth century the Venetians had their Tourist Police, to inspect hotels for cleanliness and comfort, and speed the lost visitor (in any of several languages) towards the more expensive shops.

'The piazza of St Mark's', wrote a medieval Venetian monk, with a fastidious sigh, 'seems perpetually filled with Turks, Libyans, Parthians and other monsters of the sea.' One hundred thousand visitors came in a good year to the great fair of the Ascension, the first international trade festival, when the Piazza was covered with a great marquee, and there were booths and stalls all down the Riva. Tourists from all over Europe flocked to see the annual ceremony in which the Doge, riding in a barge of dream-like elaboration, threw a ring into the Adriatic in token of perpetual domination. The carnivals of the eighteenth century, when the city was peopled with masked gamblers, courtesans, adventurers and wild hedonists – those delightful but decadent jamborees were purposely fostered by the State, partly to keep the powerless population happy, but partly to attract the tourists. Venice is perhaps the supreme tourist attraction of the world. She lives for flattery, and peers back at her admirers with an opal but heavy-lidded eye. When summer sets the city humming, the turnstiles creaking, the cash registers ringing, it feels only proper: the machine is back at work, the factory hooters blow, Sheffield is making knives again, a pit-wheel turns in Rhondda.

Well over a million foreigners came to Venice in a normal recent year. Confessions in most western languages are heard regularly in the Basilica. Americans are the most numerous visitors, followed by Germans, the French, Britons, Austrians, Swiss, Danes, Belgians, the Dutch, Canadians and (as one reference table discreetly puts it) Miscellanians. Ten thousand cars sometimes cross the causeway in a single summer day, and the buses are often so many that when they have disgorged their passengers at the Piazzale Roma they retreat to the mainland again, and you may see them parked hugger-mugger in the sunshine beneath a fly-over of the great bridge, like country coaches behind the cricket pavilion. There are 170 well-known hotels and *pensions* in Venice, and at the height of a good season they are all full. I have been outside the Basilica at three o'clock on a summer morning, and found earnest tourists consulting their guide books in the moonlight. There is an attendant at one of the garages who claims that long before he can see the registration plate on the back of the car, he can tell the occupant's nationality by the look in the driver's eye.

. Thus through the loose gilded mesh of the city there passes a cross-section of the world's spawn, and it is one of the pleasures of summer Venice to watch the sea-monsters streaming by. Germans appear to predominate, for they move in regiments, talk rather loud, push rather hard, and seem to have no particular faces, merging heavily into a jolly sunburnt Volkswagen mass. The Americans are either flamboyant to the point of repulsion, in crimson silk, or gently unobtrusive in drip-dry cotton: the one kind sitting studiously in a trattoria with its intelligent children and its large-scale map; the other vigorously *décolletée*, violently made up and slightly drunk, at a corner table in Harry's Bar.

The British seem to me to provide the best of the men (often distinguished, frequently spare, sometimes agreeably individualist) and the worst of the women (ill tempered, hair unwashed, clothes ill fitting, snobby or embarrassingly flirtatious). The French are nearly all delightful, whether they are scholarly elderly gentlemen with multi-volumed guide books, or students of existentialist sympathies with purple eyelids and no lipstick. The Japanese are almost obliterated by their mountainous festoons of photographic equipment. The Indians are marvellously fragile, exquisite and aloof. The Yugoslavs seem a little dazed (and are said by gondoliers to be the meanest visitors of all). The Australians are unmistakable. The Canadians are indistinguishable. The Russians no longer come. The Chinese have not arrived yet.

Confronted by these multitudes, in summer the character of

Venice abruptly coarsens. The cost of a coffee leaps, if you are anywhere near St Mark's, and is gradually reduced, in topographical gradations, as you take your custom farther from that avaricious fulcrum. The waiters of the Piazza brush up their brusquest manners, in preparation for the several hundred people each day who understandably believe that there must be some mistake in the bill. Souvenir stalls spring up like garish fungi, and the market is suddenly flooded with straw hats, gondoliers' shirts, maps printed on headscarves, lead gondolas, spurious antiques – *'originalissimi'*, as the old dealers used to say – a million water-colours and a thousand paperweights in the shape of St Mark's Campanile.

The unsuspecting visitor, stepping from the steamboat, is accosted by a pair of ferocious porters, who carry his bags the fifteen-odd feet into his hotel lobby and demand, as their compulsory payment for this service, the price of a substantial meal, with wine. The withered sacristans of the famous churches, brushing the dust from their cassocks, emerge eagerly from the shadows to drag you to the very last dismal pseudo-Titian of the vestry. Pampered young men pester you to visit their showrooms. The cry of 'Gondola! Gondola!' follows you like an improper suggestion down the quays. There is a queue for the lift to the top of the bell-tower. Enough people peer into the horrors of the dungeons each morning to make Casanova's head reel. There is a shop near St Mark's so well adapted to every possible shift in the balance of power that the homesick tourist may buy himself the flag of Yemen, the Ukraine, Bolivia, or even the United Nations.

And chanting a sing-song melody of triumph, the guides of Venice come into their own again. *'Guides'*, wrote Augustus Hare in the 1890s, 'are usually ignorant, vulgar and stupid in Venice, and all but the most hopelessly imbecile visitors will find them an intolerable nuisance' (though in later editions of his book he dropped the bit about the imbeciles). Nevertheless the guides of Venice flourish, the directors of itineraries boom, and many a poor holiday-maker staggers home at the end of a day's pleasure as though she has been grinding corn on a treadmill, or attending some crucial and excruciating viva voce. There are 107 churches in Venice, and nearly every tourist feels he has seen at least 200 of them: for the guides and guide books presuppose an unflagging whip-lash energy in their victims, an utter disregard for regular meals, and an insatiable appetite for art of all periods, standards and purposes.

One itinerary, for example, suggests that the unhappy visitor spends his first morning looking at the Basilica of St Mark (*the mosaics, the Treasury, the horses' gallery, the museum, the eight side-chapels, the celebrated floor, the Baptistery, the Atrium, the Nicopoeia Madonna, the Pala d'Oro, the Rood Screen and the Sacristy*); and the Piazza outside (*the Campanile, the Clock Tower, the Library, the Archaeological Museum, the columns of St Mark and St Theodore, the two Piazzettas, the Correr Museum, Florian's and Quadri's*); and the Doge's Palace (*the exterior arcades, the Giants' Staircase, the State Chambers, Tintoretto's Paradise, the Armoury, the Bridge of Sighs, the Dungeons, the Bocche di Leone*). He should move on that afternoon to the Accademia Gallery (*all twenty-four rooms*); the Scuola di San Rocco (*all sixty-two Tintorettos*); the Frari church (*the Bellini Madonna, Titian's Assumption, the tombs of Titian and Canova, the Pesaro altar piece, the Memorials and the very fine choir stalls*); the markets (*fish and vegetables*); and the small church of San Giacomo di Rialto, which well repays the trouble of a short but attentive inspection. And he should end the day with 'a quiet moment or two' upon the Rialto bridge, before returning to his hotel, so the book thoughtfully suggests, restfully by gondola. Haggard are the faces of tourists I have seen, desperately following such a course, and inexorable, unwavering, unrelenting are the voices of the lecturers so often to be heard, dogmatic but unscholarly, riding above the silences of San Giorgio or the Salute.

Alas, the truth is that most visitors to Venice, in any case, move among her wonders mindlessly, pumped briskly through the machine and spewed out along the causeway as soon as they are properly processed. An old-fashioned Englishman, once invited to produce a tourist slogan for a Middle Eastern country, suggested the cruel back-hander '*Where Every Prospect Pleases*': and there are moments in the high Venetian summer when even the lily liberal, surveying the harum-scarum harlequinade of tourism that swirls around him, must stifle some such expression of intolerance. Seen against so superb a setting, art and nature exquisitely blended, Man can seem pretty vile.

But though crowds do not suit some parts of the city – the grey districts of the north-west, the quiet canals behind the Zattere, the reaches of the inner lagoon – nevertheless the great Piazza of St Mark's is at its very best on a hot day early in summer, when visitors from the four corners of the earth are inspecting its marvels, and Venice is one great itchy palm. During Ascension week, by an old and obscure tradition, images of the three Magi, preceded by an angel-herald, emerge each hour from the face of the Clock Tower and rotate in homage around the Virgin (in any other week of the year you can see them packed away, rigid and bulge-eyed, in a glass cupboard inside the tower, near the big revolving drums that carry the figures of the clock). This is the time to inspect the Piazza. As the huge cosmopolitan crowd waits around the clock for the appearance of those quaint old sages, you can capture to perfection the summer flavour of Venice.

The great square is dressed for entertaining. The two celebrated cafés, Florian's and the Quadri – one on the south side of the square, one on the north – have arranged their chairs and tables symmetrically upon the pavement, and their orchestras string away in blithe disharmony (Florian's specializes in the sicklier musical comedy melodies, now and then graced with a popular classic, but at the Quadri you sometimes hear the drummer indulging in something precariously approaching jazz). The flags of Italy and Venice fly from the three bronze flagstaffs before the Basilica – symbolic of lost Venetian dominions, Crete, Cyprus and the Morea. Down the Piazzetta there is a glimpse of sparkling water, a flicker of gondoliers' straw hats, a shifting web of moored boats: and the shadowy Merceria, with its glittering shops, falls away out of the sunshine like a corridor of treasure.

The patterned floor of the Piazza is thick with pigeons, and two or three women at little trestle stalls are invitingly rattling their packets of maize. Round and round the arcades, cool and shaded, mills a multitude of tourists, looking for lace and picture postcards, and almost every table has its holiday couple – he reading the *Daily Mail*, she writing laboriously home. A girl in a tartan cap lounges beside her ice-cream box beneath the colonnade. The professional photo-

grapher in the middle of the square stands in an Edwardian attitude
beside his old tripod camera (which stays in the Piazza all night, like a
shrouded owl on a pedestal); and the fourteen licensed postcard
hawkers wander ingratiatingly from group to group, their trays slung
around their shoulders upon frayed and well-rubbed leather straps.
On every step or balustrade, on the ledges around the base of the
Campanile, on the supports of the two columns of the Piazzetta,
around the flagstaffs, beside the little porphyry lions – wherever
there is a square foot of free sitting space, hundreds of young people
have settled like birds, spreading their skirts and books around them.

There are faces everywhere, faces bronzed and flushed in the
cafés, faces peering back from shop windows (framed in lace napkins
and Canaletto prints), faces high in the obscurity of the Campanile
belfry, faces looking down from the Clock Tower itself, a tide of faces,
wondering, irritated, delighted, amorous, exhausted, pouring constantly from the funnel of the Merceria. And all around you before
the clock stands the core of this great daily crowd, chattering and
expectant, a turmoil of cottons, dark glasses, conical hats, guide
books, thonged sandals; a clutch of honeymooners, a twitching of
children, a clash of tongues – 'all the languages of Christendom', as
Coryat said, 'besides those that are spoken by the barbarous Eth-
nicks'; here a stiff Englishman, trying not to gape, here a jolly soul
from Iowa, every ounce a tourist, from the enamelled ear-rings
dangling beneath her bluish hair to the tips of her pink-varnished
toe-nails. All is shifting, colourful and a little sticky, as it must have
been in the hey-day of the Venetian carnival, when this city was 'the
revel of the earth, the Masque of Italy', a boast, a marvel and a show.

The preliminary bell rings on the corner of the Basilica. The Moors,
swivelling athletically from the waist, sound the hour with dignity.
The shutters open beside the strange old clock. Out come the three
Magi, led by the trumpeting angel. They bow creakily to the
Madonna, shuffle stiffly around her, and with a whirring and grating
of antique mechanisms, disappear inside. The little doors close
jerkily behind them, the cogs grind into silence, and all is still. A sigh
of amusement and pleasure runs around that gaudy crowd, and it is
the long, hot, breathless sigh of a summer in Venice. Packing away

their cameras, the Germans, Americans, Frenchmen, Yugoslavs, Japanese, Britons, Indians, Australians, Turks, Libyans, Parthians and other visiting monsters push their way towards a pink ice-cream, stoically count their money for lunch, or resume their earnest trek around the Tintorettos.

19 New on the Rialto

For Venice is a kind of metropolis, in the sense that all the world comes to visit her. If I stand upon my balcony and survey the square mile or so that lies within my vision, I can envisage the shades of an extraordinary gallery of people who have been, at one time or another, my neighbours: Duke Sforza the great mercenary, Byron and Ruskin, Réjane, Goethe, Galileo, two Popes, four Kings, Cardinal Pole, de Pisis, Chateaubriand, Barbara Hutton, Taglioni the dancer, Frank Lloyd Wright (whose house beside the Palazzo Balbi was never built), Baron Corvo (whose gondola was rowed, in his shameless last years, by a crew of four flamboyant gondoliers).

In the little square opposite my apartment Casanova was born. In the house to the right, with the flower-pots in the window, W. D. Howells lived. To my left is the palace where Wagner wrote the second act of *Tristan*, and just beyond it the terrace from which Napoleon once watched a regatta. Near by is the Ca' Rezzonico, one of the great houses of the world: Browning died in it, the Pope Clement XIII lived in it, the Emperor Francis II stayed in it, Max Beerbohm wrote about it. Across the canal is the home of the Doge Cristoforo Moro, sometimes claimed to be the original of Othello, and to my right is a palace once owned by a family so uncountably rich that it is still called Palazzo degli Scrigni – the Palace of the Money-Chests.

Around the corner is d'Annunzio's 'little red house', where he made love to Duse and wrote *Notturno* in the dark of blindness. At the Convent of La Carità, now part of the Accademia, Pope Alexander III, exiled from Rome, is said to have worked for six months as a scullion, until he was recognized by a French visitor and so completely restored to power that the Emperor himself came to Venice to beg his pardon. Don Carlos, Charles VII of Spain, used to own the house beyond the mosaic factory. In the enchanting Palazzo Dario de Regnier 'lived and wrote like a Venetian', as his memorial plaque says. La Donna of *La Donna' è Mobile* lived in the Palazzo Barbaro. In the little Corte Catecumeni, away to my right, malleable Turkish prisoners used to be confined until they had learnt their Catechism, and could embrace Christianity. Wherever I look, I can fancy the shadows of famous men – and of one obscure and pitiful woman, for it was from the balcony of the Palazzo Mocenigo that one of Byron's Venetian paramours threw herself in desperation into the canal.

Venice was an essential port of call in the Grand Tour of the eighteenth century, when fashionable English visitors awaited their audiences of the Doge as eagerly as they now queue, humming a tune from *Ancient and Modern*, to pay their respects to the Pope. Even now, until you have seen Venice there is an asymmetrical gap in your education. Not many foreigners still rent entire Venetian palaces for the season, but few famous names of the western world have not, at one time or another, appeared in the hotel registers of the city. The Venetian summer season still summons the envoys of the *haut monde*, in their yachts, Cadillacs or Pipers, to the assemblies of the Serenis-sima – the Venetians have a fine airport on the mainland for the big jets, and a smaller one on the Lido for private and chartered aircraft, more numerous every year. The most lavish ball of the 1950s, anywhere in the world, was given by a Mexican millionaire at the Palazzo Labia (some of whose previous owners, long ago, had the habit of throwing gold plate in the canal, for the show of it, and later secretly fishing it out again, for thrift).

This gallimaufry of the rich, though it sometimes conjures evoca-tive visions of eighteenth-century Venice, nevertheless does much to corrupt the spirit of the place. Unctuous sycophancy oozes from the grander hoteliers as the summer advances, and even the rhythms of the canals are sometimes shattered when there advances ponder-ously past the Salute, ensign hugely at the stern, some ostentatious motor cruiser from ports west, all cocktail bars and high fidelity. It is often only a sweeping glance that such visitors grant to the old place, for they are off to the Lido in the evening, merely returning to Venice now and then for an expensive dinner or a well-publicized party: but it is enough to tarnish the pride of the city, so patronizing does their brief survey feel, and so uncomprehending. Many an Anglo-Saxon uses Venice as a summer refuge from stricter conventions at home. Many a loud and greasy visitor brings to Harry's Bar a sudden whiff of the property developer or the take-over bid – for when you think of sudden fortunes, you often think of Venice. (But other richer men, disembarking from their schooners or swift aeroplanes, still bring to Venice some lost sense of power and worldly style.)

In its great centuries Venice was more than a mere spectacle, and the world came here not only to look at the golden horses or pay tribute to Titian, but to swop currencies, to invest funds, to rent ships, to talk diplomacy and war, to take passage, to learn the news from the East, to buy and to sell. The Fair of the Ascension attracted traders, manufacturers, financiers and even fashion designers from all Europe (a big doll, dressed in the latest fashion, was set up in the Piazza to act as a mannequin for the modes during the coming year). And the most celebrated of all Venetian institutions was the great commercial exchange of the Rialto, one of the prime facts of European history. To Europeans of the Middle Ages, the Rialto was as formidable a presence as a World Bank or a Wall Street today. It was the principal channel of finance between East and West, and the real power-house of the Venetian Empire.

The earliest of all State banks, the Banca Giro, was opened on the Rialto in the twelfth century, and for 300 years the banks of the Rialto dominated the international exchanges. From its business houses the argosies set out to the Orient, to Flanders and to England: most of the ships belonged to the State, and were built to a standard pattern (for easy servicing), but the money invested in them belonged to the merchants of the Rialto. On the walls of the Rialto colonnade a huge painted map illustrated the great trade routes of Venetian commerce – to the Dardanelles and the Sea of Azof, to Syria, Aleppo and Beirut, to Alexandria, to Spain, England and Flanders; and before it the merchants would assemble to watch the progress of their fortunes,

like staff officers in an operations room. Beside the Rialto were the
Venetian Offices of Navigation, Commerce and Shipping – the
ultimate authorities, in those days, on matters commercial and
maritime.

To the emporia of this famous place the whole world came for its
gold, its exotic textiles, its coffees and spices, sometimes brought to
Venice through countries that Europeans had never even heard of:
even Henry III of France thought it worth while to wander around the
Rialto shops incognito, in search of bargains. Throughout the
fourteenth, fifteenth and sixteenth centuries Europe asked with
Antonio: 'What's new on the Rialto?': until in the long run the seven
caravels of Vasco da Gama, rounding the Cape to India, ended the
Venetian monopoly of the Oriental trade, and laid the Rialto low. So
sensitive was the Venetian commercial sense that when, one dark
morning in 1499, the news of da Gama's voyage arrived in the city
(long before the explorer had returned to Portugal) several of the
Rialto banks instantly failed.

Today there are still banks around the eastern end of the Rialto
bridge: but the old commercial meeting-place is now a popular
market, lively, noisy, and picturesque, and only a few gnarled
reminders of its great days remain to stimulate your sense of history.
To understand the impact of the Venetian decline, there is no better
exercise than to go to the western end of the bridge, near the church
of San Giacomo, and survey the scene with one eye on the market-
women, and one on the absent magnificos.

The great enterprises have vanished. All around you now, beneath
the crooked hump of the bridge, is the animation of petty trade.
Under the arcades are the jewellers, their windows full of sovereigns,
Maria Theresa dollars, gilded ornaments, and you can see them
through their open doors, looking fearfully shrewd, weighing
minuscule gold chains (for St Christopher medallions) in desperately
delicate scales. In the passage-way is the Erberia, the vegetable
market: a jolly, pushing, hail-fellow place, its stalls loaded with
succulent peaches, onion strings, bananas, untidy heaps of fennel,
lettuces, green jagged leaves like dandelions, gherkins, rigid hares,
plucked quails in immaculate rows, spinach, slices of coconut

beneath cooling sprinklers, potatoes, dead upside-down seagulls, pieces of artichoke floating in buckets, magnificent apples, vivid radishes, oranges from Sicily and carnations from San Remo. The market men are cheerful and skilled in badinage, the shoppers earnest and hurried, and sometimes a thoughtful lawyer, in his white tabs, stalks through the hubbub towards the criminal courts.

Above the stalls stands the old church of San Giacomo, a poky but friendly little place, which is known to the Venetians familiarly as San Giacometto, and stands among the vegetables precisely as the church of St Paul's stands in Covent Garden, only awaiting an Eliza. Its big twenty-four-hour clock appears in a famous painting by Canaletto, but has had a dismal mechanical history. It went wrong several times in the fourteenth century, and had to be renewed 'for the honour and consolation of the city'. It stopped again in the eighteenth century, apparently at four o'clock. In 1914 a traveller reported that it always showed the time as three in the afternoon, and until a few years ago it was permanently stuck at midnight precisely.

Beneath this unreliable piece, hidden away among a clutter of sheds and packing cases, you will find the Gobbo di Rialto, one of the best-known images of medieval Venice. He stands now, abandoned and neglected, among a mass of boxes and old vegetables: a small hobbled granite figure of a man, supporting a flight of steps and a squat marble column. He used to be called a hunchback, but he is really only bent with burdens, for in the hey-day of the Rialto his responsibilities were great. Upon his pedestal the decrees of the Republic were promulgated, in the days when Venetian law was written in blood and enforced with fire: and to his steps men convicted of petty crimes were forced to run naked from St Mark's, hastened by a rain of blows, until at last, breathless, bleeding and humiliated, they fell chastened at his knobbly feet and embraced him in blind relief.

And around the corner, beside the Grand Canal, there lies the incomparable fish market of Venice, a glorious wet, colourful, high-smelling concourse of the sea, to which in the dawn hours fleets of barges bring the day's supply of sea-foods. Its stalls are lined deliciously with green fronds, damp and cool: and upon them are

laid, in a delicately-tinted, slobbering, writhing, glistening mass, the
sea-creatures of the lagoon. There are sleek wriggling eels, green or
spotted, still pugnaciously alive; beautiful little red fish packed in
boxes like shampoos, heads upwards; strange tube-like molluscs,
oozing at the orifice; fine red mullet, cruel pseudo-sharks, undefeated crabs and mounds of gem-like shell-fish; skates, and shoals of
small flat-fish, and things like water-tarantula, and pools of soft
bulbous octopus, furiously ejecting ink; huge slabs of tunny, fish-
rumps and fish-steaks, joints of fish, fish kidneys, innards and guts
and roes of fish: a multitude of sea-matter, pink, white, red, green,
multi-limbed, beady-eyed, sliding, senuous, shimmering, flabby,
spongy, crisp – all lying aghast upon their fresh green biers, dead,
doomed or panting, like a grove of brilliant foliage among the tundra
of Venetian stone.

By the eighteenth century the quayside beside the fish market,
once the economic centre of the western world, had become a dawn
promenade for Venetian revellers, haggard or distraught after the
night's love and gaming, and it was the fashionable thing to appear
there at first light, displaying all the proper signs of dissipation.
Today the Rialto is not even loose-living, only picturesque. There is a
sad irony to the description on the apse of San Giacomo, a memento
of its Gothic days: 'Around This Temple Let The Merchant's Law Be
Just, His Weight True, And His Covenants Faithful.' No Shylocks
now demand their securities beneath the arcades of Rialto; no
giggling courtesans sweep their mud-stained skirts through its
market in the dawn; only the greengrocers shout, the housewives
haggle, and the tourists on the bridge anxiously consult their
exposure meters. You must look at the Rialto with an inner eye: just
as, when I inspected the view from my terrace, I saw not only the
passing boatmen, and my small son stumbling across the bridge to
school, but Napoleon too, pouting on his balcony, and the lovely sick
Duse, and Othello, and Corvo, and all those poor imprisoned
infidels, desperately memorizing their articles of faith behind the
Salute.

20 Curiosities

Venice is a cheek-by-jowl, back-of-the-hand, under-the-counter, higgledy-piggledy, anecdotal city, and she is rich in piquant wrinkled things, like an assortment of bric-à-brac in the house of a wayward connoisseur, or parasites on an oyster-shell. Some are the increments of an old religion, some the bequests of history, some are just civic quirks. In Venice *'Sempre diretto!'* will always lead you to some world-familiar landmark, the Campanile of St Mark's, the Rialto, the sumptuous Piazza or the Grand Canal itself: but you must walk there crookedly, through a hall of curiosities.

Venice was always alone in the world, always unique in manners as in status. If you go to the big monastic building next door to the Frari, walk upstairs and speak nicely to the man at the reception desk, you will find yourself admitted to the State Archives of the Venetian Republic, in which are reverently preserved the records of independent Venice from its earliest beginnings until its fall. It is the most complete such State memorial on earth. Wild statistics surround its contents, born out of the secrecy of the old State, and often find their way into the most reputable guide books. Some say it contains 14 million volumes, others that it has 1,000 rooms. The nineteenth-century geographer Andrea Balbi, crazed by his theme, calculated that the separate leaves of its documents and volumes numbered 693,176,720, that placed end to end they would be 1,444,800,000 feet long and would extend eleven times round the circumference of the earth, and that they would cover so wide an area that the entire human race would stand upon their surface. Even as late as the 1850s the innermost secrets of the Council of Ten were still protected in the Archives, but now that every corner is accessible to scholars, people seem to agree that its 280 rooms contain something like 250,000 books, documents and parchments. The earliest date from 883 (when Alfred the Great was on his throne, and Charlemagne hardly dead).

Its warren of chambers, once the cells of a Franciscan monastery, are packed to the ceilings with this extraordinary documentation, file after file, quarto after quarto, huge illuminated manuscripts, hand-

drawn maps, land titles, deeds, rolls of the nobility, official proceedings of the Great Council – a vanished society perpetuated, like a
long-dead Pope in a crystal coffin, or an ear of corn from a pyramid.
There is a smell of parchment and old powdery ink: and in a small
room near the entrance a man is busy micro-filming family trees for
those modern Venetians who wish, upon payment of a suitable fee,
to confirm their descent from the pages of the Golden Book.

A sense of historical continuity also haunts the streets and
buildings of Venice. 'Yes,' said my housekeeper one day, telling me
the origins of the Salute church, 'yes, when the plague ended we all
put our hands in our pockets, every one of us, and we all gave a little
money, and built the church in gratitude.' It happened just 300 years
ago, but so strong is the sense of family in Venice, and so compressed
are all its centuries, that Emilia half-believed she had contributed a
few lire herself. Venice is full of such perpetual echoes – from the
very name of the Frezzeria, the Street of Arrow-Makers (where they
still make wicker baskets, like quivers), to the shipyards of the
Arsenal, where the tankers are repaired in the very same shipyard
that Dante visited six centuries ago. In the Campo San Zan Degola
there is a carved stone head popularly believed to represent a
legendary villain called Biagio, who chopped poor children up and
sold them as stew in his restaurant: the tale springs from the Middle
Ages, but if you visit the image you will still find it smeared with
mud, a token of Venice's long and unforgiving memory. Alongside
the Riva degli Schiavoni, the Quay of the Slavs, you may still often
see ships from Dalmatia. The sugar supplies of the city have been
unloaded at the same place – where the Alley of Sugar meets the
Zattere – since the earliest days of the Republic. The Dogana is still an
active customs house. The oldest of the *traghetti* have been in
continuous existence at least since the thirteenth century.

Here the past and the present have been repeatedly smudged, so
that the old often seems contemporary, and the new is quickly
streaked with age. They play football in the grandiose Renaissance
courtyard of the Palazzo Pisani, near the Accademia. They perform
plays in the Ridotto, once the most celebrated gaming-house in
Europe. They have exhibitions in the old School of the Shoemakers,

beside San Tomà; they make chairs in the School of the Tanners, in Santa Margherita; and if you buy yourself a glass of beer in the café that stands opposite the main door of Santo Stefano, you will be standing in the old School of the Woolworkers, once so flourishing that it possessed five Carpaccio paintings of its own. The very materials of Venice seem timeless, for often they were old already, when the Venetians stole them and brought them home to the lagoons: and even an idea like the design of the cupola came to Venice from Byzantium, and went to Byzantium from Rome.

Venice is thickly encrusted with the stranger ornaments of religion. She is one of the great reliquaries of the Christian world. Almost every Venetian church has its splinter of sacred bone, its skeleton, its nail, its piece of wood, its patriarchal stone, marvellously encased in gilt, glass and gold, kept reverently in shrines and padded boxes, or behind lush velvet curtains. The bodies of St Mark, St Stephen, St Zacharias (father of the Baptist), St Athanasius (of the Creed), St Roch, St Theodore, St Magnus, St Lucy and many another holy person lie in the churches of the city. The church of San Tomà possesses more than 10,000 sacred relics, including, so it is said, twelve complete saintly corpses (temporarily removed from the church, owing to the damp).

In San Pietro di Castello – a church founded, according to Venetian legend, by the Trojans – stands the throne used by St Peter at Antioch. In the Basilica of St Mark alone there are preserved, or so it has at one time or another been claimed, a knife used at the Last Supper; the stone on which St John the Baptist was beheaded, still stained red in the Baptistery; the skull of the Baptist; an arm of St George; a bas-relief, still wet, carved from the stone that Moses struck; a picture painted by St Luke; two small angel-shrines which once decorated Pontius Pilate's balcony in Jerusalem; a stone on which Our Lord stood while preaching in Tyre; a rib of St Stephen; a finger of Mary Magdalene; a stool belonging to the Virgin Mary; the marble stone on which Our Lord sat when He asked the Samaritan woman for water; the sword with which St Peter cut off Malchus's ear; and a manuscript of St Mark's gospel written in the Evangelist's own hand.

Scarcely less venerated than these ancient relics is the room in which the Papal Conclave of 1800 met to elect Pius VII to the Pontificate. The conclave had been banished from Rome by Napoleon (the previous Pope, asking if he might be allowed at least to die in Rome, had been told that he could 'die just wherever he liked'); and it sat in an upstairs room of the monastery of San Giorgio Maggiore, adjoining the Palladian church. The carved wooden seats are still labelled with the names of the thirty-five participating cardinals, as though they had just picked up their wide-brimmed scarlet hats and gone downstairs to the refectory; the Pope's own hat lies in a glass case, resting upon a circle of moth-balls, as if upon ball-bearings; and outside the door is the little black stove in which the ballot-papers were burnt, the tell-tale smoke of their ashes emerging through an iron chimney beside the campanile above.

The tombs of Venice, when they are not horrendous, are often wonderfully bizarre. In the church of San Giobbe, before the high altar, you may see the tomb (as we have already seen the house) of 'the original Othello', the Doge Cristoforo Moro. One theory is that Shakespeare took the tale from a scurrilous pamphlet written about this man, and its exponents like to point to a family device which is engraved upon his memorial. It represents a mulberry (*mora*) – 'and does not Shakespeare speak, or more probably Bacon, in Act IV, Scene III, of Othello's *gage d'amour* to Desdemona as "a handkerchief spotted with strawberries"? Do you need more proof, my poor friend? Are you still sunk in obsolete tradition?'

Then to the left of the high altar in the Basilica there is a heart-shaped stone set among the mosaics. Until recently nobody knew what this signified, but during the restoration of the floor the stone was lifted, and beneath it was found a small box containing a shrivelled human organ: it was the heart of the Doge Francesco Erizzo, who died in 1646 – his body lies in the church of San Martino, but he willed that his innermost being should be buried as close as possible to the patron saint of the Venetians. The Doge Francesco Morosini, who died in 1694, is buried in Santo Stefano beneath the largest funeral slab in Venice, dominating the central floor of the church, and measuring eighteen feet by fifteen. The Doge Andrea Vendramin, buried in San Zanipolo in 1478, is chiefly famous to the world at large because his effigy there was the subject of a particular scrutiny by Ruskin: convinced that the Venetian Renaissance was instinct with sham, Ruskin borrowed a ladder from the sacristan of the church and mounted the high tomb to prove that the image of the Doge was itself fraudulent, and was only carved on one side, the other being a blank slab of marble.

In the Frari, to the right of the high altar, is the tomb of the unhappy Doge Foscari, who was deposed in 1457 and died (apparently of a broken heart) a few days after his own son's execution for treason. It is a huge and pitiful edifice, to which, for five centuries, no guide had pointed without retelling the story of the family disgrace: but beneath it an inscription records a touching sequel. Two and a half centuries after the poor old Doge's death a descendant named Alvise Foscari ordered, as an act of family loyalty, that his own heart should be inserted into the tomb of shame: and so it was, in 1720. (The Doge immediately opposite, the fifteenth-century Nicolo Tron, will be seen to have a bushy beard: he grew it upon the death of a favourite son, and refused ever to shave it, as an emblem of perpetual mourning.)

And in the church of the Scalzi, the barefoot Carmelites, is the tomb of the last of all the Doges, Ludovico Manin, 120th in the succession, who surrendered his Republic with scarcely a whimper to the rampant forces of Napoleon, and died ingloriously five years later. The Manins came to Venice from Florence, flourished in commerce, and bought their nobility at the time of the wars with Genoa; but the last Doge was scarcely a stalwart figure, and his visiting card was decorated with a design of a nude Adonis asleep beneath an oak tree. There is thus an ironic melancholy to this simple tomb. It is a plain sombre slab in a side-chapel, and on it is engraved a stark inscription. '*Cineres Manini*', it says – 'The Ashes of Manin'.

Venetian art, too, is rich in curiosities. The city's pellucid feeling of delusion has always been exploited by her artists in tricks and wrinkles of perspective and proportion. Nothing is quite symmetrical in Venice – the Piazza is not only irregular, but also slopes towards the Basilica, and has a floor pattern that does not fit. Buildings are deliberately top-heavy, like the Doge's Palace, or fantastically embellished with mock draperies, like the vast church of the Gesuiti, which is so bafflingly decorated with marble drapings, curtains, carpets and tapestries that you leave it in a dizzy state of disbelief. Perspective ceilings shift heavily as you walk; writhing clumps of angels float about in the blue, reminding me of the edible frogs in the Hong Kong fish market, which are clamped together with wires, alive but congealed, and present an animated multi-limbed appearance, as though they have twelve legs apiece. Arms and ankles protrude from canvases, like Pordenone's famous horse's head in the church of San Rocco. Bells swing gaily out of painted skies. Mock Venetian blinds shade non-existent windows. If you look behind the angels that stand so triumphantly upon the portico of the Gesuiti, you will find that their buttocks are hollow, and are frankly sustained by struts of iron. The great dome of the Salute is supported by huge stone buttresses, elaborately scrolled: but they are not really necessary, for the dome is made of wood.

One winter morning, when the Doge's Palace was empty of tourists, and the custodians of the Great Council Chamber were elsewhere, I stealthily removed my shoes and mounted the steps to the Doge's Throne; and sitting there in that portentous seat, and looking at the great painted ceiling above me, I realized how carefully considered were the perspective distortions of Venetian art. All those gigantic images and symbolisms, those Goddesses and Victories and Virtues, now seemed to be performing privately for me. I could look Venezia straight in the eye, without cricking my neck. I could receive the Tribute of the Conquered Provinces without moving my head. It was as though Veronese, Tintoretto, Bassano and Palma Giovane were themselves standing before me, bowing low and awaiting my approval. This experience had an elevating effect upon me. When I had tiptoed down the steps again, and replaced my shoes, and assumed an air of innocent scholarly interest, I looked behind me to find that the footprints of my stockinged feet on the polished wooden steps of the throne were, if not twice as large as normal, at least twice as confident.

Venetian Baroque is sometimes gloriously eccentric. The façade of

San Moisè usually stops the tourists in their tracks, it is so laughably elaborate; and inside is a gigantic altar piece, built of shiny granite blocks, which reproduces, almost life-size, Jehovah, Moses, the Tablets, Mount Sinai and all. Another splendid altar is in the church of San Marziale (a divine whose legend, if I have got the right one, is described in my dictionary of saints as 'an extravagant forgery'): it seems to represent a holy hermit inside his cave, for beneath its slab there crouches, his halo just fitting in, a single forlorn and lonely sage, rather as children of artistic bent are sometimes to be seen huddled beneath grand pianos.

The façade of Santa Maria Zobenigo is notorious because not one item of its convoluted design has any religious significance whatsoever. The church was built by the Zobenigo family, but was reconstructed by the Barbaros, and its frontage is entirely devoted to their glorification. Looking from top to bottom, you will see a figure of Venice crowned, between Justice and Temperance; a double-headed eagle, the Barbaro emblem, wearing a copper crown; a vast effigy of an armoured Barbaro above the door; four Romanized Barbaros in niches; two piles of military trophies, trumpets, guns, banners, drums; and six finely sculptured plans, in stone relief, of places that figured largely in the Barbaro annals – Zara, Candia, Padua, Rome, Corfu and Spalato. (When I looked at these plans one spring evening, they were all in mint condition, but when I went back the next day I discovered that a large chunk of Spalato had been broken away in the night, leaving a pale stone scar behind it: it is odd to experience so directly the decay of a civilization.)

The Venetian artists often had a taste for whimsy and caprice, and loved private jokes, hidden allusions, undeclared self-portraits. In Veronese's famous *Feast at the House of Levi*, at the Accademia, Veronese himself is the suave major-domo figure in the left centre. He has also painted himself in the allegorical picture *Glory*, in the Doge's Palace, and in his *Marriage at Cana*, which is now in the Louvre, he not only appears himself, playing the viola, but is accompanied by his brother, Tintoretto, the Sultan Soliman, the Emperor Charles V, the Marchese del Guasto and the Marchesa di Pescara. In Gentile Bellini's *Miracle of the True Cross at San Lorenzo*, the artist's entire family kneels in smug parade on the right-hand edge of the miracle, and the Queen of Cyprus stands with her ladies on the left. In Domenico Tiepolo's odd picture *The New World*, in the Ca' Rezzonico, the artist himself is looking through a magnifying glass in the right-hand corner of the painting, with his father beside him. There is a picture of the naval battle of Lepanto, in the Sala dello Scrutinio of the Doge's Palace, in which, if you look hard enough among the carnage and the corpses, you will see a tidy little gentleman, neatly bearded, lace-collared, and perfectly calm, up to his neck in the Mediterranean: it is the artist Vicentino, undeterred by his subject.

In the adjacent picture, another naval battle, Pietro Liberi has portrayed himself as a very fat naked slave, bang in the front of the composition, brandishing a dagger. Near by is Palma Giovane's *Last Judgement*, which is supposed to contain portraits of the artist's mistress in two of her varying moods – bottom left, agonized in Hell, top right, blissful in Paradise. Next door, Tintoretto's daughter sits at the feet of St Christopher in the gigantic picture of Paradise in the Great Council Chamber. In the church of Madonna dell'Orto Tintoretto himself is seen helping to support the Golden Calf in preparation for a ritual – he has a big black beard and a complacently pagan bearing, and near by is his wife, all in blue. Palma Vecchio's celebrated Saint Barbara, in Santa Maria Formosa, described as 'the ultimate representation of Venetian beauty', is in fact the artist's daughter Violante ('an almost unique representation of a hero-woman', George Eliot once wrote of the picture, 'standing in calm preparation for martyrdom, without the slightest air of pietism, yet with the expression of a mind filled with serious conviction').

The Madonna in Titian's great Pesaro altar piece in the Frari is his own wife Celia, soon afterwards to die in childbirth. The neighbouring tomb of Canova, with its pyramidical super-structure and its suggestive half-open door, was designed *by* Canova – not for himself, but for Titian, who had his own plans for a truly Titianesque tomb, but died too soon to build it (he is buried in the Frari anyway in the grandest mausoleum of all, erected 300 years after his death by the Emperor of Austria, and surrounded by reliefs from his own works).

In the same church, the fine statue of St Jerome by Alessandro Vittoria, with its beautifully modelled veins and muscles, really portrays Titian in his old age: and the bust of Vittoria himself in San Zaccaria, representing him in dignified thought among an audience of respectful allegories, is a self-portrait. In the Scuola di San Rocco, the wooden caricature of an artist by the irrepressible Francesco Pianta mischievously lampoons Tintoretto, whose overwhelming canvases stand all around it. Five heads on Sansovino's sacristy door, behind the high altar of the Basilica, represent less than ethereal personages: they are Sansovino himself, Palladio, Veronese, Titian, and Aretino, who once endeared himself to all professional hacks by remarking that he earned his living 'by the sweat of his ink', and who is said to have died of laughing too much at an obscene joke about his own sister.

In the church of San Salvatore the fine organ-shutters were painted by Titian's brother, Francesco Vecellio: they are among his last professional works, for he presently abandoned art altogether, and became a soldier. In three Venetian buildings you may see sets of pictures that were entries in a competition, now hanging together in perpetual truce: the twelve martyrs of San Stae, the twenty-one on the ceiling of the Marciana Library, the twenty-four, all concerned with the affairs of the Carmelites, that give a cluttered but powerful distinction to the nave of the Carmini. (The stations of the Cross in Santa Maria Zobenigo were also painted by several different artists, each doing two.)

Tintoretto's last work is the picture of the titular saint in San Marziale. Titian's last is his Deposition in the Accademia, intended for his tomb: it was finished by Palma Giovane, who wrote beneath it, as you will see: 'What Titian left unfinished, Palma has reverently completed, and he dedicates the work to God.' Verocchio's last is the equestrian statue of Colleoni. Longhena's last is the Palazzo Pesaro on the Grand Canal, which he never lived to finish. Giovanni Bellini's last is his altar piece in San Giovanni Crisostomo, near the Rialto. Mantegna's last is thought to be his glorious *San Sebastiano*, in the Ca' d'Oro: it was found in his studio after his death, and at the foot of the picture, beside a smoking candle-wick, is the resigned

inscription: *'Nil Nisi Divinum Stabile Est, Caetera Fumus'* – 'Nothing
But God Endures, The Rest Is Smoke.'

Then there are the curiosities of politics and diplomacy. In the floor of
the Basilica atrium there is a small lozenge-shaped stone which
marks the point of the Emperor Frederick Barbarossa's abasement
before the Pope Alexander III in 1177. The Pope, in flight from the
Emperor's armies, came to Venice in disguise, not sure whether the
Republic was his friend or his enemy: but the Venetians, sensing
opportunities of advancement, arranged a reconciliation between the
two monarchs, and thus established the Republic's position as a
political *deus ex machina*. The Venetian legends say that the Emperor,
facing Alexander on this very spot, agreed to apologize to St Peter,
but not to the Pope, and that Alexander replied sternly: 'To Peter *and*
the Pope.' Such versions of the event have Frederick flat out on the
ground kissing the papal feet, and the loyal Venetian artists have
pictured the occasion in a great series of paintings in the Doge's
Palace, including several scenes of Venetian triumph that are utterly
apocryphal.

Many legends, too, illustrate Alexander's arrival in Venice, destitute and friendless, and several churches claim the honour of having
sheltered him in their porches on his first night in the city. Near the
Campo Sant' Aponal you will see, engraved above a small shrine at
the entrance to a narrow courtyard, the following inscription:
'Alexander the Third, Supreme Pontiff, flying from the armies of
Frederick the Emperor, coming to Venice, here reposed the first
night; and then conceded a perpetual plenary indulgence to whoever
shall say a Pater Noster and an Ave Maria in this place. Let it not be
heavy for thee to say Hail Mother. The year is 1177 and by the charity
of the devout it is lighted day and night, as is seen.' Whether this was
really the Pope's first refuge, nobody knows: but it is perfectly true
that, after some centuries of neglect and squalor, the lights do burn
there night and day, and perhaps a few passing Venetians still claim
their indulgences.

There are many mementoes of Napoleon in Venice, from the Public
Gardens to the present shape of the Piazza. Beside the church of San

Pietro di Castello, in the eastern part of the city, you may see the rambling and uncomfortable building which was, until he decreed otherwise, the palace of the Patriarch: it now provides married quarters for petty officers of the Italian Navy. If you stand with your back to the Basilica and look at the western end of the Piazza, you will see a row of twelve statues on the façade of the *Ala Napoleonica*: they represent great emperors of the past, and in the middle of them is a gap in which it was intended to erect a gigantic statue of Napoleon himself. In the meantime an enormous semi-naked effigy of him was erected in the southern Piazzetta: this was later removed to the monastery of San Giorgio, then a barracks, and it now stands in the water-entrance of the Palazzo Mocenigo at San Samuele, on the Grand Canal, where Byron once lived.

The internal politics of Venice, too, have their many peculiar memorials: the *bocche dei leoni*, the Tiepolo stone in Campo Sant' Agostin, the old crone and her mortar in the Merceria, the absent doge among the portraits in the Doge's Palace. The church of San Trovaso is a memento in itself. It lies directly on the border-line between the territories of the two ancient Venetian factions, the Nicolotti and the Castellani, and it has a door on each side of the church, one opening into Nicolotti country, the other into Castellani. If there was ever a wedding between a Castellani bride and a Nicolotti bridegroom, the wedding pair left together by the central door of the church, but their relatives stalked resolutely out in opposite directions.

But the most bizarre of all Venice's historical allusions comes from distant places and far more ancient times. Outside the main gates of the Arsenal, among a pride of peers, there stands a tall marble lion, gangling but severe. This beast was brought from Athens in 1687 by the fighting Doge Francesco Morosini (chiefly eminent in universal history because a gunner under his command blew up the Turkish powder magazine that happened to be inside the Parthenon). The lion used to guard the gateway into the Piraeus, and was so celebrated among the ancients that the port itself was known as the Port of the Lion: but when it arrived at the Arsenal, booty of war, the Venetians were puzzled to discover that engraved upon its shoulders and haunches were some peculiar inscriptions, not at all Greek in style, in characters that seemed, to the eyes of a people accustomed to the exquisite calligraphies of Arabic, rudely and brusquely chiselled.

For several centuries nobody knew what these letters were: until one nineteenth-century day a visiting Danish scholar inspected them, raised his arms in exultation, and pronounced them to be Norse runes. They were carved on the lion in the eleventh century by order of Harold the Tall, a Norwegian mercenary who fought several campaigns in the Mediterranean, conquering Athens and once dethroning the Emperor in Constantinople, only to die in 1066 as King of Norway, fighting Harold the Saxon at Stamford Bridge, Yorkshire. The inscription on the lion's left shoulder says: 'Haakon, combined with Ulf, with Asmud and with Orn, conquered this port. These men and Harold the Tall imposed large fines, on account of the revolt of the Greek people. Dalk has been detained in distant lands. Egil was waging war, together with Ragnar, in Roumania and Armenia.' And on the right haunch of this queer animal is inscribed, in the runic: 'Asmund engraved these runes in combination with Asgeir, Thorleif, Thord and Ivar, by desire of Harold the Tall, although the Greeks on reflection opposed it.'

What all this means, only the lion knows: but modern scholars have interpreted its general sense as implying that Kilroy, with friends, was there.

Other nooks of Venetian oddity are almost out of range of the guide books. Behind the Basilica there is a Lapidarium, a courtyard haphazardly studded with diverse stones and pieces of sculpture: two headless pigeons, a noseless warrior, a very old Adam in a clump of bushes, a pair of disembodied hands which have been plastered to the walls, and reach out from it creepily in perpetual distress, clutching stone rods. (As you stand before these strange objects, you may be momentarily disturbed to hear a muffled subterranean thumping, below your feet: but do not be alarmed – it is only the workmen restoring the crypt of the Basilica.)

The Palazzo Mastelli, near Madonna dell' Orto, is a house of equally esoteric quality. On its façade is a peculiar dromedary which we have already, with an unkind snigger, examined: but the inner courtyard of this place, approached around the corner, is lavishly stuccoed with souvenirs and fragments of loot, columns built high into the structure, a small Madonna in a shrine, irrelevant arches, well-heads, grilles. It is a magpie-nest of a house, secretively sheltered behind a high brick wall, and camouflaged with foliage. As you walk befuddled and enchanted from its purlieus you will not be surprised to learn that the four enigmatical Moors of the Campo dei Mori, as odd a quartet as ever stared blankly from a crumbling wall, are sometimes supposed to have been among its ancient residents.

On the ground floor of the Fondaco dei Turchi, which is now the Natural History Museum (and has Faliero's coffin in its loggia), there is a courtyard that is part boat-house, part menagerie, part Pantheon. Around its walls are affixed a series of portrait statues, once kept in the Doge's Palace: there are admirals, painters, scholars, poets, architects, Sebastian Cabot, Marco Polo, Galileo and Admiral Emo, with Dante thrown in for respect and affection. These mouldering images, now unvisited from one year to the next, gaze down thoughtfully upon the boats and apparatus of the chief collector of the Museum, who spends half his time gathering specimens in the reedy wastes of the lagoon, and half the time stuffing and mounting them upstairs. Four or five black *sandoli* lie there on the flagstones, with oars and planks and an outboard motor: and here and there among the jumble you may find little living creatures, recently plucked from their nests or burrows, and now kept in doomed but kindly confinement until they are the right age to be, as the American taxidermists say, eternalized.

A pair of baby seagulls, perhaps, lives beneath the poop of one boat, stamping angrily about on their infinitesimal webbed feet, and sometimes plodding across to the courtyard fountain for a dignified circuit of its pool – four times round precisely, no more, no less, before returning to their nest beneath the protruding eyes of one of the lesser-known philosophers. A young duck inhabits a nearby sarcophagus. In a wire cage in the shadow of Titian two green snakes are moodily coiled, and huddled beneath the earth of a wooden box are three leathery salamanders. Upstairs the Museum of Natural History, impeccably organized, breathes the spirit of rational inquiry:

but there is something delightfully hare-brained to the courtyard below.

The naval museum at the Arsenal is similarly intriguing, with its bits of ships, banners, figure-heads, lions galore and remains of the Bucintoro; so is the Scuola di San Giovanni, with a beautiful Renaissance courtyard and staircase, and a main hall that is half museum and half carpenter's shop; so is the tiny Oratory of the Annunciation, twenty feet square, in the Campo Sant' Angelo; and the carved stone girl on the Zattere who has tied her long hair beneath her chin, like a muffler; and the boatyards of the city, and its innumerable cloistered courtyards, its unsuspected churches, its quirks and idiosyncrasies of architecture, its topsy-turvy street plan.

There is a column-head among the arcades of the Doge's Palace that tells, for no apparent reason, the sad life story of a child – love at first sight between its mooning parents, courtship, conception (in a double bed), birth, childhood, early death, tears. In any other city this sequence of images might strike you as perfectly inexplicable, bearing as it does no relation to anything else in the palace, containing no apparent historical or religious allusion, and conveying no recognizable moral. Here, though, it does not seem untoward: for when you have wandered around this city for a time, and examined a few of its crooked displays, and inspected some of its paradoxes and perplexities, you will realize that much the most curious thing in Venice is Venice herself.

21 To the Prodigies

If you imagine Venice as an oil painting, then the basis of its colour is provided by this twisted gnarled ambience of the city, crowded, aged, nonconformist. Before the highlights of the place are grandly daubed upon it, there is a gentler layer of fine tinting, giving richness, variety and strength to the composition. This is provided by a multitude of modest but wonderful monuments in the city, well known but not world-renowned, which are as essential to its flavour as are the picture postcard marvels.

Consider first the ward of Cannaregio, the northernmost section of the city. Here is the entrancing Gothic church of Madonna dell' Orto, named for the miraculous image found in a neighbouring garden and now lumpishly deposited in the right transept: there is a radiant Cima Baptism in this building, and a Giovanni Bellini altar-piece, and Tintoretto's admired Presentation, and a photograph (in a side-chapel) of a recent vicar of the church who seems to me to have one of the finest faces in Venice. Very near is the church of Sant' Alvise, almost ignored by the mass itineraries, with Tiepolo's mighty *The Way to Calvary*, and the appealing little knightly pictures known as the Baby Carpaccios – which do look as though they might have been painted by some artist of genius in his nursery days, and in fact bear (not altogether convincingly) Carpaccio's signature.

To the east is the church of the Misericordia, with two cherubs on its façade so genuinely mournful that their small faces are swollen with tears; to the south is San Giovanni Crisostomo, with its lovely Bellini altar-piece and a picture in which the elusive Giorgione is thought to have had a hand. The monumental Gesuiti has its mock draperies and Titian's awful picture of the martyrdom of St Lawrence. The exquisite funeral church of San Michele stands on its island in a perpetual obsequial hush, like a very aristocratic undertaker.

On the Grand Canal stands the Ca' d'Oro museum, which possesses Mantegna's wonderful *San Sebastiano*, and also Guardi's well-known picture of the Piazzetta, more often copied, perhaps, than any other landscape painting on earth. Not far away is the Labia Palace, the scene of many voluptuous celebrations, which is decorated in apposite magnificence with Tiepolo frescoes depicting the career of Cleopatra. The three dismal courtyards of the Ghetto stand among their tenements. The church of San Giobbe is tucked neatly away near the slaughter-house. If you arrive by aircraft or car, it is worth visiting the railway station, if only to marvel at the ingenuity by which so lavish and functional a building can be designed without providing a single place for the weary traveller to sit down without paying for the privilege.

Consider secondly the ward of Castello, the eastern part of the city.

The church of Santa Maria Formosa contains an altar-piece by Alvise Vivarini that is startlingly reminiscent of Stanley Spencer, besides Palma Vecchio's renowned *Santa Barbara*: and almost next door, in the Querini Stampalia gallery, is a fascinating collection of eight-eenth-century Venetian genre paintings, illustrating everything from a bull-baiting to a nun's reception room. The main altar-piece in San Giovanni in Bragora is a masterpiece by Cima, now well displayed, once so badly placed that, as one old English guide book robustly advises, 'the best way to see it is to stand upon the altar'. There is a famous Giovanni Bellini in San Zaccaria, and a glister of ikons in San Giorgio dei Greci, and an ornate but gentle Madonna by Negroponte in San Francesco della Vigna.

Above the main door of Sant' Elena is a masterly figure of a man in supplication, by Antonio Rizzo. The Scuola di San Marco, the hospital, contains some of the most opulent assembly rooms in Venice. Hidden away in the heart of the *sestiere* is the church of the Knights of Malta, San Giovanni, with elegant quarters for the Grand Prior of the order, and a cosy house for the chaplain. Among the plane trees of the Public Gardens there stand self-consciously the elaborate pavilions of the Biennale, and the whole eastern region of Castello is dominated by the grim uncompromising walls of the Arsenal, blocking many a quaint vista, and bringing to this poor neighbourhood a vision of the city's iron days.

Consider third, in this survey of second-class sights, the ward of San Marco, clustering around the Basilica. Here is the Correr Museum, with famous pictures by the Bellinis, Lotto and Carpaccio, not to speak of the original blocks for Barbari's famous Venetian map, and many surprising curios of Venetian life and history, like banners from captured Turkish warships, and shoes with twelve-inch heels. Around the corner in the Piazzetta, the Marciana Library displays in a glass case the illuminated Breviario Grimani, one of the most beautiful and valuable of books, the pages of which are turned over daily, with infinite caution, by a permanently awestruck curator.

The Baroque extravaganzas of San Moisè and Santa Maria Zobe-nigo are both in this *sestiere*. So is the church of San Salvatore, which has a Renaissance interior of great distinction, and a white marble image of Pius X, and in Easter week is transformed by the brilliance of a magnificent silver altar-screen. Santo Stefano has a big comfortable nave and a haughty campanile, San Giuliano a good Sansovino carving above its door – it represents the rich physician from Ravenna who paid for the church. The Fenice Theatre has a delightfully evocative series of eighteenth-century banqueting rooms, still echoing to the clip of buckled shoes and the swish of crinolines. If you walk up a side alley from the Campo Manin, on the southern side of that square, you will come across the fine spiral staircase, said to defy all the proper constructional laws, which is called *Scala dal Bovolo* – the Staircase of the Snail. If you wander down the dazzling Merceria, the Venetian Fifth Avenue, you will come in the end to the statue of Goldoni the playwright, which stands in the Campo San Bartolomeo, gently and quizzically smiling, and seems to me as happy a memorial as any man could ask for.

Consider next the southern ward of Dorsoduro, the 'Hard Back', with its attendant island of Giudecca. It extends from the Dogana at one end, with the bronze figure of Fortune holding his sail of chance, almost to the car park at the other. The Salute is its most ponderous monument: in this vast church, besides its Titians and its Tintorettos and the pillars brought from the Roman amphitheatre at Pola, you may notice that the great lamp hanging on a chain from the centre of the dome is two or three inches out of true. Near by is the quaint little cluster of buildings around San Gregorio, from where, in the war-like days of the Republic, they used to throw a defensive chain across the Grand Canal. The factional church of San Trovaso is in Dorsoduro; its real name (in case your guide book is of pedantic leanings) is Santi Gervasio e Protasio, far too large a mouthful for the Venetian vernacular. Near it is the church of the Gesuati, on the Zattere waterfront, which has a gay Tiepolo ceiling, floating with pantomimic angels.

In the church of the Carmini you may see another entrancing Cima, one of the rare Venetian pictures of Lorenzo Lotto (who deserted the city, driven out by jealous rivals), and some interesting bas-reliefs of ships, near the main door. The neighbouring Scuola dei Carmini glows, and sometimes shrieks, with the talent of Tiepolo.

There are organ-shutters painted deliciously by Guardi in the church of Angelo Raffaele, besides two agreeable saints, one on each side of the altar, whose haloes are tilted rakishly at opposing angles to give symmetry to the *ensemble*. San Sebastiano is magnificently decorated by Veronese, who is buried there. San Pantaleone is notable for a gigantic painting, as much engineering as art, that covers its concave ceiling. The Ca' Rezzonico museum has a quaint little puppet theatre in its attic, and out towards the docks there is a weird, shadowy, barbaric, gleaming, candle-lit church called San Nicolo dei Mendicoli – it has a solemn figure of the Virgin in a dark red velvet dress, and two cherubs of herculean measurements. Across the waters on Giudecca there broods the famous Palladian church of the Redentore, an antiseptic fane that nobody loves.

Consider fifthly San Polo, the district that lines the Grand Canal between Ca' Foscari and the Rialto – or, if you are of modernist tastes, between the fire station and the Post Office. Here are the vivid splendours of the markets, bustling around the law courts and San Giacomo di Rialto, and the meshed networks of old houses, converging upon the Rialto, that used to be the stews of Venice. The church of San Rocco is in this ward, and so is the café of Nini the cat: and on the left-hand wall of San Giovanni Elemosinario, near the Rialto, there is a wonderful old Chartres-like carving of the Nativity, rescued from the ruins of an earlier building, with a gentle recumbent Madonna and an ox who gently licks, in a manner of dreamy devotion, the little face of the Christ-Child.

Sixthly Santa Croce, the westernmost *sestiere*, whose pace and atmosphere is increasingly dictated by the presence of the Piazzale Roma, buzzing with buses and ablaze with neon signs. If you knock on the door of a convent near Campo San Zan Degola, a very old nun will produce a very large key and take you into the church of her order, San Giovanni Decollato: and leading you carefully through its damp and peeling nave, she will show you, high on the wall of a side chapel, the remains of some Byzantine frescoes that are said to be the oldest works of art in Venice, and which, though not in themselves very beautiful, have a certain hypnotic allure to them, like the goggle-eyes that peer at you out of the middle of cuckoo-spit.

In San Giacomo dell' Orio there is a queer and beautiful green pillar, made of Greek marble, and a wooden roof built precisely like the hull of a boat. Santa Maria Mater Domini is an unjustly neglected Renaissance church by the Lombardi brothers, of clean but gorgeous line. San Cassiano has a noble Titian Crucifixion. The back of San Nicolò da Tolentino looks like an Edwardian battleship, with barbettes, bulwarks, flying bridges and catwalks. In the church of San Simeone Grande there is a breathtaking statue of St Simeon in death, in the chapel to the left of the high altar: his mouth is slightly open, his eyes stare, his hair is long and tangled, and the whole is carved with such strength and certainty that you may feel the presence of that dead saint lingering beside you still, long after you have left the dark little church and joined the crowds that press perpetually towards the station.

What depth and richness and variety of colouring these minor monuments of the *sestieri* contribute to the masterpiece of Venice herself! There are palaces to see everywhere, and precious churches, and bridges, and pictures by the thousand, and all the criss-cross pattern of antiquity that is picturesque Venice, mocked by the materialists, sentimentalized by the Romantics, but still by any standards an astonishing phenomenon, as fruity as plum pudding, as tart as the brandy that flames about its holly.

But when all is said, and nearly all is done, it is the diapason sights you come to see. You may meander through your curiosities, your shy churches and your unobtrusive geniuses. You may follow the wandering canals from San Giobbe to Sant' Elena. You may inspect the dustbin barges, and wonder at the leaning campaniles, and tickle the cats' whiskers, and sample the roast eel, and sniff the burnt straw of the boat-yards, and breathe the spices of the Orient, and listen to the tread of the great ships' screws, and count the trains on the causeway, and attend an Armenian Mass, and look a dozen lions in the eye, and hold your nose beside a drained canal, and examine the Archives of the Republic, and haggle with the gondoliers, and buy an Afghan flag, and peer over the wall of the Servite convent, and ride the *vaporetti* like a connoisseur, and wave a brisk good morning to

Signor Dandolo, as he leans from his window with a commanding presence, like a generalissimo speeding a parting fleet. The time will necessarily come, though, when you obey the injunctions of the generations, and follow the stream of traffic to the superlatives of Venice. They will be as familiar to you as the Pyramids or the Great Wall of China: but the most marvellous of the Venetian spectacles are still the ones that get their well-worn stars in Baedeker.

No little building in the world is more fascinating than the Renaissance church of Santa Maria dei Miracoli, hidden away behind the Rialto like a precious stone in ruffled satin. It has all the gentle perfection, and some of the curious dull sheen, that marks a great pearl from the Persian Gulf, and it seems so complete and self-contained that it might be prised from the surrounding houses and taken bodily away, leaving only a neat little church-shaped cavity, not at all unsightly, in the fabric of the city. Its choir stalls are decorated with adorable figures, its altar is raised high and holy above its congregation, and the miraculous picture that it was built to honour is still reverenced inside it. I cannot imagine the most truculent of atheists failing to remove his hat as he enters this irresistible sanctuary.

Nothing anywhere is more piquantly charming than the Scuola di San Giorgio degli Schiavoni, which Carpaccio decorated, long ago, with a small series of masterpieces. It is no bigger than your garage, and its four walls positively smile with the genius of this delightful painter, the only Venetian artist with a sense of humour. Here is St George lunging resolutely at his dragon, which is surrounded horribly by odd segments of semi-digested maidens; and here is St Tryphonius with a very small well-behaved basilisk; and here the monks of St Jerome's monastery, including one old brother on crutches, run in comical terror from the mildest of all possible lions; and here, in the most beguiling of all these canvases, St Jerome himself sits in his comfortable study, looking out of his window in search of a deathless phrase, while his famous little white terrier sits bright-eyed on its haunches beside him.

No art gallery in Europe is more exuberant than the Accademia, the distillation of Venetian civilization. There are better collections of pictures elsewhere, grander Titians, finer Bellinis, more numerous Guardis, Canalettos and Giorgiones: but the glory of the Accademia is that all this grand variety of beauty and taste, ranging from the toy-like to the overblown, has been inspired by the small city that lies about you, from the crystal Cimas and the quaint Carpaccios to Tintoretto himself and Veronese's tremendous *Feast at the House of Levi*, to my mind the most endlessly fascinating picture of them all. You are standing in the middle of the paintbox. You can see one of Titian's studios from the window of the building, and Veronese's house is 200 yards away across the Grand Canal.

No collection of sacred pictures is more overwhelming of impact than the immense series of Tintorettos in the Scuola di San Rocco – often dark, often grandiose, often incomprehensible, but culminating in the huge masterpiece of the Crucifixion, which Velazquez humbly copied, and before which, to this day, you may still see strong men moved to tears. (And around the walls of this great school are the impudent satirical carvings of Francesco Pianta, wonderfully witty and original: there is a mock miniature library all of wood, an explanatory catalogue in microscopic writing, and an enormous blaze-eyed Hercules at the end of the hall.)

Nothing is cooler, and whiter, and more austerely reverent than Palladio's church of San Giorgio Maggiore, standing with such worldly aplomb among its peasantry of convent buildings. Somebody once defined this group of structures as 'on the whole, a great success': and it does have a feeling of high accomplishment, as of a piece of machinery that clicks silently into its appointed grooves, or an aircraft of unimpeachable line. The proportions are perfect, the setting supreme, and from the top of the campanile you get the best view in Venice (a smooth Swiss lift will take you there, and the Benedictine monk who operates it is almost as proud of its plastic buttons as he is of his historic monastery).

No two churches are starker, pinker, loftier, nobler than the two Friars' churches of Venice – the Frari on one side of the Grand Canal, San Zanipolo on the other. The Frari is like a stooping high-browed monk, intellectual and meditative, with its two great Titians, its lovely altar-pieces by Giovanni Bellini, the Vivarinis, Basaiti, its tall

tombs of artists, rulers, statesmen, generals, its carved choir stalls
and its air of imperturbable calm. San Zanipolo has more of a flourish
to it, a more florid style, suave but curled: its tombs are myriad and
illustrious – forty-six Doges are buried there – its roof is high-vaulted,
and outside its walls stands the unrivalled equestrian statue of
Colleoni, the most famous horseback figure in the world. If you stand
upon the campanile of one of these churches, you can see the
campanile of the other: but they carefully ignore each other, like rival
dogmatists at an ecclesiastical congress.

Nothing is more stimulating, on a gleaming spring day, than the
kaleidoscopic Basin of St Mark, the pool that lies directly before the
Piazzetta, bounded by the incomparable curve of the Riva degli
Schiavoni. It reminds me often of Hong Kong, without the junks,
so incessant is its traffic and so limpid its colouring. In the day-time
the basin is never calm, however still the weather, because of the
constant churning of ships and propellers: but at night, if you take
your boat out there through the lamplight, it is as still and dark and
luscious as a great lake of plum-juice, through which your bows
seep thickly, and into whose sickly viscous liquid the dim shape of
the Doge's Palace seems to be slowly sinking, like a pastry
pavilion.

Nothing on this earth is grander than the Grand Canal, in its great
doubling sweep through the city, jostling with boats, lined by the
high old palaces that form its guard of honour: secretive buildings
like the Granary of the Republic, and dazzling ones like the Ca'
d'Oro, and pompous piles like the Prefecture, and enchanting
unconventional structures like the little Palazzo Dario, loaded with
marble and inset with verd-antique. They look almost stagy, like the
Victorian sham-façades of one-horse Western towns, but they are
rich with the realities of history. There is a church with a green dome
at the station end of the canal, and Desdemona's villa at the other,
and there are Byzantine arches, and Gothic windows, and Renaissance flowerings, and the whole is plastered with a thick increment
of romance and literature. As your boat churns its way towards the
lagoon, all these improbable palaces fall away from your prow like so
many fantasies, as though they had been erected for some forgotten

exhibition, the Crystal Palace or the Brussels World Fair, and had been left to rot away in splendour until the next display.

And so at last we come, like an army of pilgrims before us, into the central complex of St Mark's, which many a proud Venetian, dead and living, has fondly regarded as the heart of the world. We are among the prodigies. We take a cup of coffee in the music-laden, pigeon-busy Piazza, beside the bronze flag-poles and the great kindly Campanile, where the sun is brighter than anywhere else on earth, the light clearer, the crowds more animated, and where more people congregate on a Sunday morning in July than in all the other piazzas of the world put together. We labour through the gigantic halls of the Doge's Palace, beneath the battles, the fleshy nymphs and the panoramic parables – Venice Triumphant, Venice Holding A Sceptre, Venice Conferring Honours, Venice Accepting Neptune's Trident, Venice Breaking her Chains, Venice Receiving Gifts from Juno, Venice Ruling the World, The Conquered Cities Offering Gifts to Venice, Venice Receiving the Crown in Token of her Power, The Apotheosis of Venice, The Victories of Venice over Franks, and Greeks, and Sicilians, and Turks, and Albanians, and Genoese, and Paduans – and on to the Bridge of Sighs, Titian's bewitching St Christopher, the gleaming armoury, the dreadful dungeons – a swollen, beringed, nightmare palace, pink outside, ominous within.

We watch the Moors of the Clock Tower clanging their big bell; we inspect the two squat little lions near the tomb of Manin; and thus we pass into the old cavern of the Basilica, golden with mosaics, its pavement heaving in elaborate patterns, its dim-lit spaces pierced with figures, gleaming with treasure, dusty and drab and opaque with centuries of incense, cluttered with chapels and galleries and unsuspected altars, with the legendary Pala d'Oro a golden sheet of jewels behind the high altar, and the great organ reverberating above us, mingled with the thumping of the café drums outside, and an endless movement of priests, sight-seers, vergers, groups of country folk, children, nuns, and a haze of dust sliding across the open doors, and a solitary proud pigeon strutting angrily away across the crooked floor towards the sunshine of the Piazza.

22 Purposes

'We are not' (swore d'Annunzio) 'and will not be a museum, a
hostelry . . . a sky painted Prussian blue for honeymoon couples.'
You may conclude, as you wander intoxicated among these spectacles, that Venice has happily found her modern *métier* as the
greatest of all museums; but you may sometimes have the feeling, as I
do, that this is in some sense a prostitution of a great city, a
degradation, a shame. Venice has always been an exhibitionist, and
has always welcomed her lucrative sight-seers, but she was built for
trade, power, and empire. She is still the seat of a prefecture, the
capital of a province, the headquarters of many business enterprises:
but it is a far cry, all the same, from a Quarter and A Half-Quarter of
the Roman Empire.

Nobody will deny that tourism is part of the Venetian mystique.
The Piazza is better, livelier, lovelier for its garish summer crowds.
Venice handles her visitors, if not exactly kindly, or even delicately,
at least efficiently: her methods have been tried and tested over many
generations. Her output of pleasure-per-customer-per-month is
high, and I think it probable that all in all you can have a better
holiday in Venice than anywhere else on earth – especially if you hire
yourself a boat, and see the place in its prime and original perspective. Venice devotes herself diligently and understandably to a
very profitable monopoly: Venice.

Nor is she as fossilized as her detractors claim, and as a certain kind
of devotee, often foreign and elderly, would like her to be. She has
probably changed less in the last three centuries than any other city in
Europe, even resisting the triumphant town-planners of the Napo-
leonic age: but she has changed more than you might suppose.
Several new artificial islands have radically altered her outline – in the
area of Sant' Elena, at the western end of Giudecca, around the docks
– and more are constantly being prepared (the mud-banks are staked,
reinforced with concrete, and stacked with rubbish). Within living
memory whole new housing areas have arisen at Sant' Elena, on
Giudecca, and north of the Ghetto. The vast new railway station has

been completed since the Second World War. There is a big new hotel near the station, and a plain but desperately exclusive one on Giudecca, and a large ugly extension has been built to the Danieli on the Riva degli Schiavoni.

Quaysides have been repeatedly widened, as you can confirm by examining the structure of the Riva, upon which little plaques record its limits before it was widened in 1780. Since the eighteenth century scores of canals and ponds have been filled in to make streets: every Rio Terra, every Piscina is such a place, and very pleasant they are to walk in, with space to swing your shopping bag about, or play with your balloon. Two big new streets have been cut through the buildings, one leading to the station, one on the edge of he Public Gardens. Above all, the building of the motor causeway has brought a bridgehead of the machine age to the fringe of Venice, and has made the region of the Piazzale Roma a raucous portent of the future: for shattering is the transition that separates the ineffable small squares of Dorsoduro from the diesel fumes, blinding lights, myriad cars and petrol pumps of the Piazzale, one of the nastiest places I know.

If you want to consider the modern purposes of Venice, have a Cinzano at a café by the car park, and do your meditating there.

'Venice has to fight', says a handbook published by the Tourist Department, 'against the pressing threat of the rhythm of modern life'; and this gnomic statement, if scarcely disinterested, puts the Venetian problem in a nutshell. Venice poses an insoluable dilemma. If they compromise with modernity, fill in her canals and take cars to the Piazza, then they wreck her absolutely. If they leave her alone, she potters down the years as a honeymoon city, part art gallery, part burlesque, her mighty monuments mere spectacles, her wide suzerainties reduced for ever to the cheap banalities of the guides.

Two schools of thought grapple with this conundrum. (I do not count the rigid advocates of the *status quo*.) One believes that Venice proper should be regarded purely as a lovely backwater, preserved in artistic inutility, while commerce and industry should be confined to the mainland suburb of Mestre, technically part of the Municipality.

The other school wishes Venice herself, her city and her lagoon, to be given new meaning by an infusion of modern activities. Fierce newspaper controversies rage around these opposing conceptions; personal enmities are cherished; plan is pitted against plan, statistic against statistic; and Venice herself stands waiting, half-stultified, half-modernized, part a relic, part a revival.

The first school does not object to tourism, so long as the city is not further vulgarized, but its proponents cherish their Venice chiefly as a centre of art and scholarship. They enthusiastically support the Biennale, the International Music Festival, the Film Festival, the great periodical exhibitions of Venetian art. They think the future of the Serenissima is well represented by Peggy Guggenheim's collection of modern paintings in the Palazzo Venier, which is gauntly but spectacularly contemporary, and softened only by the youthful indiscretions of masters who adopted the principles of the Dada Movement or the Suprematists relatively late in their careers. They send visitors helter-skelter to the Fondazione Cini which has recently been established on San Giorgio, and which is partly a sea school, partly a technical college, but chiefly a magnificently equipped centre of scholarship, ablaze with purpose and idealism. They are earnest, devoted, anxious people: and as they shake their heads over the rhythm of modern life, and analyse the threats to their beloved Venice, it sometimes feels as though they are dissecting, with infinite care and the latest possible instruments of surgery, an absolutely rock-bottom dead cadaver.

The other school points out impatiently that the population of the city proper, tourists or no tourists, Klees or no Klees, has long been declining. Many Venetians have moved to Mestre altogether and work in its shipyards and factories. Many more (including several gondoliers) live on the mainland, where houses are more plentiful and conditions less cramping, and commute to Venice each day down the causeway. Others again have moved to villas and apartments on the Lido, and pour off the steamers each morning at St Mark's precisely as the Guildford stockbrokers flood into Waterloo. This trend (say the advocates of city development) will continue, unless Venice is herself modernized. Business houses will move to the mainland, leaving the social life of the city stagnant and its palaces neglected. Venice will become ever more artificial, ever more degraded, until the tourists themselves, sensing the shamness of her heart, will take their holiday allowances elsewhere. Such men want to revive the industries of the lagoon – lace, glass, shipbuilding, mosaics. They want to establish new industrial communities on the bigger islands, with underground roads to the mainland. They want to extend the Piazzale Roma complex further into the city, filling in canals for motor traffic, and taking cars directly to the quays of the Zattere. They would like to build a metro. They once proposed a world fair in Venice to celebrate the arrival of the twenty-first century. They talk of Venice in tones of bouncing angry gusto, as you might discuss converting some dreamy country house into flats (paying proper attention, of course, to its undoubted architectural merits).

Do we not know them well, whenever we live, the aesthetic conservers on the one hand, the men of change on the other? Which of their two philosophies is the more romantic, I have never been able to decide.

The prime advantages of Venice lie, as both sides agree, in her position upon the frontiers of east and west. This is handy for tourists, stimulating to art and scholarship, and good for business. In particular, it sustains the importance of Venice (and her subsidiary, Mestre) as a world port. If you are attacked by pangs of distaste in Venice, look along the side canals, and you can nearly always see a ship.

Venice is still the third largest port in Italy. Crippled by Vasco da Gama's discoveries, she revived a little when de Lesseps cut the Suez Canal – a project she had herself vainly proposed to the Sultan of Egypt several centuries before. Since then the port has been, with fluctuations, steadily expanding. Today big ships are always on the move in Venice, and at the quays of Giudecca there are usually vessels tied up for painting and repairs, their power cables wound casually round the antique Jerusalem buttresses that support the waterside structures. There are active repair yards behind the

Arsenal, and even within the ramparts of that old fortress you sometimes see the glare of welding upon a tanker's hull. (The envious Trevisans used to call the Arsenal a 'gondola factory': the Venetians retorted that whatever its functions, it was big enough to contain the whole of Treviso within its walls.)

Most ships sail clean through the city down the broad dredged canal to Mestre and the oil terminals of Porto Marghera and Sant' Ilario. Still, many do use the docks of Venice proper, either to discharge passengers, or to unload cargoes that will later be taken by train or truck to the awkwardly limited hinterland served by the port – not too far to the west, because of Genoa, not too far to the south, because of a vigorously expanding Rimini, not too far to the east, because of poor old Trieste. The big docks at the western edge of the city, whose derricks welcome you grimly as you drive along the causeway, are entirely modern. Their great grain elevator has become, from any mainland viewpoint, the principal landmark of the city, and the freighters of the world have painted their names and slogans upon their quaysides.

More spectacularly noticeable, though, are the cruise ships which day after day sweep with such beautiful panache into the city, sometimes to tie up at the Zattere, where the old transatlantic liners used to embark their passengers, sometimes to lie beside the Riva degli Schiavoni. They fly many flags – Greek, Russian, Turkish, British – and after a couple of days in port, having unleashed their passengers upon the tourist sights, they steal away again like fugitives on the tide, often before the city is awake: away through the sea-gates to Istanbul, or the Black Sea, or Egypt, or to slip from island to island, from temple to temple, from lecture to lecture of the blue Aegean.

The Venetians have also built themselves an international airport, administered by the port authorities, on the northern shore of the lagoon. They used to rely upon a small and inconvenient field on the Lido, and on the airport at Treviso, an hour away by bus, and unsuitable for big jets. The present airfield can handle the very biggest. Its runways lie parallel with the lagoon, rather as those at Nice run beside the Mediterranean, and it is linked with Venice by a deep-water canal, and a road connecting it with the causeway. Its runways are almost as long as the city of Venice itself, and it is called (for it cost several million pounds) the Aeroporto Marco Polo.

Do not suppose, then, that the mummy has twitched its last. Argue they may about the purposes of Venice, the dangers that threaten her, the opportunities that are hers: but there are many Venetians who see her future clear, and who, looking well ahead into the twenty-first century, envisage her as the south-eastern gateway of united Europe.

For myself, I think she deserves even more. I admire the rampaging go-getters of Venice, and I sympathize with the gentle conservatives: but I believe the true purpose of Venice lies somewhere between, or perhaps beyond, their two extremes. For if you shut your eyes very hard, and forget the price of coffee, you may see a vision of another Venice. She became great as a market city, poised between East and West, between Crusader and Saracen, between white and brown: and if you try very hard, allowing a glimmer of gold from the Basilica to seep beneath your eyelids, and a fragrance of cream to enter your nostrils, and the distant melody of a café pianist to orchestrate your thoughts – if you really try, you can imagine her a noble market-place again. In these incomparable palaces, East and West might meet once more, to fuse their philosophies at last, and settle their squalid bickerings. In these mighty halls the senate of the world might deliberate, and in the cavernous recesses of the Basilica, glimmering and aromatic, all the divinities might sit in reconciliation. Venice is made for greatness, a God-built city, and her obvious destiny is mediation. She only awaits a summons.

But if you are not the visionary kind – well, pay the man, don't argue, take a gondola into the lagoon and watch her magical silhouette sink into the sunset: still, after a thousand years, one of the supreme sights of civilization.

THE LAGOON

23 Seventh Sea

Sometimes in a brutal winter night you may hear the distant roar of
the Adriatic, pounding against the foreshore: and as you huddle
beneath your bedclothes it may strike you suddenly how lonely a city
Venice remains, how isolated among her waters, how forbiddingly
surrounded by mud-banks, shallows and unfrequented reedy
places. She is no longer a true island, and the comfortable mainland is
only a couple of miles from your back door: but she still stands alone
among the seaweed, as she did when the first Byzantine envoys
wondered at her gimcrack settlements, fourteen centuries ago. Time
and again in Venice you will glance along some narrow slatternly
canal, down a canyon of cramped houses, or through the pillars of a
grey arcade, and see before you beneath a bridge a tossing green
square of open water: it is the lagoon, which stands at the end of
every Venetian thoroughfare like a slab of queer wet countryside.

Several sheltered spaces of water, part sea, part lake, part estuary,
line the north-western shores of the Adriatic: in one Aquileia was
built, in another Ravenna, in a third Comacchio, in a fourth Venice
herself. They were known to the ancients as the Seven Seas, and they
were created in the first place by the slow action of rivers. Into this
cranny of the Mediterranean flows the River Po, most generous of
rivers, which rises on the borders of France, marches across the
breadth of Italy, and enters the sea in a web of rivulets and marshes.
Other famous streams tumble down from the Alpine escarpment,
losing pace and fury as they come, until at last they sprawl sluggishly
towards the sea in wide stone beds: the Brenta, which rolls elegantly
through Padua out of the Tyrol; the Piave, which rises on the borders
of Austria, and meanders down through Cadore and the delectable
Belluno country; the Sile, which is the river of Treviso; the Adige,
which is the river of Verona; the Ticino, the Oglio, the Adda, the
Mincio, the Livenza, the Isonzo and the Tagliamento. This congregation of waters, sliding towards the sea, has made the coastline a
series of estuaries, interlinked or overlapping: and three rivers in
particular, the Piave, the Brenta and the Sile, created the Venetian

lagoon. If you look very hard to the north, to the high Alpine valleys in the far distance, lost among the ridges and snow peaks, then you will be looking towards the ultimate origins of Venice.

When a river pours out of a mountain, or crosses its own alluvial plain, it brings with it an unseen cargo of rubble: sand, mud, silt, stones and all the miscellaneous bric-à-brac of nature, from broken tree-trunks to the infinitesimal shells of water-creatures. If the geological conditions are right, when its water eventually meets the seas, some of this material, buffeted between fresh water flowing one way and salt water pushing the other, gives up the struggle and settles on the bottom, forming a bar. The river forces its way past these exhausted sediments, the sea swirls around them, more silt is added to them, and presently they become islands of the estuary, such as litter the delta of the Nile, and lie sun-baked and turtle-haunted around that other Venice, the southernmost village of the Mississippi.

Such barriers were erected, aeons ago, by the Brenta, the Piave and the Sile, when they met the currents of the Adriatic (which, as it happens, sweep in a circular motion around this northern gulf). They were long lonely strips of sand and gravel, which presently sprouted grass, sea-anemones and pine trees, and became proper islands. Behind them, over the centuries, a great pond settled, chequered with currents and counter-currents, a mixture of salt and fresh, an equilibrium of floods: and among the water other islands appeared, either high ground that had not been swamped, or accumulations of silt. This damp expanse, speckled with islets, clogged with mud-banks and half-drowned fields, protected from the sea by its narrow strands – this place of beautiful desolation is the Venetian lagoon. It is thirty-five miles long and never more than seven miles wide, and it covers an area, so the most confident experts decree, of 210 square miles. It is roughly crescent-shaped, and forms the rounded north-western corner of the Adriatic, where Italy swings eastward towards Trieste and Croatia. Its peers among the Seven Seas have long since lost their eminence – the lagoon of Ravenna silted up, the lagoon of Aquileia forgotten: but the lagoon of Venice grows livelier every year.

Very early in their history, soon after they had settled on their islands and established their infant State, the Venetians began to improve upon their bleak environment. It was a precarious refuge for them. The sea was always threatening to break in, especially when they had weakened the barrier islands by chopping down the pine forests. The silt was always threatening to clog the entire lagoon, turning it into a vulnerable stretch of land. The Venetians therefore buttressed their mud-banks, first with palisades of wood and rubble, later with tremendous stone walls: and more fundamentally, they deliberately altered the geography of the lagoon. Until historical times seven openings between the bars – now called *lidi* – connected it with the open sea, allowing the river water to leave, and the Adriatic tides to ebb and flow inside. The Venetians eliminated some of these gaps, leaving only three entrances or *porti* through which the various waters could leave or enter. This strengthened the line of the *lidi*, deepened the remaining breaches, and increased the scouring force of the tide.

They also, in a series of tremendous engineering works, diverted the Brenta, the Sile, the Piave and the most northerly stream of the Po, driving them through canals outside the confines of the lagoon, and allowing only a trickle of the Brenta to continue its normal flow. The lagoon became predominantly salt water, greatly reducing (so the contemporary savants thought) the ever-present menace of malaria. The entry of silt with the rivers was virtually stopped: and this was opportune, for already half the lagoon townships were congealed in mud, and some had been entirely obliterated.

Thus the lagoon is partly an artificial phenomenon; but although it often looks colourless and monotonous, a doleful mud-infested mere, it is rich in all kinds of marine life. Its infusions of salt and fresh water breed organisms luxuriantly, so that the bottoms of boats are quickly fouled with tiny weeds and limpets, and the underneaths of palaces sprout water-foliage. The lagoon is also remarkable for its biological variety. Each *porto* governs its own small junction of rivulets, with its own watershed: and wherever the tides meet, flowing through their respective entrances, there is a recognizable bump in the floor of the lagoon, dividing it into three distinct regions.

It is also split into two parts, traditionally called the Dead and the Live Lagoon, by the limit of the tides. In all these separate sections the fauna and flora vary, making this a kind of Kew Gardens among waters; it used to be said that even the colour of the currents varied, ranging from yellow in the north by way of azure, red and green to purple in the extreme south.

In the seaward part, where the tides run powerfully and the water is almost entirely salt, all the sea-things live and flourish, the mud-banks are bare and glutinous and the channels rich in Adriatic fish. Farther from the sea, or tucked away from its flow, other organisms thrive: beings of the marshes, sea-lavenders, grasses and tamarisks, swamp-creatures in semi-stagnant pools, duck and other birds of the reeds. There are innumerable oysters in these waters, and crusta-ceans of many and obscure varieties, from the sea-locust to the thumb-nail shrimp; and sometimes a poor flying-fish, leaping in exaltation across the surf, enters the lagoon in error and is trapped, like a spent sunbeam, in some muddy recess among the fens.

A special race of men, too, has been evolved to live in this place: descended partly from the pre-Venetian fishing communities, and partly from Venetians who lingered in the wastes when the centre of national momentum had moved to the Rialto. They are the fittest who have survived, for this has often been a sick lagoon, plagued with malaria, thick and unwholesome vapours, periodically swept by epidemics of cholera and eastern disease. Like the rest of the fauna, the people vary greatly from part to part, according to their way of life, their past, their degree of sophistication, their parochial environ-ment. Inshore they are marsh-people, who tend salt-pans, fish among grasses, and do some peripheral agriculture. Farther out they can still be farmers or horticulturists, if they live in the right kind of island; but they are more likely to be salt-water fishermen, either taking their big boats to sea, or hunting crabs, molluscs and sardines among the mud-banks of the outer lagoon.

Their dialect varies, from island to island. Their manners instantly reflect their background, harsh or gentle. They even look different, the men of Burano (for instance) tousled and knobbly, the men of Chioggia traditionally Giorgionesque. The lagoon islands were much more independent in the days before steam and motors, with their own thriving local governments, their own proud piazzas, their own marble columns and lions of St Mark: and each retains some of its old pride still, and is distinctly annoyed if you confuse it with any neighbouring islet. 'Burano!' the man from Murano will exclaim. 'It's an island of savages!' – but only two miles of shallow water separates the one from the other.

The lagoon is never complacent. Not only do the tides scour it twice a day, the ships navigate it, the winds sweep it coldly and the speed-boats of the Venetian playboys scud across its surface in clouds of showy spray: it also needs incessant engineering, to keep its bulwarks from collapsing or its channels silting up. The Magistracy of the Waters is never idle in the lagoon. Its surveyors, engineers and watermen are always on the watch, perennially patching sea-walls and replacing palisades. Its dredgers clank the months away in the big shipping channels, looming through the morning mist like aged and arthritic elephants. The survival of Venice depends upon two contradictory precautions, forming themselves an allegory of the lagoon: one keeps the sea out; the other, the land. If the barrier of the outer islands were broken, Venice would be drowned. If the lagoon were silted up, her canals would be dammed with mud and ooze, her port would die, her drains would fester and stink from Trieste to Turin (it is no accident that the romantic fatalists, foreseeing a variety of dramatic ends for the Serenissima, have never had the heart to suggest this one).

So when you hear that beating of the surf, whipped up by the edges of a *bora*, go to sleep again by all means, but remember that Venice still lives like a diver in his suit, dependent upon the man with the pump above, and pressed all about, from goggles to lead-weighted boots, by the jealous swirl of the waters.

24 The Office of a Moat

The Venetians first filtered into the lagoon because it offered an obvious place of refuge, safe from landlubber barbarians and demoralizing heresies. They fortified it from the start, building tall watch-towers, throwing defensive chains across its waterways, erecting high protective walls along its quays. As early as the sixth century the people of Padua were complaining that the Venetians had militarized the mouth of the Brenta, to prevent alien shipping entering the lagoon. Nine centuries later the traveller Pero Tafur vividly described the war-readiness of the Venetian Navy. As soon as the alarm sounded, he records, the first warship emerged from the gate of the Arsenal, under tow: and from a succession of windows its supplies were handed out – cordage from one window, food from another, small arms from a third, mortars from a fourth, oars from a fifth – until at the end of the canal the crew leapt on board, and the galley sailed away, fully armed and ready for action, into the Canale San Marco. For many centuries the lagoon served the Venetians admirably in the office of a moat, and it stands there still, in the nuclear age, as a wide watery redoubt, studded with antique forts and gun-sites.

No enemy has ever succeeded in taking Venice by storm. The first assault upon it was made by Pepin, son of Charlemagne, in 809; and the legend of his rebuff symbolizes the Venetians' canny sense of self-defence. When they first came into this waste, established their tribunes in its various islands, and painfully coalesced into a single State, their original capital was the now-vanished island of Malamocco, half a mile off the reef. They were afraid of enemies from the mainland, not from the Adriatic, and so set up their Government as deep in the sea as possible. Pepin, though, in pursuance of his father's imperial ambitions, determined to humble the Venetians, and attacked the settlements from the seaward side. His forces seized the southern villages one by one, and finally stood before Malamocco itself. The Government then abandoned its exposed headquarters, and withdrew across the mud-flats, through intricate shallow channels that only the Venetians understood, to a group of islands in the very centre of the lagoon, called Rivo Alto – Rialto.

Pepin seized Malamocco triumphantly, and prepared to cross the lagoon in pursuit. Only one old woman, so the story goes, had stayed behind in Malamocco, determined to do or die, and this patriotic crone was summoned to the royal presence. 'Which is the way to

Rivo Alto?' demanded Pepin, and the old lady knew her moment had come. Quavering was her finger as she pointed across the treacherous flats, where the tide swirled deceitfully, and the mud oozed, and the seaweed swayed in turbulence. Tremulous was her voice as she answered the prince. '*Sempre diritto!*' she said: and Pepin's fleet, instantly running aground, was ambushed by the Venetians and utterly humiliated.

The next major enemies to enter the lagoon were the Genoese, the prime rivals of Venetian supremacy throughout the fourteenth century: but they too were kept at arm's length by its muddy presence. At the most threatening moment of their protracted campaigns against the Venetians, in 1379, they captured Chioggia, the southern key to Venice, and settled down to starve the Serenissima. Their warships burnt a Venetian galley within sight of the city, watched by hundreds of awestruck citizens, and some of their raiders may even have crossed the reef and entered the lagoon proper. The Venetians were hard-pressed. Half their fleet, under the dashing Carlo Zeno, was away in distant waters. The other half was demoralized by past setbacks, and its commander, Vettor Pisani, was actually released from prison to assume his duties. Cannon were mounted in the belfry of St Mark's Campanile, just in case, and the Doge himself volunteered to go into action, a desperate step indeed.

Pisani thus sailed out to battle with a scratch fleet of warships, a ramshackle army, most of the male population of Venice in patriotic tumult between decks, and this hell-for-leather potentate beside him on the poop. Yet in a few weeks he had so exploited the tactical advantages of the lagoon that the Genoese were placed critically on the defensive. They dared not station their ships outside the *lidi*, to face the buffeting of the winter sea and the possible return of Zeno, so they withdrew inside the Porto di Chioggia, the southernmost entrance to the lagoon: and there Pisani, swiftly deploying his vessels, promptly bottled them up. He closed the main Porto di Lido, to the north, with an iron chain, guarded by fortress guns. He closed the Porto di Malamocco, the central gate, by sinking two old ships, filled with stone. Four more blockships closed the entrance to

Chioggia itself, and two others blocked the main channel from the town towards Venice. A wall was built across the mud-flats at the approaches to the city, in case these successive obstacles were overcome, and for miles around every signpost and marker stake was removed, making the entire lagoon a slimy trap for alien navigators.

Thus the Genoese were caught. Venetian troops were landed near Chioggia, and the Genoese tried helplessly to get out to sea, even cutting a channel through the sand-bank that separated their ships from the Adriatic: but it was hopeless. Their supply routes were cut, and they were presently reduced, so their chroniclers say, to eating 'rats, mice and other unclean things'. They were doomed already when, in a day famous in Venetian history, the topmasts of Zeno's hurrying squadrons appeared over the horizon, and the victory was clinched. As a last straw for the poor Genoese, a campanile in Chioggia, hit by a stray shell when all was almost over, collapsed in a heap of rubble and killed their commander, Pietro Doria.

No other battles have been fought within the lagoon. Four hostile forces have, at one time or another, penetrated to the city of Venice, but they have never had to force their way across these waters. The first was a vagabond pirate commando, scum from Dalmatia, who decided one day in the tenth century to raid Venice at a moment when a mass wedding was to take place in the church of San Pietro di Castello. They sidled into the city at night, pounced upon the ceremony, kidnapped the brides with their handsome dowries, ran to their ships ('their accursed barks', the poet Rogers called them), and sailed exultantly away. The infuriated Venetians, led by the men of the Cabinet Makers' Guild, followed in furious chase: and presently skilfully using their knowledge of the lagoon, close-hauled and black with anger, they overtook the pirates, killed them every one, returned with the fainting brides to Venice, married them hastily and lived happily ever after.

It was eight centuries before the next enemy set foot in Venice, and by that time simpler citizens believed their lagoon to be divinely impregnable, so securely had it protected their city through all the switchbacks of Italian history. The mainland of the Veneto had long been a cockpit of European rivalries, and in 1796 Napoleon entered it with his heady slogans, his battle-stained infantry, and his volunteer legion of Italian liberals (some of whom, so Trevelyan tells us, had re-entered their native country by sliding down the Alpine slopes on their stomachs, their horses glissading behind them). Venice carefully looked the other way – by then she was the weakest State in Europe, besotted with hedonism. Even when it became clear that Napoleon was not going to spare her, and that war was inevitable, the emergency orders given by the Republic to her Proveditor General merely enjoined him to 'maintain intact the tranquillity of the State, and give ease and happiness to its subjects'. One hundred and thirty six casinos still flourished in the city. Five thousand families, we are told, received company every evening. The Venetians were no longer men of war: when the last Doge heard the news of his election, in 1789, he burst into tears and fainted.

This enervated and gangrenous organism Bonaparte had already promised to the Austrians, under the secret agreement of Leoben: and presently he picked his quarrel with the Serenissima. One day in April 1797 a French frigate, *Libérateur d'Italie*, sailed through the Porto di Lido without permission, an appalling affront to Venetian privilege. Such a thing had not happened for five centuries. The fort of Sant' Andrea opened fire, the ship was boarded and looted, the French commander was killed. This was Napoleon's *casus belli*. He refused to treat with the Venetian envoys sent to plead for peace, and blamed the Republic for a massacre of French troops that had occurred in Verona. The Venetians were, he said, 'dripping with French blood'. 'I have 80,000 men and twenty gunboats . . . *io sarò un Attila per lo Stato Veneto*.'

On 1 May 1797 he declared war. The Venetians were too disorganized, too frightened, too leaderless, too riddled with doubts, too far gone to offer any resistance: and two weeks later forty of their own boats conveyed 3,231 French soldiers from the mainland to the Piazza of St Mark – 'lean forms', as a French historian has described them, 'shaped for vigorous action, grimy with powder, their hats decked only with the cockade'. '*J'ai occupé ce matin*,' the French general reported prosaically to Napoleon, '*la ville de Venise, avec la 5e demi-brigade de bataille, et les îles et forts adjacents*.' He was the first commander ever to report the capture of Venice, and as he sealed this matter-of-fact dispatch he ended an epoch.

The Austrians were the next to take Venice. In the vagaries of their relationship with France, they had first been given the city, then lost it after Austerlitz, then regained it after Waterloo: until in 1848 the Venetians themselves, rising under Daniele Manin, expelled them and restored the Republic. This time the citizens, hardened by ignominy and suffering, defended their lagoon with tenacity against imperial blockade. They garrisoned its innumerable forts, breached its newly-completed railway bridge, and even made some successful sorties on the mainland. The Austrians invested the city fiercely. They floated explosives over Venice on balloons, like the balloon-bombs flown over California by the Japanese; and when these operations proved a laughable fiasco, they dismounted their field-guns, to give them more elevation, and shelled the city heavily. Everything west of the Piazza was within their range.

Battered, starving, short of ammunition, ravaged by cholera, without allies, Venice resisted longer than any of the other rebellious Italian cities, but in August 1849 Manin surrendered. The Austrians entered the lagoon without fighting. Their commander, that indomitable old autocrat Marshal Radetzky, whose last illegitimate child was born in his eighty-first year, rode up the Grand Canal in triumphant panoply: but not a soul was there to greet him, scarcely a maidservant peered from the windows of the palaces, and when he reached the Piazza he found it empty but for his own soldiers. Only one obsequious priest, so we are told, ran from the atrium of the Basilica and, throwing himself before the conqueror, fervently kissed his hand.

The last invading force to enter Venice was British. In 1945, when the world war was clearly ending and the German armies were retreating through Italy in a demoralized rout, the partisans of Venice seized the city from the last of the Germans, gave them a safe conduct to the mainland, shot a few of their own particular enemies, and awaited the arrival of the Allies, then storming across the Po. Two New Zealand tanks were the first to arrive: they raced each other down the causeway neck and neck, and one New Zealander reported that as his vehicles clattered pell-mell over a fly-over near Mestre, he looked down and saw the Germans racing helter-skelter in the opposite direction underneath.

The New Zealanders had specific orders from their commander, General Freyberg, to capture the Danieli Hotel – he had stayed there before the war, and wanted to reserve it as a New Zealand officers' club, even sending a special reconnaissance party to undertake the mission. They were received enthusiastically by the Venetians, and presently the British infantry arrived too, every boat in the place was requisitioned, the Danieli, the Excelsior, the Luna were turned into officers' clubs, and so many soldiers' canteens were established that you can still see the blue and yellow NAAFI signs mouldering upon Venetian walls among the other graffiti of history. Three days later the armistice was signed, and the war in Italy was over.

Thus the city has been spared the worst of war, and there have never been bazookas in the Piazza, or tommy-gun bursts across the Grand Canal. No bomb has ever fallen upon the Basilica of St Mark. In none of the several assaults was much damage done to Venice. In the 1848 revolution, though several thousand Austrian shells fell in the city, it is said that only one house was completely destroyed. In the First World War, when Venice was an active military base, she was repeatedly bombed – the bronze horses were removed for safety, the Basilica was heavily reinforced with bags full of seaweed, and night watchmen shouted throughout the night: *'Pace in aeria!'* – 'All quiet in the sky!' In several churches you may see unexploded missiles hung as *ex votos* upon the walls: but among all the treasures of the city, only the roof of the Scalzi church, near the station, was destroyed. In the Second World War Mestre was heavily bombed, but Venice never. The tower of San Nicolò dei Mendicoli was struck by a stray shell during the German withdrawal, and the Tiepolo frescoes in the Palazzo Labia were damaged when a German ammunition ship blew up in the harbour: but apart from broken windows, nothing was destroyed. Venice was, I am told, the very first city on both the German and the Allied lists of places that must not be harmed. Not everybody has welcomed this immunity. In 1914, when a bomb almost hit the Basilica, the crazy Futurist Marinetti, who wanted to pull down all the Italian masterpieces and begin again, flew over the city in an aeroplane dropping leaflets. 'Italians, awake!' they said. 'The enemy is attempting to destroy the monuments which it is our own patriotic privilege to demolish!'

The lagoon has saved Venice. She has stood aside from the main currents of war, and has fought her battles, like England, chiefly in distant places. She stands upon no vital cross-roads, controls no crucial bridge, overlooks no strategic position, commands no damaging field of fire. You could, if you happened to be another Napoleon, take the whole of Italy without much feeling the exclusion of Venice: and the innumerable wars of the Italian mainland, though they have often involved Venetian troops, have always passed the city by. Even the ferocious Turks, whose armies were so near in 1471 that the fires of their carnage could be seen from the top of St Mark's Campanile – even those implacable hordes never entered the lagoon. No city on earth is easier to spot from the air, framed by her silver waters, and no city has fewer cellars to use as air-raid shelters: yet almost the only civilian casualties of the two world wars were the 200 citizens who walked into canals in the black-out and were drowned. In the official histories of the Italian campaigns of the Second World War, Venice is scarcely mentioned as a military objective: and one British regimental diary, recording the hard slog up the peninsula, observed in reviewing the battles to come that all ranks were 'eager to get to grips with Jerry again, and looking forward, too, to some sightseeing in Venice'. In war as in peace, Venice stands alone, subject to none of the usual rules and conventions: like the fashionable eighteenth-century priest who, though courted by the greatest families of the Serenissima, chose to live in a rat-infested garret, and collected spiders' webs as a hobby.

But though nobody much cares nowadays, the lagoon is still a formidable military barrier. Napoleon himself apparently thought that if the Venetians decided to defend it, he would need as many men to beat them as he had at Austerlitz in the greatest battle of his career; but the Austrians were perhaps the last to survey it with a serious strategic eye. It was the main base for their imperial fleet, which was largely Italian-manned, and partly built in the old Arsenal of Venice. They made the lagoon a mesh-work of strong-points – in 1848 there were sixty forts (though visiting British officers were, as usual, not greatly impressed by their design). In the First World War it was a naval base, an armoury, and the launching site for d'Annunzio's dashing air raids against the Austrians. In the second it was a refuge for many a hunted partisan and prisoner-of-war, lurking in remote and vaporous fastnesses where the Germans never penetrated: and many Venetians hid there too, escaping conscription into Nazi labour forces. The German Army made a short last stand, until blasted out by the guns of the New Zealand armour, on the north-eastern edge of the lagoon, and they used barges to withdraw some of their troops along its water-ways. Before the rot set in they had prepared a defence system along the line of the Adige river, from Chioggia in the east to Lake Garda in the west: and some strategists believe that this line, embedded at its left flank in the impassable mud-flats of the lagoon, might have been the toughest of all the successive barriers that delayed the Allied advance through Italy.

The warlike propensities of the Venetian lagoon are still inescapable. If you come by train, almost the first thing you see is the big mainland fort of Marghera, a star-shaped earthwork outside Mestre, now covered in a stubble of grass and weed, like a downland barrow. Half-way up the causeway there stands the exposed gun platform beside the railway which was, for a few perilous weeks, the outermost Venetian stronghold in the 1848 revolution; and near by is the odd little island called San Secondo, shaped like a Pacific atoll, which is now a municipal stores depot, but was once an important fort and magazine. To the south of the causeway, near the docks, you may see the minute Isola Tresse: this is crowned by a concrete bunker, and on its wall there still stands a black swastika – painted, whether in irony or ignorance, the wrong way round.

All about the city there stand such relics of a military past – shuttered little islands and abandoned barracks, fine old forts and aircraft hangars. The distant Sant' Angelo della Polvere – St Angelo of the Gunpowder – looks like a fairy island, crowned with towers, but turns out to be, when you approach it in disillusionment, only an old powder factory, clamped and padlocked. San Lazzaretto, on the other side of the city, was once the quarantine station of Venice, then a military detention depot. In the seventeenth century, when Venice was threatened by Spanish ambitions, a division of Dutch soldiers, hired direct from Holland and brought to the lagoon in Dutch ships, was quartered on this island: they got so bored that they mutinied, and to this day the sentries still pace the grim square ramparts of its barracks with an air of unutterable ennui, waiting for an enemy that has never in all the 1,500 years of Venetian history chosen to come this way.

From the windows of San Giacomo in Palude – St James in the Marshes – to the north of Venice, cheerful soldiers in their shirt-sleeves, doing the washing-up, still grin at you as your boat chugs by, and a notice sternly forbids your presence within fifty yards of this vital outpost. Half a mile away, on the islet of Madonna del Monte, stands a huge derelict ammunition building, littered with rubble but still bound about with iron cables, to keep it standing in case of an explosion: it is a sun-soaked but eerie place – I once found six dead lizards lying side by side on a stone there, with a swarm of locusts performing their obsequies round about, and in the winter the dried pods of its little trees jingle metallically in the wind like the medals of long-dead corporals. Another barred and abandoned powder-island is Santo Spirito, away beyond Giudecca. From here Pisani's engineers built their protective wall to the *lidi*, but it later became a famous monastery, with pictures by Titian and Palma Vecchio, and a church by Sansovino. The church was despoiled when its monastic order was suppressed, in 1656, but as they were at that moment building the great new church of the Salute, the pictures were opportunely taken there, and they hang still in the Sacristy.

Out beside the great sea-gates, you may see the Adriatic defences of the lagoon. At the southern *porto* there stands behind high grass banks, still flying its flag, the fortress of La Lupa – the She-Wolf – medieval in masonry, eighteenth century in embellishment: and near by a little stony settlement by the water, now inhabited by a few fisher-families, is the remains of the powerful Fort Caromani, itself named for a much older strong-hold still, Ca' Romani – the House of the Romans. Two big octagonal fortresses, rising sheer from the water, guard the central *porto* of Malamocco. They are overgrown and deserted nowadays, and look rather like the stilt-forts that the British built in 1940 to protect their sea-approaches; but not long ago a passing fisherman, observing me raise my camera towards these dilapidated defences, told me gently but firmly that photography of military works was, as I surely ought to know, strictly forbidden.

At the northern end of the lagoon, near Punta Sabbione, there stands Fort Treporti, a comical towering construction, all knobs and tessellation, that looks like a chess-board castle. Not far away is the old seaplane base of Vignole, now a helicopter station, and the Italian Air Force still occupies the rambling slipways, hangars and repair shops of the amphibians, haunted by D'Annunzio's flamboyant shade. If you are ever silly enough to charter an aeroplane at the Lido airfield, you will learn (during your long and fruitless hours of waiting) how often the airspace of the lagoon is monopolized by military manoeuvres. And four-square before the Porto di Lido, the principal gateway of the lagoon, glowers the magnificent castle of Sant' Andrea, on the islet of Certosa; from its mighty ramparts they used to stretch the iron chain that blocked the channel to enemy ships, and it still stands there undefeated, the senior sentinel of Venice.

So the old lagoon still bristles. Its forts may be, as those visiting officers reported, 'not up to British standards'; its great navies have vanished; its guns are mostly spiked; its prickles are blunted; the jets that whistle overhead have come here in the twinkling of an eye from airfields on the Lombardy flat-lands. But sometimes, as your boat potters down the Canale San Marco, you may hear an ear-splitting roar behind your stern; and suddenly there will spring from the walls of the Arsenal a lean grey torpedo-boat, with a noble plume of spray streaming from her stern, and a shattering bellow of diesels; and she will disappear thrillingly towards the open sea, the rumble of her engines echoing among the old towers and ramparts of the place, the fishing boats bobbing and rolling in her wash.

25 Navigation

The lagoon is a trap for enemies, a work-ground and thoroughfare for friends. The Venetians first appeared in history when Narses the Eunuch, satrap of the Byzantine Emperors, asked them with flattery and circumspection to transport his troops across its wastes; and they began their satisfactory career as middle-men by carrying cargoes across it from Aquileia to Ravenna. Its presence gave the Venetians the best natural port in Italy, spacious and sheltered. Its tides kept them healthy, its fish fed them. Its nearer waters have always served them as a pleasure-park – 'we will go', wrote the deposed Doge Foscari to a friend, after his removal from office,' – we will go and amuse ourselves in a boat, rowing to the monasteries'.

It has always been, though, an atrocious place to navigate. Its tides are fierce, its storms blow up suddenly and dangerously, and most of it is treacherously shallow. Sometimes the *bora* sweeps devastatingly across its mud-banks – in 1613 it blew down two of the bronze flagpoles in the Piazza. (Two of the *valli* – vales, or reaches – into which the fishermen have divided their lagoon are called the Small Vale of Above the Wind and the Small Vale of Below the Wind.) The lagoon is full of secret currents, shoals, clinging water-weeds. Over most of its expanse, if you lie in the bows of your boat in the sunshine, with a hamper beside you and an arm around your waist, you can see the slithery foliage of its bottom scudding obliquely beneath your keel: until, rashly taking a short cut, you find yourselves soggily aground, your propeller churning the mud around you and your idylls indefinitely postponed.

The lagoon can be an uncommonly lonely place. Its water, as the Venetians would say, is very wet. Its mud is horribly sticky. On many evenings, even in summer, a chill unfriendly wind blows up, making the water grey and choppy, and the horizons infinitely distant. Often, as you push your crippled boat laboriously across the flats, the mud gurgling around your legs, there is nothing to be seen but a solitary silent islet, a far-away rickety shack, or the long dim line of the mainland. It is no use shouting. There are monasteries and forts in this wide lagoon, fishing villages and shooting lodges, fleets of boats and companies of stalwart fishing people; but the empty spaces are so wide, the high arch of the sky is so deadening, the wind is so gusty, the tide so swift, that nowhere on earth could feel much lonelier, when you are stuck in the ooze of the Venetian lagoon.

The Venetians have always been terrified of going aground. Storms, demons, pirates, monsters – all figure in the folklore of Venetian seamanship: but low water more dreadfully than any of them. The St Christophers of Venice, as often as not, are depicted conveying the infant Christ across the shallow hazards of the lagoon, and many a sacred legend secretes a mud-bank among its pieties – even the ship carrying the body of St Mark, hastening home from Alexandria, went ashore in the middle of the Mediterranean, and had to be miraculously refloated. 'I should not see the sandy hour-glass run', says Salarino to Antonio in the very first dialogue of *The Merchant of Venice*, 'But I should think of shallows and of flats, And see my wealthy Andrew docked in sand.'

Very early in their history, urged by these apprehensions, the Venetians surveyed and charted their lagoon, marking its safe passages with wooden poles. Today its entire expanse is criss-crossed with these *bricole*, a multititude of stakes driven into the mud, from Chioggia in the south to the marshy morasses of the extreme north. Some are elaborately prepared, with tripod piles and lamps; at night the channels around the big mud-flat in the Basin of St Mark are brilliantly illuminated with orange lamps, like the perimeters of a fairground. Other channels demand more of your waterman's instincts, for they rely upon a few sporadic and sometimes rickety poles, offering no very clear indication which side you are supposed to pass, and often confused by bits of tree and bramble which fishermen have stuck in the mud to mark their fish-traps or demarcate some private shoal.

If you keep very close to the *bricole*, you are usually safe: but not always, for sometimes their positioning is disconcertingly precise, and if you are a few inches on the wrong side – splosh, there you are again, up to your knees in mud, and pushing from the stern. There are said to be 20,000 *bricole* in the Venetian lagoon. Some are precariously rotting, and look as though generations of water-rats have nibbled their woodwork. One or two have little shrines upon them, dear to the artists and poets of the nineteenth century ('*Around her shrine no earthly blossoms blow, No footsteps fret the pathway to and fro*'). Many are used by lovers, anglers and bathing boys as mooring piles for their boats: and one of the most curious sights of the lagoon is offered by those gondoliers who, to while away a blazing holiday, run their gondolas upon a convenient mud-bank and take their families paddling, leaving their queer-prowed craft gasping and stranded upon the mud, fenced by the gaunt stockade of the *bricole*.

Like the canals of the city, the navigational channels of the lagoon are mostly based upon natural runnels and rivulets, sometimes dredged and deepened. There are entrance channels through each of the three surviving *porti*. There are transverse channels along the outer edge of the lagoon, close to the inside shore of the *lidi*. There are innumerable channels meandering through the shallows to the inner recesses of the lagoon, sometimes unmarked and known only to local fishermen, sometimes haphazardly signposted with old poles. Some such water-ways link Venice with the canals and rivers that lead into the Lombardy plain: you can sail directly from the lagoon to Treviso, to Padua, to Mantua and Cremona, and even up the Po and its affluents to Turin. Some are the delivery routes of the city, linking the Rialto markets with the vegetable gardens and orchards of the lagoon: at the turn of the century, when there were still civic levies on vegetable produce, floating customs houses commanded each approach to Venice, and armed excise-men patrolled the mud-banks at night. The greatest channel of all ushers the big ships through the Porto di Lido and, striding in majesty past St Mark's, runs away bathetically as the Canale Ex-Vittorio Emmanuele III to the workaday quays of Mestre.

These channels have played their immemorial parts in Venetian history. The broad Canale Orfano, which you will see to your right as your ferry-boat approaches the Lido, owes its name – the Orphan Canal – to its sanguinary past. In the first days of Venetian settlement, when the various lagoon colonies were still fighting each other, two factions squabbled so violently that the Canale Orfano ran 'red with blood' (and according to some chroniclers, this particular dispute was the origin of the Nicolotti-Castellani feud). Later the bulk of poor Pepin's army was hacked to pieces on the shoals beside this canal, only a mile or two from its objectives on the Rialto islands: some Franks were drowned, some suffocated in the mud, some had their throats cut, and only the most agile managed to flounder away across the flats.

In the Middle Ages the Canale Orfano became the scene of judicial drownings, a watery Tyburn. Criminals were not generally drowned in Venice, and an awful secrecy surrounded such occasions. The unhappy prisoner, languishing in his dark cell beneath the Doge's Palace, was paid a last visit by the duty monk, and a first visit by the duty executioner – 'bountifully hired by the Senate', so Coryat tells us. The terms of the sentence were read to him – that he should be 'conducted to the Canale Orfano, with his hands tied behind his back and weights tied to his body, and there drowned, and let him die'. Then at dead of night, bound and muffled, he was led into a barge beside the Bridge of Straw and softly rowed across the lagoon, past the sleeping San Giorgio Maggiore, to the Orphan Canal: and there, with a grunt and a splash, they threw him overboard. His death was never publicly announced. Only the State registers of deaths and judgements have since revealed that, for instance, between 1551 and 1604 there were 203 punitive drownings. The last criminal was tossed into the water early in the eighteenth century: but until the end of the Republic a grim old statute forbade any kind of fishing in the ominous Canale Orfano, on pain (obviously) of death. For myself, when I go bathing there to this day I sometimes still fancy ancient skeletons tickling my toes in the mud, and see the masked faces of the executioners peering at me darkly from the passing *vaporetti*.

New channels are still being cut through the lagoon. One leads direct to the new oil port of Sant' Ilario, south of Mestre, avoiding the city of Venice altogether. It enters the lagoon by the Porto di Malamocco, which was the chief Venetian port of entry in the days of Austrian rule; and slashing through a web of minor channels, islets and swamps, ends among the oil-tanks in what used to be one of the queerest and loneliest reaches of the lagoon – where centuries ago the powerful abbey of Sant' Ilario, suzerain of the surrounding flat-lands, maintained its private port of entry at the mouth of the River Lama. The new canal is deep enough (as no other channel is) to take ships of 100,000 tons and the passage of its super-tankers from Kuwait or Tripoli, has profoundly altered the hushed and dejected character of the south-western lagoon.

Another new canal, to the north of Venice, links the city with the Marco Polo airport, and conveys arrivals theatrically, in scudding high-powered motor boats, directly from the customs sheds to the Piazza of St Mark, by way of the municipal cemetery. Like Venice herself, the lagoon is changing: fight though the conservatives may to ensure that its peculiar aureole, as one Victorian poet expressed it

> . . . *burns and blazes*
> *With richest, rosiest hue,*
> *Where red San Giorgio raises*
> *Its belfry in the blue*

– struggle manfully though they may, the world is overtaking these solitary but dramatic places.

I am only half-sad about it, because for me the excitement of the lagoon lies less in its pale or lurid silences than in its sense of age-old activity. One of the best places I know to watch the ships go by is the wide free channel of the Porto di Lido, where the Canale San Marco sweeps out to sea. Bulbous black buoys mark this tremendous water-way, and two long stone moles protect it, extending to the twin lighthouses that mark the extremity of Venice. On the Lido shore stands the old tower of San Nicolò, from which the first of all weather-cones was hoisted five centuries ago. To the east, a wide, calm, empty water-way leads to Treporti, and you can just see, far away among the haze, one lonely white house on a distant promon-tory. At the junction of the waters, scowling and vigilant, the castle of Sant' Andrea awaits another impudent frigate, or peers through its gun-slits towards the ruffians of Dalmatia.

Here you switch off your engine, allow your boat to rock with the sea-swell, and let the traffic of the lagoon stream past you. A squadron of fishing boats lies idle and becalmed upon a sand-bank, waiting for the tide or the shell-fish. A dredger thumps away behind you, surrounded by dirty lighters, like acolytes. The ferry-steamer for Treporti, steering clear of the big Sant' Erasmo mud-bank, sweeps in a spacious curve around the marker buoy and swings away towards the shore. Over the mole you can see the riggings of fishing smacks, meandering to and fro off the Lido sands; and sometimes a tangled crabman's boat, a riddle of nets, ropes and buckets, slides swiftly past you with an air of intense and urgent preoccupation. A dapper little speedboat hurries towards some unfrequented bathing beach; a languid yacht tacks between the lighthouses; eight jolly men, seven portly women, twelve children, three dogs and a picnic basket lollop hilariously by in a motor boat with a cotton canopy, keeping close inshore and all talking at once.

And through them all the big ships sail, as they have for a thousand years: the cruising liners, the elegant white tankers from the Persian Gulf; a submarine from Malta, spouting jets of water from the base of its streamlined conning-tower; a succession of limping old freighters, rust-streaked and beery; and sometimes, if you are lucky, a great white cruise ship, proud and beautiful, pounding by in the misty sunshine like another old argosy, its passengers crowding the sun-decks and clustered on the forecastle, its crew bustling about the companion-ways, and its captain just to be seen upon his bridge, gazing grandly through his binoculars, as though he is awaiting a signal flag from St Mark's to welcome him home from Cathay.

26 On the Edge

It is ninety miles around the perimeters of the lagoon, but it is still all Venice: tempered, watered, vulgarized, often neglected, but always tinged with the magic of the place – 'a breath of Venice on the wind'. Only fifty years ago most of the lagoon shore was untouched by progress, sparsely inhabited, scarcely visited by tourists from one decade to the next. The old guide books speak tantalizingly of unspoilt strands and virgin beaches, and make it sound as though a trip to the villages on the rim of the lagoon required a sleeping-bag and a bag of beads.

Today Herr Baedeker would find it much more suitable for delicate constitutions, and could safely advise that stomach pills, portable wash-basins and topees will not be required. Wherever the car can go, modernity has followed. Of the perimeter of the Venetian lagoon, only the *lidi*, the central bulwarks against the Adriatic, are inaccessible by road – and you may even take your Lancia there, if you load it on a car ferry. The other seaward barriers, the Littorale di Cavallino and the Lido di Sottomarina, are in effect protrusions of the mainland, and you can drive all the way along them – on Cavallino, indeed, to a point within three miles of the Piazza itself. There are still places on the mainland shore that are remote and unfrequented, if only because nobody much wants to live there, but they are disappearing fast. In the middle of the lagoon you can still feel uncomfortably isolated: on its edge you are seldom very far from a telephone, a parish priest or a Coca-Cola.

The *enfant terrible* of the lagoon, and some would say its new master, is Mestre. Until the First World War it was no more than a castle-village, surrounded by forts and scratchy farmland. Today it is a hideous industrial city, straggling, unkempt, dirty, shapeless and nearly always (or so it seems) blurred in drizzle. Its docks at Porto Marghera are, in hard commercial terms, the new Venice. When people speak of Venice as the oil port of Europe, they really mean Mestre. Its shipyards are among the most important in Italy, and the half-built ships on their slipways loom patronizingly over the Venice causeway. Its factories employ 30,000 men, producing chemicals, aluminium, zinc, coke, plate-glass, paint, canned foods, instruments, and millions of gallons of refined oil. In Mestre the roads and railways converge upon Venice: and the place is spreading so fast and frowardly that before long we may expect to see its drab tentacles extending along half the mainland shore of the lagoon, from the new oil port in the south to the new airport in the north. Administratively, Mestre is part of Venice, and many of the guide books list its hotels together with those of the Serenissima. There are no sadder people on earth than those unfortunates who inadvertently book rooms there, or accept some claptrap advice about its advantages, and are to be seen emerging from their hotel lobbies, spruced and primped for an evening's gaiety, into the hubbub, traffic jams, half-completed streets and dowdy villas of this dismal conurbation.

This particular stretch of shore, nevertheless, has always been the classic point of embarkation for Venice. Nearby the remains of the diverted Brenta enter the lagoon, and it was at Fusina, the little port at its mouth, that generations of travellers boarded their gondolas and were slowly paddled, as in a dream, towards the distant pile of the city. From Fusina, by 'the common ferry which trades to Venice', Portia travelled from Belmont to her seat of judgement: Shakespeare called it 'the tranect', a word that has baffled generations of commentators, and may perhaps be a corruption of *traghetto*. From here, too, the heavy-laden barges used to take fresh river water to the city. In Montaigne's time it was also a portage: barges were lifted from the Brenta by a horse-powered pulley, wheeled across a spit of land, and lowered into the canal that crossed the lagoon to Venice. Later a little railway line was built to Fusina, and today the buses come down there from Padua to connect with the Venice ferry boats.

It is only two or three miles from the centre of Mestre, but it is still suggestively calm and ruminative, like a place on the edge of great mysteries. Herds of sheep wander about its grassy river-banks, guarded by laconic shepherds in cloaks and floppy tall-crowned hats. There is a quaint little landing-place, with a stuffy café, and the remains of the old railway rot away beside the river levee. The road wanders through wide water meadows, and ends abruptly at the edge of the lagoon; and there, sitting lazily upon a bollard, you will often find a grey-clad sentry with a rifle, gazing absently across the water. 'The object which first catches the eye', wrote Ruskin at the climax of a magnificent descriptive passage, 'is a sullen cloud of black smoke . . . which issues from the belfry of a church. It is Venice.' Today, if you catch your first glimpse of the city from this classic foreshore, the first thing you will see is the big grain elevator, and the second is the untidy iron silhouette of the port. It may remind you of Cardiff docks or Jersey City: but it is Venice.

North-east of Mestre the line of the lagoon shore curves, through marshy and once malarious flat-lands, past salt-pans and water-meadows and duck-flown swamps, to the promontory of Cavallino, a long sandy spit which doubles back upon itself, and reaches almost to Venice. It has seen some bumpy fluctuations of fortune. Its towns have risen, fallen, risen again. Its pine forests were destroyed, and are now growing again. It was once intersected by two important gateways into the Adriatic: one where the Piave entered the sea, now a mere creek, the other the Porto di Treporti, now closed altogether. For centuries Cavallino remained neglected, inhabited only by poor farmers and fishermen, visited only by a few adventurous sports-men: and there are still sections of this narrow shore that remain infinitely bucolic, rich in birds and earthy vegetables, with frogs croaking in miasmic ditches and pleasant country inns. The ancient village of Treporti still gazes in whitewashed simplicity across the marshes, and some of the creeks of the place are so like the Cherwell that you almost expect to encounter punt-loads of undergraduates, with parasols and gramophones, or hear the distant stroke of Tom.

Progress, though, has recently struck Cavallino with a jazzy vengeance: for not long ago the speculators, eyeing this long line of sandy beaches, built there the brand-new town of Iesolo. Its sands are immensely long and exquisitely fine, flecked with grass and scented with pine-cones. Its hundreds of new buildings are instantly reminiscent of Tel Aviv. It has a race-course, two roller-skating rinks and a psammato-therapic establishment (if you know what that is). It is a big, booming, rip-roaring, highly successful holiday resort, one of the most popular on the Adriatic, and you may see its gaudy posters beckoning you to the lagoon everywhere from Milan to Vienna. Gradations of activity ripple away from it into nearly every part of Cavallino. There are petrol stations, and garages, and excellent bus services. Bulldozers rumble and rip the days away. If you penetrate to the very tip of the promontory, Punta Sabbione, where you may look across the water to the half-hidden pinnacles of Venice, a notice in German will tell you where to park your bicycle, a fizzy drink is awaiting you in its little red ice-box, and presently the car ferry will arrive impatiently from the Lido to ship you away to the Film Festival. If you want a taste of the old Cavallino, a sniff of its dank fragrances, a stroll along its empty sand-dunes, you must make haste: it cannot last much longer.

There is a resort, too, at the other extremity of the lagoon, where the multi-coloured sunshades stand in mathematical patterns on the sands of Sottomarina, and the young bloods ride their motor scooters helter-skelter along the foreshore. The guardian of the southern lagoon, though, and the traditional key to Venice, is still a place of horny and homely instincts. There is a stumpy winged lion on a pillar at Chioggia which has long been a joke among the Venetians – they like to call it the Cat of St Mark: and a streak of pathos, an echo of ridicule, seems to infuse the life of this ancient fishing town, which still feels palsied, scabrous and tumble-down, and sunk in morbid superstition.

A rabble of touts, car-park men, beggar boys and assorted obsequious attendants greet you as you step upon the quayside at Chioggia, or open the door of your car: and the wide central street of the place always seems to be either totally deserted, or thick with fustian youths and flouncy groups of girls. Chioggia is a place of stubborn, sullen character. Its people have a cast of feature all their own, broad-nosed and big-eyed, and their incomprehensible dialect is said to be the language of the early Venetian settlers, with Greek overtones. Their town is rigidly symmetrical, without the endearing higgledy-piggledy intricacies of Venice. Two unwavering causeways connect it with the neighbouring mainland, and it consists of one main street and three canals, all running in parallel, with nine bridges in rectangular intersection.

For all its sense of degeneracy, it is the greatest fishing port in Italy, its fleets ranging the whole Adriatic, and its catch travelling each day in refrigerated trucks as far as Milan, Rome and Innsbruck. Its narrow canals are crammed and chock-a-block with shipping, thickets of masts and sails, packed so tightly hull to hull that you can often walk from one quay to another, and getting a boat out must be at least as difficult as putting one in a bottle. The wharfs and alley-ways of Chioggia are always crowded with fishermen's wives, wearing black shawls and faded flowered pinafores, sitting at trestle tables, chattering raucously, and doing obviously traditional things with needles, pieces of wood, nets and pestles. The musty churches of Chioggia are hung with the votive offerings of fishermen – crude and touching storm scenes, with half-swamped boats agonizingly in the foreground, and benignant helpful Madonnas leaning elaborately out of the clouds.

Chioggia lives, dreams, talks, and eats fish. Its streets are littered with fish scales. Its fish market is startlingly polychromatic. Its principal restaurant offers an incomparable variety of fish-foods. (A surprising number of tourists come to Chioggia nowadays, and a Swiss visitor to the town once told me, munching a particularly succulent polypus, that he was not even bothering to go on to Venice.) At the hotel boys will come to your breakfast table selling you sponges fresh from the sea-bed, and from your window you may watch the sturdy snub-nosed fishing-boats steaming away to work. Chioggia faces the Adriatic, where the big fish swim, and has its back to the lagoon: and though it is often a disappointment to visitors, I have grown to like the place and its rude people, and feel there is something deep-sea and salt-swept to its manners (even the touts on the quayside are a genial kind of riff-raff, once you have tipped them, or bought one of their desiccated sea-horses). Its reserve is really less surly than phlegmatic, and its people have a local reputation for positively English stolidity. 'Help! I'm drowning!' says one Chioggian in a beloved Venetian anecdote. 'Hang on a minute,' says the other, 'I'm just lighting my pipe.' In the lagoon one day I gave a tow to a boat-load of tattered Chioggian sardine-fishers, and I remember the encounter with a midsummer pleasure: for when they left me in the approaches to Chioggia, they waved good-bye with such dazzling smiles and such indolent, graceful, airy gestures that I felt as though a crew of Tritons were slipping the tow.

Such are the towns of the lagoon shore, from the blatant Mestre to the decadent Chioggia. For the rest, the perimeter is flat, monotonous and often dreary; and to be honest, though there are some interesting places upon it, and some haunting relics of old glories, it is astonishing to me how so drab a frame can contain so glittering a masterpiece: for wherever you stand upon this coast, whether the juke-boxes are screaming beside you at Iesolo, or the fisher-children intoning their shrill catechism in the cathedral at Chioggia, the trolley-buses spitting sparks at Mestre, the oil tanks stinking at Porto Marghera, the flocks of sheep and donkeys trailing absent-mindedly towards Fusina – wherever you are, you are never more than ten miles from Venice herself.

27 Island Towns

But it is not always Venice that you first see from the mainland, for the old Venetians built many island towns before they moved to the Rialto archipelago. There is a hamlet called Altino, east of Mestre, that is the site of the Roman Altinum. It has a little museum beside its church, and a vague air of lost distinction. If you walk from the village across the Trieste road, to the marshy edge of the lagoon, you will see across the fens and puddles (part sea, part land, part salt-bog) a solitary tall campanile. You cannot quite make out what lies around it, for the light of the lagoon is delusive, and is sometimes crystal clear, but sometimes veiled in shimmer: all you can see among that muddle of marshland is the single red-brick tower, a talisman in the waste. It looks very old, and very proud, and very lonely, and abandoned. It is the campanile of Torcello.

When the frightened ancients left the mainland, they had not very far to go – though in those days the lagoon seems to have been, if dryer, rather wider than it is now. In the course of their successive emigrations, spread over many decades, some went to the Adriatic shore, but many stayed within a few miles of the mainland, within sight of their enemies. In all twelve major settlements were established, from Clugies Major (Chioggia) in the south to Grado, which lies in the next lagoon to the north, and has long since lost all connection with Venice. The people of Altinum, a proud and prosperous city, walked to the edge of the lagoon, as we have done, and chose the island that is now Torcello; or, in another version of events, they were divinely ordered to climb the city watch-tower, and from its eminence, seeing a vision of boats, ships and islands, deduced that they were intended to move into the corner of the lagoon. They took everything they could with them, even to building stone, and around Torcello they built five townships, each named pathetically after a gateway of their lost city. This became the richest and most advanced of the lagoon colonies, in the days when the islets of Rivo Alto were still rude fishing hamlets. 'Mother and daughter,' cries Ruskin from the top of Torcello campanile, 'you behold them both in their widowhood – Torcello and Venice.'

The weeds of Torcello are much the more poignant. The city flourished and grew for some centuries, and by the 1500s is said to have had 20,000 inhabitants, a score of splendid churches, paved streets and many bridges. Torcello contributed three completely equipped galleys to the Chioggia wars, and sent 100 bowmen for service in the fifteenth-century Dalmatian campaigns. The two pious merchants who stole the body of St Mark from the Egyptians were both citizens of Torcello. Torcello had her own gateway to the sea, through Cavallino, and was a flourishing mart and shipping centre in her own right, even after the move from Malamocco to Rialto. In the oldest woodcuts and maps of Venice she usually appears formidably in the background, a mound of turrets and towers in the water. In the twelfth century one commentator wrote respectfully of the '*Magnum Emporium Torcellanorum*'.

She then entered a disastrous decline. Her canals were clogged up with silt from the rivers, not yet diverted from the lagoon, and her people were decimated by malaria and pestilent fevers. Her trade was killed at last by the rising energy of the Rialto islands, better placed in the centre of the lagoon, near the mouth of the Brenta. Torcello fell into lethargy and despondence. Her most vigorous citizens moved to Venice, her merchant houses folded and were forgotten. Presently the island was so deserted and disused that the Venetian builders, when they were short of materials, used to come to Torcello and load the remains of palaces into their barges, scrabbling among the rubble for the right size of staircase or a suitably sculptured cornice. Through the centuries poor Torcello rotted, crumbling and subsiding and declining into marshland again. When Napoleon overthrew the Republic she proclaimed herself, in a moment of frantic virility, an autonomous State: but by the middle of the nineteenth century a visit to Torcello was, for every romantic visitor, a positive ecstasy of melancholia.

Today about a hundred people live there: but Torcello is that fortunate phenomenon, a ghost with a private income, like the dead mining towns of the American West, or even Pompeii. It is still an island of exquisite nostalgia. A sad stone Madonna greets you when you land there, behind a tangle of old barbed wire, and a narrow muddy canal leads you through green fields to the decayed Piazza, once the centre of city life, now no more than a village green. Nowhere in the lagoon can you feel the meaning of Venice more pungently, for this place has an inescapable air of hunted determination, and it is all too easy, as you gaze across its empty water-ways, to imagine the fires of terrible enemies burning on the mainland shore, or hear the frightened Te Deums of exiles.

The island is green, and is planted with fields of artichokes and scrubby orchards. Small farmhouses stand here and there, with boat-houses made of thatched wattle, and skinny barking dogs. A wide sluggish canal, more like a great river than a creek, separates Torcello from the patchy mud-islands that run away to the mainland: on this listless channel I once saw a tall white yacht that had sailed from Norway, and was slipping away to Venice in the first dim light of dawn, like a spirit-ship among the marshes. The city of Torcello has utterly vanished: but the little lanes of the place, last vestiges of the Fondamenta Bobizo, the Campo San Giovanni, the Fondamenta dei Borgogni, and many another lost thoroughfare – all these dusty small paths lead, as if by habit, towards the Piazza. It is only a little grassy square, but it still has a suggestion of pomposity, passed down from the days when the Tribune met there, and the patrician palaces stood all about. It stands beside a canal, and around it are grouped a trattoria, a little museum in a Gothic palace, two or three cottages, the octagonal Byzantine church of Santa Fosca, and the cathedral of Santa Maria Assunta, which a learned man once described as the most moving church in Christendom.

Certainly it is a building of symbolic significance, for at this spot, with the founding of Venice, the tides of Rome and Byzantium met. Torcello marks a watershed. To the west there extends the ribbed and vaulted architecture we call Gothic – Rome, Chartres, Cambridge and the monasteries of Ireland. To the east stand the domes: Mount Athos, Istanbul, the bulbous churches of Russia and the noble mosques of Cairo, Samarkand, Isfahan and India. On one side of Torcello is the Palace of Westminster, on the other the Taj Mahal.

It is a spiritual watershed, too. At Torcello the theologies overlap, and the rival ideals of Christianity met here, half-way between the old Rome and the New. The cathedral of Torcello is part Byzantine, part Gothic, partly eastern, partly western. It was built badly, by scared men in a hurry – some say in a panic, because they thought that the end of the world would occur in the year 1000. It is simple and sophisticated at the same time, bold and tremulous too. Its campanile is grandly defiant (and was grander still, before lightning lopped off its top in 1640); but enormous stone shutters, swinging on stone pegs, protect its windows from the furies of elements and enemies. Tall and aloof it stands there, with nothing warm or welcoming to its spirit, and it still feels almost makeshift, barn-like, as if it is uncompleted, or only temporary.

At one end of the nave is a vast mosaic, covering the entire west wall, and illustrating in profuse and often grotesque detail the Crucifixion, the Resurrection of the Dead and the imminent Day of Judgement – an illustrated manual of dogma, from St Michael conscientiously weighing the souls, like an apothecary, to the poor damned sinners far below. At the other end of the church, above the stalls of the rounded apse, there stands something infinitely more magnificent: for there against a dim gold background, tall, slender and terribly sad, is the Teotoca Madonna – the God-Bearer. There are tears on her mosaic cheeks, and she gazes down the church with an expression of timeless reproach, cherishing the Child in her arms as though she has foreseen all the years that are to come, and holds each one of us responsible. This is the noblest memorial of the lagoon. Greek craftsmen made it, so we are told: and there are some who think that the Venetians, through all their epochs of splendour and success, never created anything quite so beautiful.

Beneath that sad and seer-like scrutiny, a host of tourists mills about the church: popping into Santa Fosca if they have a moment to spare; buying postcards from the women who have set up their stalls on the grass outside, like village ladies at a fête; posing for photographs in the great stone chair, called obscurely the Throne of Attila, that stands in the middle of the Piazza (even the soul-struck Victorians, on their shaky progressions through the remains, allowed themselves this moment of tourist levity, and many a faded snapshot shows them, in their flowered hats and mutton-chop sleeves, posing as to the manner born in this imperial seat).

Some of these people, but not many, have come on the regular ferry service from Venice, and are going to have a picnic beside a muddy rivulet somewhere behind the cathedral, while their children catch crabs and prawns among the pools and their wine grows steadily hotter in the sun. Most of them, though, have come to Torcello primarily for lunch at the trattoria: for this simple-looking inn, with its rustic tables beside the door, its complement of picturesque pedlars – this unpretentious hostelry is one of the most famous restaurants in Italy, where you can eat splendidly, drink from tall frosted glasses, and bask the afternoon away among flower gardens in the shadow of the campanile.

Harry's Bar owns and runs this inn, and provides comfortable motor boats to take you there, and spares you half an hour or so before lunch to look at the cathedral: and it has all the pretensions of its celebrated progenitor (mock-modesty, mementoes of the great, fancy cocktails) and all the considerable attractions (admirable food, excellent service, and a certain simplicity of spirit that is not all spurious).

I have eaten many a delicious dish there, and have enjoyed my ham and eggs among the sighing of the laurels, the creaking of old timbers, the splashing of small ducks and amphibious dogs, and the early-morning chatter of the island women, washing their smalls upon the quay. And by a swift adjustment of the imagination, I find it easy still, when I stand upon the mainland shore, and see that distant campanile in the mud, to fancy Torcello as deserted, desolate and abandoned as she used to be, when the wind blew through empty ruins, and only a dim rustic lamp burnt in the bar-room of the inn. I dismiss the gin-fizzes and the *filet mignon* from my mind: and I think of the haunted water-ways of the island, that silent white ship among the marshes, the great stone shutters of the cathedral, the soft rustle of trees in the night, and the lanky image of the Teotoca Madonna, tear-stained and accusing, which a child once gravely described to me as 'a thin young lady, holding God'.

Many other islands of the lagoon have had their eras of urban glory, before fading, like Torcello, into bleached obscurity, for the life of a lagoon town is beset with inconstancy. It is always rising or waning, sinking or abruptly reviving: either being slowly sucked into the subsoil, or converted at great expense into a little Coney Island. Two islands only have survived as living townships from times immemorial, and both lie in the melancholy expanse of the northern lagoon, on the water-route between Torcello and Venice.

Burano you will see first, and remember longest, as a sheer splash of colour. A wide brackish waste surrounds it, exuding dankness. A mile or two away is the solemn tower of Torcello; to the east a small island is clad in cypress trees; to the north the marshes trail away in desolation. It is a muted scene, slate-grey, pale blue and muddy green: but in the middle of it there bursts a sudden splurge of rather childish colour, its reflections spilling into the water, and staining these lugubrious channels like an overturned paint-pot. This is the island town of Burano. Its campanile leans at a comical angle, and it is packed tightly with hundreds of bright little houses, like a vivid adobe village in a dismal desert: red and blue houses, yellow and orange and blazing white, a jumble of primary colours shining in the mud.

It lives by fishing and by lace-making, an old Venetian craft which was revived in the nineteenth century. In its hey-day Venetian lace was the best in the world, sometimes so delicate that a collar ordered for Louis XIV was made of white human hair, no spun thread being fine enough for the design. Later the industry languished so disastrously that when they came to resuscitate it, only one very old lady survived who knew how to make Venetian point: they muffled her in woollies, stuffed her with pills, and gently filched her secrets before she died.

The lace industry is now conducted with an air of profound charitable purpose, but at a pleasant profit for its sponsors. There is a school of lace-making near the church, where tourists are more than welcome, and may even be allowed, if they press hard enough, to make some trifling purchase; and every Burano cottage doorway has its demure lace-maker, stitching away in the sunshine, eyes screwed up and fingers flickering (if the tourist season is bad, she may have abandoned lace, and be devoting her talents to the production of coarse net curtains). Only a hint of tragedy sours the spectacle: for no occupation looks more damaging to the eye-sight, except perhaps writing fugues by candle-light.

While the women stitch, the men go fishing, as in an allegory, or an opera. Wild-eyed fishermen stalk the streets of Burano, carrying cork floats and enormous shoes, and there are nets hanging up to dry on the wall of the church. The fishermen sail their boats to the very doors of their houses, to be greeted with soups and fond embraces: and this suggestion of ideal domesticity, the quintessential femininity of the women, the shaggy masculinity of the men, the gaudy little houses, the soups and the nets and the flashing needles – all this makes Burano feel like one protracted amateur theatrical. Until recently the island was very poor indeed, and you will still find Hammers and Sickles upon its walls, until the tidy housewives wash them off: but the place does not seem real enough to be hungry. It is an island of absurd diminutives: tiny canals, toy-like homes, miniature bridges, infinitesimal stitches. Nothing very much has ever happened in Burano (though there can scarcely be a town on earth that has more memorial plaques to the square mile) and life there feels flaky and insubstantial. The lace-makers bend over their frames, the fishermen paddle out to the mud-banks, the tourists take a quick look round on their way to Torcello, and the hours pass like the first act of an obvious play, or a rousing opera chorus.

Water surrounds it, though, and it lies embedded like a trinket in the lagoon. Its canals are silted and blocked with mud, making it extremely difficult to sail a boat into the town – '*Scavate Canale!*' says a slogan painted angrily on one wall. The drainage of Burano is the filthiest and smelliest in the lagoon, pouring visibly into the shallow

canals around you, and its streets are thick with muck. It looks gay
and operatic in summer, but in winter its colours wilt before the grey
gust of the wind, and its old women huddle about in their long black
shawls, like undernourished eagles.

I once turned into Burano as a refuge, driven back from Venice by a
rising storm, and deposited my crew of five hilarious and ill-
disciplined children upon a quayside. They were soaked to the skin,
splashed with mud and very cold, and they ran about the place in a
frenzy of excitement, burbling inexplicable English slang. Observing
this minor emergency, the Buranese threw off their pose of fancy
dress and demonstrated how deep were their island instincts, for all
their manner of stage-struck flippancy. In a trice those children were
silenced and muffled in the back rooms of cottages, wrapped in
towels; in a moment there emerged from unknown kitchens bowls of
an aromatic soup; in five minutes a crowd of skilled bystanders had
stripped my boat of its gear and stacked it away neatly in cubby-holes
and sheds; in half an hour our night's programme was arranged for
us; and through it all two or three old ladies in black, crouched on
stools beside their doors, continued blandly with their needle-work,
clickety-click, clickety-click, as though they were waiting for the
water-tumbrils.

Very different is the spirit of Murano, the most curmudgeonly of the
Venetian communities, where it always feels like early-closing day.
Once upon a time this big island, only a mile from the Fondamenta
Nuove in Venice, was the gentlemen's playground of Venice, a kind
of private Vauxhall, where the aristocrats of the time, lapped in
everything exquisite, strolled beneath their vines and fruit trees,
discussing poetry and philosophical conceptions, and conducting
discreet but delicious amours. Successive English Ambassadors had
sumptuous apartments on Murano, and by all accounts made
excellent use of them.

The island then became the glass foundry of Venice, in the days
when the Venetians held a virtual monopoly of the craft, and were
the only people in Europe who knew how to make a mirror. So many
disastrous fires had ravaged Venice that in the thirteenth century all

the furnaces were compulsorily removed to Murano, which became the principal glass manufactory of the western world, with a population in the sixteenth century of more than 30,000. In envious foreign eyes Murano was imbued with almost mystical technical advantages. It was true that particular qualities of the local sand, and deposits of marine vegetation in the lagoon, made it a convenient place for glass-making; but many visitors thought, like the sixteenth-century James Howell, that the superiority of Venetian glass was due to 'the quality of the circumambient Air that hangs o'er the place'. So beneficient was this air, so it was said, that the best Venetian tumblers would break instantly into fragments if the merest drop of poison were poured into them.

In fact Venice owed her supremacy to the ingenuity of her artisans, the knowledges she filched from the East, and the strict protectionist policies of the State. Like the steel-makers of Stalin's Russia, the glass-men of Murano became pampered wards of Government. Nothing was too good for them, so long as they worked. They even had their own nobility, and you may see its Golden Register in the Museum of Glass, among a wide variety of Murano products, and portraits of eminent glass-makers. All kinds of civic privileges were granted to Murano. The island coined its own money, and the ubiquitous spies of the Republic were forbidden to set foot there, so important to the national economy were its crafts and secrets. (But if a glass-maker took his knowledge out of Murano, and set himself up in business elsewhere in the world, inexorable and pitiless were the agents of State sent to find him out, wherever he was, and kill him.)

Glass is still the *raison d'être* of Murano, its pleasure-gardens having long ago been buried beneath brick and paving-stones. The glass industry, like the lace industry, withered with the Republic, but was revived in the nineteenth century and now dominates the island. A handful of imposing patrician palaces remains, and Murano's own Grand Canal has a grandeur still not unworthy of its great progenitor. There is an elegant mouldy Piazza, and one excellent trattoria, and two great churches survive – a third, at the western end of the Grand Canal, has been turned into a tenement block, its high chancel stuffed with layers of ramshackle dwelling-places, a grubby line of washing strung from the remains of its porch. For the rest, Murano is a clutter of small glass factories, rambling, messy, uncoordinated places, built of red brick or dingy stonework, with tall blackened chimneys and wooden landing-stages. All along the canals these slipshod establishments stand, and scarcely a tourist comes to Murano without visiting one (though you can watch the processes much more comfortably, if not caught unawares by tout or hall porter, within a few hundred yards of St Mark's).

The important thing to know about the Murano glass-makers is that almost everything they make is, at least to my taste, perfectly hideous. This has always been so. Only one nineteenth-century designer, in all the hundreds whose work is displayed in the museum, seems to me to have evolved any elegance of line. When the Emperor Frederick III passed through Venice, on the occasion when he rode his horse up the Campanile of St Mark's, he was given an elaborate service of Murano glass: but he took such an instant dislike to the pieces, so the story goes, that he tipped off his court jester, in the course of his buffooneries, to bump into the table on which they were displayed, shattering them into a thousand merciful fragments. The Venetians still profess to find Murano glass lovely, but sophisticates in the industry, if you manage to crack their shell of salesmanship, will admit that bilious yellow is not their favourite colour, and agree that one or two of the chandeliers might with advantage be a little more chaste.

All this is a pity, for the making of glass is an activity of unfailing fascination, and there is still a fine fiery mystery to what Howell called 'the Furnaces and Calcinations, the Transubstantiations, the Liquefactions that are incident to this Art'. Inside the drab work-shops of Murano the Transubstantiations still occur, every working day of the year. Here stands the master glass-blower beside his furnace, grand and self-assured, with a couple of respectful appren-tices to hand him his implements, and his long pipe in his hand like a wand. With a flourish he raises it to his lips, and with a gentle blow produces a small round bubble of glass. A twist, a chip, another delicate breath, and there appears the embryo of an ornament. A twiddle of the pipe follows, a slice with an iron rod, a dollop of molten glass, a swift plunge into the fire, a gulp or two, a flourish in the air, a sudden snap of iron shears – and abruptly the blower lays down his work with a gesture of artistic exhaustion, as Praxiteles might rest his trowel, leaving the apprentice boys around him silent with respect, and the tourists, sweating in the heat, clustered awestruck about a huge glass harlequin, beady-eyed and multi-coloured, whose long spindly legs, swollen stomach, drunken grin and dissipated attitude breathe a spirit of unsurpassable vulgarity.

Upstairs the products of the factory are laid out horribly for your inspection, as in some nightmare treasure cave: feathery candlesticks, violent vases, tumblers of awful ostentation, degraded glass animals, coarse images of clowns and revellers. Beside the door stands a pile of crates, carefully pointed in your direction, and stamped with improbable addresses: 'Messrs. John Jones, Piccadilly', 'Alphonse Frères, Place de la Concorde', or 'Elmer B. Hoover and Company Inc., Brooklyn Bridge, U.S.A.' – 'we send our beautiful traditional wares', remarks the guide educationally, 'to all parts of the civilized world, travellers' cheques accepted.' Dazed are the faces of the more sensitive tourists, as they shamble through these blinding arcades: and sometimes you will hear the man from the glass factory shouting through the window to a pair of husbands who have evaded the tour, and are sitting comfortably on the quay outside. 'Gentlemen! Gentlemen!' he calls reprovingly. 'Sirs! Your charming ladies are awaiting you in the Vestibule! All the prices are marked!'

The people of Murano are not prepossessing. They scowl outside their pubs on Sundays. They look shabby and surly, and have none of the gentle courtesy of the city Venetian. Long years of poverty and tourism have soured them – 'bowed down', so Ruskin described a Murano church congregation, 'partly in feebleness, partly in a fearful devotion, with their grey clothes cast far over their faces, ghastly and settled into a gloomy animal misery'. The fringes of their island trail away into rubbish dumps and cess-pools, and only one great monument remains to take away the taste of it. The cathedral of San Donato stands upon a crooked canal, behind a string of glass factories. Its splendid red-brick colonnaded apse overlooks a wide piazza, and it is a structure of great presence: broader in the beam than the Gothic friars' churches of Venice, and therefore somehow more queenly – less like a great commander than an influential consort, in a fox fur and a toque.

This great church has had a chequered history, for its supremacy on the island was long challenged by the now-vanished church of Santo Stefano. The two foundations were rivals in the possession of sacred relics. First one acquired a kneebone or a hair, then the other, each producing more marvellous sanctities, until the cathedral was able to announce one glorious day that it had been given the body of St Donato himself, Bishop of Euboea, which had been brought home in triumph by Venetian crusaders. This eminent prelate had killed a dragon in Cephalonia by spitting at it, and his body was received in reverent triumph and placed in a marble sarcophagus. The clergy of Santo Stefano were discountenanced: but they fought back strongly down the decades, and nearly 200 years later they made a brave last bid for the hegemony. On 14 April 1374 the abbot of Santo Stefano announced that he had discovered in the vaults of the church not one sacred limb, nor even one unhappy martyr, but nothing less than a cache of 200 holy corpses – which, being of 'infantile form and stature', were soon identified by unimpeachable scholars as the Innocents murdered by King Herod.

It was a dramatic coup, but unavailing. San Donato was unabashed, and has remained the undisputed cathedral of Murano ever since. It is one of the greatest churches of Venice, and the principal reason for visiting this froward island today. It has a wonderfully entertaining mosaic floor, a series of creepy faceless images beside the main door, and a mosaic of the Madonna, high in the apse, that is less accusatory, but hardly less breath-taking than the Teotoca at Torcello. It has even more. When the Doge Domenico Michiele returned from the East with the corpse of Bishop Donato, he presented two separate containers to the abbot of the church: and if you go to the east end of the building, behind the high altar, and raise your eyes to the wall above you, there you will see, neatly stacked, like antlers, the bones of the dragon that Donato slew, in the dim sunshine years of long ago, when saints and martyrs frequented the islands of the lagoon, and pious spittle could still work miracles.

28 Holy Waters

In those days these were holy waters, speckled with monasteries, and almost every islet had its devout but often comfortable community. Many an old print depicts now desolate islands of the lagoon in their days of consequence, with classical porticoes and shady palms, and monks in nonchalant worldly attitudes upon their water-steps. The convents of the Venetian lagoon were famous throughout Christendom, and possessed great treasuries of art and religion. In the later days of the Republic they were often places of gaiety, too, where fashionable society nuns received visitors in an atmosphere of gossip, frivolity, flirtation and even downright salacity. When Charles de Brosses visited Venice in the 1730s three convents were cattily disputing the right to supply a mistress for the new Papal Nuncio. This is the title assumed by one Venetian aristocrat, when she humbly took the veil: '*Sua Eccellenza Abbadessa reverendissima donna Maria Luigia principessa Rezzonico.*'

Life, nevertheless, was not always easy for the monasteries. They were often closed, when Venice's relations with the Papacy demanded it, and often revived, and sometimes transferred from one brotherhood to another, so that by the time Napoleon suppressed the orders most of them had changed hands several times, and some had already fallen into disuse. Their works of art were neglected or dispersed. When the monastery of San Cristoforo was closed (its island now forms part of San Michele) its pictures and sculptures disappeared all over the world, and the only work left in Italy is a painting by Basaiti that hangs in the church of San Pietro in Murano. The hey-day of the island monasteries was long past, when the new Attila scourged Venice; and today only two survive.

Beside the channel to the Lido, within sight of St Mark's, lies San Lazzaro, a small, comfortable, well-kept, rather suburban sort of island, with groves of cypresses, a neat little campanile, arbours, terraces and waterside gardens – just the place, you might think, for a languorous but not very sinful dalliance. This is the home of the

Mechitar Fathers, members of an independent Armenian order, observing the eastern rites of the Roman Catholic Church. The Mechitarists, with their founder Mechitar ('The Comforter'), were expelled from their monastery in Modone when the Turks overran Morea in 1715. They were granted asylum in Venice, and given the deserted island of San Lazzaro, in those days an austere and unpromising islet off the lonely reef of the Lido. There they prospered. Mechitar himself supervised the building of their monastery; they acquired productive lands on the mainland; and as the Armenian nation was decimated by persecution, its scholarship suppressed and its energies emasculated, so San Lazzaro became a repository of the national learning and religion. Today the monastery is one of the three principal centres of Armenian culture in the world, the others being Vienna and Etchmiadzin, the religious capital of the Armenian Republic.

San Lazzaro is one of the most genial spots in Venice, not by and large a Dickensian place. Its twenty or so monks, heavily bearded and dressed in voluminous black cassocks, are at once gentle, welcoming and urbane, and though they eat in silence in their dark-panelled refectory, and recite their long offices three times each day, and meditate each evening for a good half-hour, and have a reputation both for scholarship and for piety – nevertheless they somehow give the impression that the pleasures of the world are at least not beyond their powers of imagination. They run a school for Armenian boys on the island, to which pupils come from all over the Mediterranean. They have another school in the city of Venice. Their monastery is the seat of the Academy of Armenian Literature, and they are frequently engaged in learned disputation of dogma or etymology. But the duties of these engaging Fathers are never menial, for as the official guide book to the monastery explains, 'lay brothers and Italian servants attend to the cooking, cleaning and gardening'.

Everybody has been nice to the Mechitarists, since they arrived in Venice. Their culture, a fusion of East and West, appealed to the Venetians from the start, and the Republic treated them very generously. Even Napoleon reprieved them, when he closed the other monasteries: they had sent their delegates to Paris itself to plead for his favour. Their splendid collection of manuscripts and books has been supplemented, at one time or another, by a mass of miscellaneous gifts, making the whole island a store-house of esoteric curios. A banana tree, a palm tree and a cedar of Lebanon flourish in the central cloister; there are rooms full of quaint paintings, and corridors hung with rare prints. The Duke of Madrid gave a collection of mineralogical and oceanographical objects. Pope Gregory XVI gave a marble figure of himself. Canova gave a plaster cast of a statue of Napoleon's son. An eminent Armenian of Egypt gave his collection of Oriental books, including signed copies of some not altogether suitable works by Sir Richard Burton. The Patriarch of Venice gave a reliquary divided into fifty compartments, with a small sacred relic in each.

In the museum upstairs there is a fine Egyptian mummy, with some of its teeth still in the jaw, and the rest carefully stowed away in a little linen bag (its covering of beads was restored in the nineteenth century by the glass-makers of Murano). There is some manna in a box, and a telescope trained through a window upon the Campanile of St Mark. There is a collection of books about the Armenian language in languages other than Armenian. There is a Buddhist ritual found by an Indian Armenian in a temple in Madras. There is a collection of wooden carvings from Mount Athos, and another of Chinese ivories, and a small armoury of antique weapons, and a machine for making electric sparks, and a passage from the Koran in Coptic, and a German set of medals depicting the heads of British monarchs, including a fine portrait of King Oliver I. There are autograph letters from Browning and Longfellow, and a visitors' book reserved (the Fathers have a healthy respect for temporal achievement) 'for princes and celebrities'. There are signed photographs of statesmen, bishops, sultans and Popes – 'all presented', says the official handbook with a sniff, 'personally'.

Above all there is Lord Byron. In 1816 the poet, anxious to while away the daylight hours of the Venetian winter, decided to learn Armenian – '*something craggy*' to break his mind upon; and making the acquaintance of the kindly Mechitarists, he used to row across to San Lazzaro three times a week and study the language in their library. For four months he was a regular visitor. The Armenians were enchanted, and have never allowed the memory of their improbable pupil to die, so that many people in Venice, asked to think of San Lazzaro, think first of Byron, and only secondly of the Armenians. Byron's spirit haunts the island. We see the trees he helped to plant, the summer-house he meditated in, the desk he sat at, the pen he wrote with, the knife he used to cut his pages. We are shown a splendid painting of his first arrival on the island, almost an *ex voto*, glowing with aristocratic romance; another shows him sprawling in indolent grace upon the terrace, attended by venerable but respectful monks, with the sun falling poetically into the lagoon behind him, and a big dog lying at his feet. We are given a copy of the Armenian Grammar which he compiled, as a very minor collaborator, with a scholar of the monastery (and in which, in my copy anyway, some sober-side has brusquely amended in red ink a passage referring inadvertently, but inoffensively, to 'the curtain that hangs over the back-side of the tabernacle').

Byron is not always happily remembered in Venice, but good priests are often attracted by dashing and gifted reprobates, and at San Lazzaro only his better nature is recalled. He seems to have been genuinely liked by the Fathers, and to have treated them with honesty and respect. When the centenary of his death was commemorated, in 1924, a now forgotten poet named Charles Cammell was asked to write some verses, for translation into the Armenian. He addressed them to the Mechitarist Fathers themselves, and ended his poem with the lines:

> If England holds his body, Greece his heart,
> You surely of his spirit hold a part,
> Perhaps the highest, for with you remain
> The Friendship and the Peace, but not the pain.

Certainly the Armenians of San Lazzaro will not soon forget Lord Byron. Of his stay among them, as the monastery handbook rightly says, they have kept 'ample and particular record' (though I have some doubts, all the same, about his eventual proficiency in their language – a 'Waterloo of an alphabet', as he put it himself).

Armenians are practical people. The Mechitarists lead lives of great devotion on their island, and there is something infinitely appealing about the little piles of vestments, each neatly capped with its biretta, that you see trimly folded on a chest in the vestry of their chapel. But the engine-room, the money-vault of their island, is its famous printing press. The first Armenian press in western Europe was established in Venice, then the world capital of printing, in 1512: and soon after the Mechitarists arrived from Greece, they founded one of their own. Its machines are modern and cosmopolitan – some from Germany, some from America, some from Britain – and will print you almost anything, in almost any language. They used to print a book on San Lazzaro that consisted of the prayer of St Nerses divided into twenty-four sections, one for each hour, and translated into thirty-six languages. This entailed printing in twelve scripts – Arabic, Aramaic, Armenian, Chaldean, Chinese, Ethiopian, Greek, Hebrew, Japanese, Latin, Russian and Sanskrit, not to speak of Scandinavian aberrations of the alphabet, and such subtle variations as differentiate the Russian from the Serbian. It is a confusing book. Some of the prayers read backwards, some from top to bottom, and some apparently upside down. It includes prayers in Greenlandish and Gaelic, and in the English section at least (I have not examined the Amharic very carefully) there is not a single misprint.

Today the press is still polyglot, but it also specializes in glossy picture postcards, posters and shiny commercial labels. You may feel agreeably elevated by your visit to San Lazzaro, and sail away with the music of its immemorial chants ringing like a benediction in your ears: but when you buy a bottle of Italian Vermouth in Venice, the chances are that its slick coloured label rolled off the printing presses of the Armenians.

San Lazzaro is always on the move. The very structure of the island has trebled in size since the foundation of the monastery, as you may see from a plaque on the landing-stage. The orginal buildings are cracking – the Abbot Mechitar, though a versatile man, was no architect – and there are plans to rebuild the whole place, illustrated in a plaster model near the electric-spark machine. The Armenians are on familiar terms with the authorities of Venice (which one lay brother solemnly insists upon calling the Serenissima – 'The Serenissima has been most helpful with the drainage', or 'We have made the necessary application to the Serenissima'). San Lazzaro never feels far from the great world, and takes modernity easily in its stride.

The other island monastery of the lagoon shares none of this sophisticated bounce, but lies becalmed in perpetual peace, among the northern marshlands. San Francesco del Deserto is a small and captivating island in the fens to the east of Burano, and beckons you shyly across the waters with a row of cypresses and tall umbrella palms, waving and buckling in the breeze like a line of Tibetan prayer flags. A tortuous shallow channel takes you there, and you step from your boat on to grass as green as an English lawn, speckled with Wiltshire daisies, beneath trees as rich as Connecticut elms, to a scent of Mediterranean flowers and rich tilled earth. A crucifix stands guardian above the landing-stage, and a notice on the wall gives you grave warning that games, dancing, profanity and loud voices are all equally prohibited. San Lazzaro is a plump little Riviera, but San Francesco is Shangri-la.

They say that St Francis was shipwrecked here during a voyage from the East in a Venetian ship – perhaps, so some indulgent hagiographers suggest, after his attempt to evangelize the Muslims in 1219. They show you a piece of tree that sprouted miraculously from his staff, and a coffin in which it was his practice to lie as acclimatization for the tomb (the friars of the island, I am told, have now adopted the system for themselves). Certainly the place is full of the Poverello's friends. A friar will meet you as you walk towards the convent from the creek (he is sure to speak excellent English and French, and probably German too, and is one of those who hear the confessions of foreigners in St Mark's Basilica, three days a week); and as he guides you through the green bowers of this Arcadia, he will introduce you to the beasts of the garden, posed among the shrubberies as in an illuminated Breviary. Here on a grassy bank struts a pair of peacocks. Here is a brood of ducklings, scuttling away towards the water's edge, and here a flutter of scraggy hens. Everywhere there are swallows, most Franciscan of creatures, and the island is loud with bird song. There are even two cows, munching hay in a barn among the vegetable gardens.

It is a novice house. There are thirty friars, all Italian, of whom fourteen are novices. Their cloisters are old and serene, their church is ugly but peaceful, and the most striking thing about their island is its silence. Nobody indeed dances, plays games, utters profanities or talks in a loud voice. Nobody lives there but the friars. A few motor boats bring tourists in the summer months. A jet sometimes flashes overhead, or an airliner lowers its flaps for a landing. Otherwise not a disharmony disturbs the convent. The friars row themselves silently about in *sandoli*, and you may often see their bent brown figures, labouring at the oar, far away among the flats. The fishermen of the surrounding islets are mostly too poor for motor boats, and the din of Venice (which seems, in this context, positively diabolic) is hours away across the water. The only sounds of San Francesco del Deserto are bells, chanting male voices, sober conversation, the singing of song birds, the squawking of peacocks, the clucking of ducks and hens, and sometimes a deep dissatisfied bellow, as of a soul sated with Elysium, from the ruminating cattle in the cow-house.

The friars seem content with these arrangements. The happy text of San Francesco's pieties is 'O beata solitudo, O sola beatitudo', and my cicerone there once quoted the words to me with an expression in his eye not exactly smug – he was much too meek for that – but at least tinged with grateful complacency.

29 Dead and Alive

Many a smaller flowering island lies in these wide waters. Some are little more than shooting-lodges, places of Roman temperament, directly descended from the first pleasure-houses of the lagoon: big four-square buildings on isolated marsh-banks, self-contained as castles, with taciturn slow-witted custodians and angry watch-dogs, and spacious loggias on which, at the right time of year, the duck-hunters assemble in carousal. Others are small fishing settlements, such as the little Isola Tessera, beyond Murano, where a boisterous community of fisherfolk lives in hugger-mugger fellowship, like the jolliest of all *kibbutzim*: their boats lie bobbing about their water-gate, thick foliage decorates their houses, and when it is foggy, or dinner-time, a big bronze bell rings out from their little campanile, calling the men home across the mud. Most such islets though, are places of decay, decline, or desertion, and stand as sad reminders of the lagoon's greater days.

A cordon of such doleful relics surrounds the archipelago of Venice proper. The Venetians call them *Isole del Dolore*, because until recently they all used to be what the guide books tactfully describe as 'hospital centres' – that is to say, sanatoria, isolation hospitals and lunatic asylums. A special steamboat service linked them with the Riva degli Schiavoni: the boat was marked *Ospedale*, and it was usually full of patients' relatives and nurses (who spent four days of each week at their island posts, and three on holiday in Venice). Some of these sad islets will probably soon be revivified as holiday resorts ('Caribbean-style Beach Complexes') but for the moment most of them are abandoned. A sombre silence surrounds them, and sometimes makes them feel less like inhabited places than sea-rocks protruding savagely from the lagoon. They have melancholy and sometimes peculiar histories, too. The most cheerful of them, the former tuberculosis sanatorium called Sacca Sessola, is an artificial island, and has no mournful connotations. The others are all tinged with regret.

La Grazia, for instance, which lies only half a mile beyond San Giorgio Maggiore, used to be a hospice for pilgrims going to the Holy Land – in the days when the Venetians, astutely battening upon this source of income, organized it so thoroughly that they even had teams of multi-lingual officials, precisely like tourist police, always on duty in the Piazza to guide visitors to the glass factories. The island then became a monastery, to honour a miraculous figure of the Virgin which was brought from Constantinople and was said to be the handiwork of St Paul himself. It had a splendid Gothic church with a campanile, but when Napoleon suppressed the monastic orders, it became a powder magazine: and during the 1848 revolution some-body lit a match inside it, and blew the whole place up. It stands there now looking distinctly subdued: for it ended up as the isolation hospital of Venice, where children with pimpled faces gazed wanly towards the distant merry-go-rounds of the Riva fairground.

Farther out is San Clemente, a huge whitish block of masonry, cold and heavy-shouldered. This, too, has been a monastery in its time, and still possesses a handsome seventeenth-century church, decor-ated with marble mock-draperies, and a pleasant little tree-shaded garden, to soften its severities: but it has a barred and shrouded air, because for a century and more it was a lunatic asylum. It is only two or three miles from St Mark's, like Alcatraz from Fisherman's Wharf, but it might be in the middle of a grey ocean, so shuttered does it seem, and so self-sufficient. During the Second World War two young Venetians evading German conscription hid in the boat-house of this gloomy island: their parents brought them provisions once a week by boat, and they lived there in the shadows undisturbed until the end of the war, when they emerged blinking into the sunshine and went home rejoicing.

The other ex-asylum, if less forbidding, is much more celebrated. San Servolo (or San Servilio, as non-Venetians would call it) was a Benedictine monastery as early as the eighth century, and played a curious part in the history of the Republic. In 1001 the Western Emperor Otto III, observing the growing power of Venice, visited the city incognito, partly for curiosity, partly for reasons of policy: and it was to this island that he was secretly ushered, muffled in black, at dead of night, upon his arrival in the lagoon. (He was met at the monastery by the Doge Pietro Orseolo II, who promptly deluded the unfortunate young man, so some historians say, into granting all kinds of quite unpremeditated concessions.)

For several centuries San Servolo flourished with the Benedictines, assuming various medical and charitable functions until, in 1725, it became a hospital for the insane – but only, by order of the Council of Ten, 'maniacs of noble family or comfortable circumstances': less fortunate lunatics were left at large in the city, or shut up in prison. Napoleon's arrival ended this fearful injustice, and presently Shelley made San Servolo the most famous madhouse on earth – 'a window-less, deformed and dreary pile', as Julian thought with Maddalo, 'such a one as age to age might add, for uses vile'.

Poor San Servolo! The very presence of the island, its past and its purpose cast a chill upon the passer-by; and there are still people who claim to hear, from the transient *vaporetto*, those same 'yells and howlings and lamentings keen' that made Julian shudder that evening, looking across the lagoon with Maddalo.

Other inshore islands are less haunted, though still often wreathed in nostalgia. On the channel to Fusina there is an islet called San Giorgio in Alga – St George In the Seaweed – to which Baron Corvo liked to row his *sandolo*, in his days of Venetian watermanship, and from where Ruskin considered you could get the best view in all Venice. This little place has also had its moments of consequence. Here, it is said, the unlucky Doge Faliero, sailing through a mist to take up office in his palace, ran ashore in his Bucintoro: it was regarded as an ill omen for his reign, and sure enough, only eight months later he was decapitated for treason (he also made the foolish mistake, when at last he stepped ashore at the Piazzetta, of walking between the two columns on the Molo, than which, as any fish-wife knew, nothing was more certain to bring a man bad luck).

Here too, in the island's monastic days, there lived a humble but learned monk named Gabriele Condulmer. One day, when this man was doing his turn of duty as monastery porter, an unknown hermit rowed himself to the water-gate. Condulmer welcomed him kindly, took him into the church and prayed with him, and when the visitor returned to his boat, he turned to the monk and made a solemn prophecy. 'You, Gabriele Condulmer,' he said, 'will become first a Cardinal, then a Pope: but in your pontificate, I prophesy, you will suffer many and grievous adversities.' The hermit then rowed himself away, and was never seen again. The monk became Eugenius IV, one of the unhappiest and most ill-used of all the Popes.

His monastery has long fallen into disuse and dereliction. It was half-destroyed by fire in 1717. Its campanile had its top lopped off to serve as an observation post in the 1848 revolution, and was later demolished altogether. The remains of its buildings became first a powder magazine, then a fort, and are now the home of a fisherman's family. Two vicious dogs bark at you ferociously if you approach too closely, even splashing into the water to get to grips with you. Only a stone plaque of St George, and a sweet figure of the Madonna, modestly standing beneath a stone canopy at an angle of the wall, remain as reminders of old sanctities.

Or there is Poveglia, away beyond San Servolo, a low huddle of buildings on a flat islet, with a single tall campanile in the middle. It is like a stylized Venetian island, such as you see drawn, with a few deft strokes of the air-brush, in the background of the travel posters. This was once Popilia, named for its abundance of poplars, an autonomous community with its own vigorous Government. It played an heroic and blood-thirsty part, so we are told, in the defeat of Pepin – the Poveglians, living at the end of the Canale Orfano, are said to have pushed more Franks under the mud than any other body of combatants. In the war against the Genoese, so the official chronicles record, Poveglia was devastated by its own inhabitants 'by public order'. Romantics say this was an early example of 'scorched earth' policies: cynics with a nose for euphemisms suspect that a party of Genoese raided the island, and devastated it for themselves.

Poor Poveglia declined sadly down the centuries – it became a quarantine station first, then an isolation hospital, and finally a home for aged indigents: aged people, who were to be seen sunning themselves happily upon its lawns, or aged ships, which are still laid up in a neighbouring channel, hull to hull, funnel to funnel, pitifully streaked with rust and salt, their only attendants the skeleton crews who maintain their engines and the marine surveyors who now and then, clambering up their quavering gang-planks, shake their heads doubtfully upon their forecastles. Poveglia is shaped like a fan, and is cultivated to the water's edge with vines and maize, with a fringe of small trees running around its perimeter as a hem. At its apex there is a small octagonal stone fort, covered with shrubberies, in which there lives, so somebody recently assured me, a colony of several hundred plump rabbits, tastily varying the diet of crabs and stewed mussels on which I had always assumed the old people next door to subsist.

To the east two big agricultural islands, intersected by shallow canals, form the market garden of Venice, fertilized by her manure, sustained by her appetite, but scarcely visited by her citizens from one year to another. Sant' Erasmo and Vignole extend almost from the tip of the city itself to the island of San Francesco del Deserto – five miles of damp but fertile vegetable-bed, inhabited only by gardeners and fishermen.

They are interesting but dowdy islands. Nosing your way down their brown waterways, you might be in the heart of some fecund but dilapidated countryside – Carolina, perhaps, or Kildare. The water is overhung with trees and thick tangled shrubberies, and in the summer a layer of country dust lies heavily on the leaves like chalk. The cottages are clean but tumble-down, the gardens scrubby but productive. You may pass a fishermen's slipway among the fields, with their boats high and dry among their nets: or you may moor your boat beside a rickety white clapboard chapel, like a fundamentalist shrine in the American South, so that you almost expect to hear the whine of piccaninny hymn tunes from their windows, or the fruity acclamations of Holy Rollers.

A farmyard smell hangs in the air of these places, heavily freighted with mud and manure. Their gardens are rich with onions, asparagus, potatoes, cabbages and artichokes – for which, so the islanders gloomily complain, they are meagrely underpaid by the middle-men who convey this produce to the markets of the city. These are the islands upon which the bolder Venetian planners hope to erect brand-new industrial communities, swamping their onion-patches in apartment blocks and power-stations; and already their earthy dereliction seems doomed and transient, like the crannies of countryside that you will sometimes find, hemmed in by housing estates, on the outskirts of London and Los Angeles.

There is only one village in these islands – the area of which, put together, is substantially greater than Venice herself. It stands on the western shore of Sant' Erasmo, looking vapidly across to the cypresses of San Francesco and the patchwork muddle of Burano. It has a café with striped parasols propped pathetically outside it, and an old black landing-stage where the ferry-steamers stop, and a white barn of a church, cold and characterless. No history seems to be attached to these places – they are not even surrounded, as an estate agent once said to me of a peculiarly repellent half-timbered house, 'by the amenities of tradition'. The most conscientious guide books scarcely mention them. So resolutely has the world ignored them that some obscure medieval by-law, so I am assured, even forbids dancing on them. The people of Vignole and Sant' Erasmo strike me as a grumpy lot; and who can blame them?

Mazzorbo is a backwater of quite another kind. It lies west of Burano, to which it is connected by a footbridge, and it consists of a church, a cemetery, a fine broad canal, a few fields, a long stone wall always scrawled with politics, a handful of houses and an excellent trattoria where, if the wind is right, they will roast you a wild duck in the twinkling of an eye, or pull a fat wriggling eel from the bog at the bottom of the garden. The Mazzorbo people are simple but expansive, and will welcome you genially to their tables in the inn, and happily share your white wine and spaghetti: and this is unexpected, for if Sant' Erasmo is moribund, Mazzorbo is a living elegy.

Once it was very grand. Even in Roman times it was the site of a celebrated shrine to the god Belenus, and its very name means *major urbs*. In the Middle Ages it became the Venetian port of entry for the great German trade route – the *Alemagna* – and almost all imports from central Europe passed through the Mazzorbo customs. Particularly well-endowed, racy and upper-crust convents flourished there; rows of stylish palaces lined the canals of the place; a comfortable society of patricians and merchants made it one of the liveliest social centres of the lagoon. My oldest Venetian guide book, published in 1740, depicts the island dignified by eight campaniles, and still rich in gardens and palaces.

But long before that the rot had set in. Malaria had enervated the citizens of Mazzorbo, the rise of the Rialto had ruined its commerce, its thoroughfares were blocked with sludge and water-weed. By the eleventh century most of the people of Mazzorbo had decided to emigrate. Taking their houses carefully to pieces, as peripatetic Americans sometimes still do, they loaded the bricks and stones into barges and sailed away to Venice – many of the little houses still standing around the Rialto bridge, once the vortex of the Venetian stews, are immigrants from old Mazzorbo. Today there is almost nothing left, and Mazzorbo is only a market garden, the cemetery of Burano, and a staging-post on the ferry-boat route to Torcello (splendidly do the *vaporetti* churn their way down the long straight stretch of its Grand Canal, the waves of their wake rippling along the towpaths, like stern-wheelers sweeping past Natchez on their way to New Orleans).

But if you look through the window of the trattoria, shifting your eye past the red Coca-Cola sticker, you will see a small square house across the canal that still retains some distant suggestion of grandeur. It has Gothic windows and a solid square doorway. A rotting wall protects it from the water, and a *sandolo* is tied up beside its landing-stage. In the garden, among some stunted fruit trees, one or two defaced statues moulder the decades away. This is a house out of the past, like a coelacanth among fishes. Today it is all alone. Once it stood bravely among a line of peers, gleaming with life and luxury, padded boats at its steps and pampered courtesans in its salons. It is the Ca' d'Oro – the House of Gold, a last defiant relic of Mazzorbo's forgotten hey-day.

And far off in the northern lagoon there lies the loneliest and saddest of all the Venetian islets, Sant' Ariano. It was originally a suburb-island of Torcello, forming with the neighbouring Constanziaca yet another famous and flourishing community. Now it is inhabited only by the dead, for in the seventeenth century, when its living glories had long vanished, it became the bone-house of Venice, and thus it is coldly marked on the map: *Osseria*, with a small black cross. They no longer take the bones there from Venice, preferring to tip them into a common grave upon San Michele: but it is only a few years since the monthly bone-barge ploughed its slow way to Sant' Ariano, freighted with anonymous remains, and a guide book to the lagoon published in 1904 observes darkly that 'modern industry makes use of its unnamed skeletons, without scruple, for the refining of sugar'.

They do not, I think, make sugar from its bones nowadays, but it remains a queer and curdling place. I went there once from Mazzorbo, threading my boat through the treacherous channels behind Torcello, in a landscape that seemed uneasily deserted. A few sea-birds flew furtively above me. Far, far away across the marshes I could see a solitary fishing-boat. Torcello looked lifeless, and beyond it the swamps stretched away in dejection towards Altino. The channel to Sant' Ariano twists and winds incessantly through the flats, so that for half an hour or more you can see the distant white rectangular wall of the bone-yard, all alone among the grass: and when at last I reached it the sun was high, the wind had dropped, the lagoon was deathly calm, and all was sunk in heat and silence. There were lizards on the water-steps of the island. As I disembarked a rat jumped from the mud and dived into the water with a splash. The white gate of the *osseria* shone cruelly in the sunlight, and looking through its grille I could see in the shadows of the porch a stark staring head of Christ, unsmiling and emaciated.

The gate was locked, but walking around the corner I jumped up to the top of the wall, and peered into the enclosure. There was nothing to be seen but a mass of tangled bushes, entirely filling the place, and growing thickly to the very walls. Not a memorial was there, not a bunch of flowers, not a touch of humanity, only this dense green jungle of shrubbery. I scrambled down the wall into the enclosure, slithering through the spiky foliage, and pushing aside the brambles I looked down at my feet to see what I was standing on.

Beneath those bushes, I discovered, the ground was made of bones. These were bone-bushes. There was not a square foot of soil to be seen, only bones: thigh-bones and finger bones, crumpled bones and solid bones, and a few tilted skulls shining like phosphorescence in the shade of the undergrowth. I leapt over that wall like a steeplechaser, and was home, believe me, well before dark.

30 The Sacred Bulwarks

A sixteenth-century Venetian decree speaks of the lagoon, its waters and its islands, as 'sanctos muros patriae' – the 'sacred bulwarks of the fatherland'. Now as then, the outermost rampart of all is formed by the islands of the *lidi*, whose fragile and sometimes shifting strand is all that shields Venice from the sea. Not so long ago poets and people of that kind used to go to the Lido to ride horses, meditate, and ponder the 'peaked isles' of the Euganean Hills in the sunset. Doges went a-hawking there. The 30,000 soldiers of the 4th Crusade were quartered there while their leaders haggled over costs and payments. In the fourteenth century every able-bodied Venetian male between the ages of sixteen and thirty-five had to practise cross-bow shooting there. Byron wanted to be buried there, beneath the inscription *Implora Pace*, in the days when the sands were empty and washed in delicious melancholy.

Today the name of the place is synonymous with trendy glamour. All the myriad Lidos of the world, from Jamaica to the Serpentine, a million ice-cream parlours, a thousand gimcrack pin-table saloons, are named for this ancient place. This is a dual paradox. It is paradoxical first because *lido* is merely the Italian word for a shore or beach, and the *lidi* of Venice was a generic title for all the thin islands, part mud, part sand, on the seaward perimeter of the lagoon. There are two such reefs today, for the semi-promontory of Sottomarina is now virtually part of the mainland. The southern island is called the Littorale di Pellestrina. The other, and especially the northern end of it, is called by common custom the Lido.

The second paradox is this: that though the world thinks of the Lido as a place of expensive pleasure-making, the cultural guide books dismiss it with a grimace, the loftier tourists claim never to have set foot there, nevertheless these reefs are places of drama and romance, soaked in history as well as sun-tan lotion, and still the sacred bulwarks of the Serenissima.

They begin with a bang at the Porto di Lido, the principal gateway of

Venice, which was formed by the union of three smaller breaches in the *lidi*, but later fell into such neglect that under the Austrian régime only small ships could use it. It was revived when the Italian Kingdom took over Venice, sheltered by the two long moles which now stretch out to sea, and restored to all its old splendours. Few of the world's sea-gates have such noble memories. Generations of argosies sailed for the East through this passage, and here for eight centuries the Doges of Venice, in a celebrated ceremonial, married the Adriatic.

The custom began when the Doge Pietro Orseolo, in the year 997, took a fleet this way to defeat the first sea-enemies of the Republic, the Dalmatians (unfailingly described by the Venetian historians as 'pirates'). For decades the Venetians had paid them tribute, but in that year the Doge announced that he 'did not care to send a messenger this time, but would come to Dalmatia himself'. He annihilated them, and over the years the ceremony at the *porto*, which had begun as a libation before battle, came to be symbolic of Venetian naval power. A vast cavalcade of ornamental barges sailed to the Lido each Ascension Day, with the Doge supreme in the stern of his *bucintoro*, and a cluster of tourist craft milling about behind. The great fleet hove-to at the sea-gate, and there was handed to the Doge a glittering diamond ring, blessed by the Patriarch. Holy water was poured into the sea, and the Doge, standing in his poop, cried in a loud voice: 'O sea, we wed thee in sign of our true and everlasting dominion!' – and to the singing of choirs, the prayers of priests, the acclaim of the people, the rumble of guns, the back-paddling of oars, the slapping of sails, the roaring of the tide, he threw the ring ceremoniously into the water. For twenty generations this ritual was one of the great sights of Europe. Several hundred rings were thrown into the sea (though their value, we may assume, progressively declined as the mercenary instincts of the Venetians developed). One was found later inside a fish, and is now in the treasury of the Basilica, looking grand but corroded in a glass case. The others are somewhere below you in the mud, souvenirs of divorce: for when, that fatal April day in 1797, the guns of Sant' Andrea opened fire upon the *Libérateur d' Italie*, Venice's wedlock with the sea collapsed in bitter tears.

Beside the *porto*, and visible far out to sea, stands the magnificent old church of San Nicolò di Lido, an ancient weather-station, lighthouse, watch-tower and sailors' talisman. It is named for a lie, for the body of Santa Claus does not, as the old Venetians claimed, in fact lie inside it. In the eleventh century Bari, then under Norman domination, set itself up in rivalry to Venice as a mart between East and West, and wished to emulate the Serenissima in the possession of some awe-inspiring relic. Its citizens acccordingly acquired the corpse of St Nicolas of Myra, patron saint of pawn-brokers, slaves, virgins, sailors, robbers, prisoners, owners of property and children. This saint was particularly revered by the Venetians, if only because at the Council of Nicaea he had soundly boxed the ears of the theologian Arius, from whose very heresy, adopted by the Lombards, some of the earliest of the Venetians had fled into the lagoon. Since he was also the patron of seafarers, they much resented his adoption by Bari, especially as it occurred during the years when their own great St Mark was lost inside his pillar of the Basilica.

They therefore invented the fiction that a party of Venetian adventurers had raided Bari and stolen the corpse, and the church on the Lido was renamed as its shrine. Great ceremonies were held there on the saint's feast day, and even in the last years of the Republic it was still claimed that his body lay there, 'together with another St Nicholas, uncle of the first'. The uncle, indeed, may really be there: but Bari has long re-established itself as the undoubted resting-place of Santa Claus, for the silver reliquary of St Nicholas there is one of the principal miracle shrines of Italy, and has for nine centuries consistently exuded a liquid Holy Manna of such purity as to be indistinguishable from the clearest spring water. San Nicolò di Lido thus has an abashed, hang-dog air to it, and the more houseproud of the guide books prudently circumvent its history, and linger with unbalanced emphasis among its fine carved choir stalls.

Down the road is the tree-shaded cemetery of the Venetian Jews, once a place of mockery and contumely, now munificently restored. Near it is a Catholic burial-ground, and in an overgrown corner of the latter, locked away among rickety walls, are the remains of the celebrated Protestant burial-ground of the Lido. In the old days *acattolici* who died in Venice were denied burial in consecrated ground, and were instead dismissed to a field on this lonely island. The penultimate British Ambassador to Venice was buried there, and so, I believe, was Shelley's Clara: but when the airport was built at the end of the island, their graves were engulfed, and their remains were bundled together and placed in one aristocratic sarcophagus. Today this memorial stands in the corner of the cemetery, and on it you may just discern, like a gentlemanly whisper from the past, the lordly name of Sackville.

All around it, weedy and decayed, lie the other uprooted tombstones, some flat, some upside down, some piled like paving-stones. The little garden is difficult to find, and hardly anyone visits it. When I was there, guided through the maze of Catholic tombs by an obliging gardener, I idly brushed away the dust and pine-needles from a slab that lay beside my hand, and found it to be the tombstone of Joseph Smith, the British Consul who first recognized the talent of Canaletto and founded the splendid royal collection of his pictures now at Windsor Castle. 'This man', said I to my companion, 'was once much honoured in England.' The gardener smiled sympathetically, groping for words that would be at once honest and undeprecating, for he had never heard of Joseph Smith, but did not want to hurt my feelings. 'I imagine so,' he said at last, 'I imagine so.'

Among these old and mellowed things, the new world of the Lido coruscates. Vast, glittering and costly is this famous beach resort, and only a prig or a recluse could call it altogether dull. Its hotels range from the orchid to the aspidistra; its shops are full of outrageous clothes and gorgeously sticky cakes; its streets are lined with wistaria and bougainvillea; its Casino is lavish, its discotheques well frequented; its strings of fairy-lights, in loops and gaudy cascades, provide a piquant and sometimes comforting contrast to the dim medieval outline of Venice across the water. You can travel about the Lido by bus, by car or barouche. You can gamble there, or spot celebrities, or ride, or eat over-priced ill-cooked ostentatious moonlit meals. You can even, if it is the depth of winter, or if you are a person of forcible temperament, sometimes push your way down the bathing beaches for a mediocre swim (assuming you have a ticket, of course, for that particular stretch of foreshore).

There are some lovely villas on the lagoon side of the Lido – long white creeper-covered houses, such as might stand above Carthage in Tunisia, or recline among the blossoms in Marakesh. There are also many modest houses and blocks of flats, for an increasing number of Venetians prefer to live in the easy space of this modern town, and commute each morning to the crooked Serenissima. The Lido is a well-planned, well-kept, comfortable place, and even in the winter, when its promenades are deserted and its restaurants closed, it still feels fairly cosy. Its seaside is second rate – 'after our English seas', says Mr Edward Hutton bravely, 'the sluggish Adriatic might seem but a poor substitute': but its indescribable views across the lagoon, to the *Isole del Dolore* and the dim Euganean Hills, and the high façades of Venice herself – this consummate prospect makes the resort uniquely privileged among the holiday places of the earth.

Its influence, like Iesolo's, is creeping inexorably southwards, and the southern tip of the island is already occupied by Alberoni, a kind of embryo Lido, with a fashionable golf course, a couple of hotels, and numbers of hospitals, rest camps and sanatoria strewn among its sands like blockhouses. These two outposts of sophistication, though, are not yet united, and between them there are still reaches of the Lido shore that are silent and simple, meshed in weeds, tree-trunks and creepers, and littered with sea-shells (among which, on summer evenings, you may sometimes see eccentric enthusiasts, in baggy trousers or gypsy skirts, energetically scrabbling). The lagoon shore is lined with vegetable gardens and obscure rustic outhouses, and the little creeks that sidle into the island are so rich and steamy, so thickly fringed with reeds and coarse grass, that they might be brown backwaters of the Mississippi, in Huck Finn's country.

Amidst all this, with its face towards Venice, stands the fishing town of Malamocco, one of the friendliest places in the lagoon. The original Malamocco, the first capital of the united Venetians, has entirely vanished: scholars believe that it stood off-shore, on an island in the sea, and that it was overwhelmed by a twelfth-century cataclysm – every now and then an expedition puts on its goggles and flippers, and dives in search of its ruins. Modern Malamocco, all the same, feels very old indeed. It has its own miniature piazza, three churches, and an old gubernatorial palace. A canal runs behind the town, between the lagoon and the sea, and here the vegetable barges set up shop each morning, announcing their arrival with ancient wailing hawking cries, apparently in Arabic. The women meander back to their houses carrying their potatoes in outstretched aprons, and the small boys stand on the quayside licking ice-creams. Green wet water-meadows stretch away to the sea-wall, and the streets of Malamocco are (so a notice kindly tells us) paved with sea-shells.

There is a trattoria near the waterfront at Malamocco where you may eat your *scampi* and female crabs in a garden, and survey the translucent lagoon before you as from a napkinned terrace. Helpful loafers will look after your boat for you, and from the neighbouring bowling-alley you may sometimes hear guttural cries of triumph or despair, and the thudding of wooden balls. Away to the right, over a parade of little islands, you can see the towers of Venice. To the left there stands the disused lighthouse of Spania, surrounded by thickets of fishermen's poles. Near by old ships sometimes lie in pathetic dignity, high and rusty in the water: in Evelyn's day Malamocco was the 'chiefe port and ankerage' for English merchant-men, but now it is only a haven for unwanted vessels. Now and then the trolleybus from the Lido slithers to a stop beside the quay, and occasionally a trim little Fiat scurries by: but there is an air of sun-soaked, slap-happy repose to Malamocco. The excitements of the *plage* have not yet reached it, and the exertions of old Venice have long been forgotten. You may bask here in the sunshine undisturbed and unembarrassed, and even the small female crabs, fried in fat and garnished with oily segments of octopus, have a tranquil, soothing flavour to their shrivelled pincers.

The gusto of the Lido fades as you sail southwards down the reef, and this easy-going feeling withers. The northern stretch of the *lidi* is prosperous and hospitable; the southern is threadbare and penuri-ous. A slow serene ripple from the sea sways your progress as you

pass Alberoni and cross the Porto di Malamocco, the second of the
Venetian sea-gates, where the Austrian fleet used to lie at anchor,
and the super-tankers pound down to Sant' Ilario; but on the other
side the Littorale di Pellestrina lies harshly, a poor, cluttered,
ramshackle litter of villages, straggling along the ever-narrowing line
of the reef.

By now it is hardly an island, and the villages huddle together as
though they spring directly from the water – the sea at their back
doors, the lagoon lapping at the front. Where San Pietro in Volta
ends, Porto Secco begins, and Sant' Antonio merges into Pellestrina,
so that as you pass by their successive unkempt quaysides the reef
beside you is like one long water-side street. There are churches now
and again, and a *piazzetta* or two beside the water, and a café with
tables outside its door, and sometimes a poor arid garden. The
cottages are gaily painted but peeling, and are intermingled with
tattered sheds, warehouses, boatyards, wood-piles. There are great
oil barges, high and dry on piles, having their bottoms scraped; there
are fleets of fishing boats in endless lines along the quays. At Porto
Secco you may see the desiccated creek that is a dried-up *porto* to the
sea, at Pellestrina there is a medieval fortress-tower: but mostly the
villages dissolve before your eyes into a muddle of tumbled structures, and look as though they have been not merely swept and
bleached by the elements, but positively scraped.

This is the poorest of the Venetian shores. It has no shine or
glamour, and even its people seem wizened. They are the inhabitants
of a precarious sand-bank, and slowly, as you journey southwards,
the line of their island contracts. Now, looking between the houses,
you can see a strip of green and a glimmer of sea; now the green has
vanished, and there is only a grey line of masonry beyond the
piazzetta; now the houses themselves peter out, and there are shacks,
raggety lines of bathing huts, boat-houses, rubbish yards; until at
last, passing the final gravestones of Pellestrina, you find that only a
great stone wall represents the ultimate bulwark.

Here you moor your boat carefully at an antique iron ring, and
climbing a flight of steps you find yourself poised between the
waters. You are standing upon the Murazzi, the noble sea-walls that

were the last great engineering works of the dying Republic. Without these great ramparts, 6,000 yards long and immensely strong, the Adriatic would by now have burst the Pellestrina strand, and flooded the lagoon. The Murazzi are made of huge blocks of Istrian granite, so beautifully put together that Goethe praised them as a work of art. It took thirty-eight years to build them. Upon the wall a big bronze slab, erected in 1751, records the purpose of the construction: *'Ut Sacra Aestuaria Urbis Et Libertatis Sedes Perpetuum Conserventur Colosseas Moles Ex Solido Marmore Contra Mare Posuere Curatores Aquarum.'* Nearly two centuries later, though, the Venetians erected another plaque, which better expresses the proud spirit of these magnificent works. *'Ausu Romano,'* it says, *'Aere Veneto.'* A truly Roman venture it was, achieved by the Venetians in their last years of independence.

A narrow path runs along the top of the Murazzi, and here you may sit, dangling your legs, and consider the sacredness of the *lidi*. On one side there heaves the Adriatic Sea, cold, grey, restless, very deep, rolling across to Trieste, Pola, Dubrovnik, and away to Albania, Corfu and Cephalonia. On the other side, a few feet away, the Venetian lagoon lies pale and placid. Its waters are still and meditative; a host of little craft moves perpetually across its wide expanse; and below you, where your boat lies motionless at its moorings, the small silver fish twitch and flicker among the seaweed.

31 Lost

But the lagoon is doomed, for its essences are too vaporous to survive. It is a place of vanished glories, lost islands and forgotten palaces – Malamocco drowned, Torcello deserted, Murano degraded, Mazzorbo moribund, Sant' Ariano sepulchral, monasteries dispersed and campaniles toppled. Soon the speculators, the oil-men and the bridge-builders will dispel its last suggestions of secrecy.

On the chart of the lagoon, away among the shambling marshes in the south-west, there is an islet marked Cason dei Sette Morti – the House of the Seven Dead Men. It commemorates a legend. The Cason, an isolated stone house among the waters, was used by fishermen, in the days before motor engines, as a base for their operations; they would sleep, eat and rest there during intervals between fishing, caulk their boats and mend their nets, while one of their number went off to market with the catch. Several such lonely fishing lodges litter the emptier reaches of the southern lagoon – Cason Cornio Nuovo, Caso di Valle in Pozzo, Cason Bombae, Cason di Valgrande – mere specks in the mud, named for medieval master fishermen, or forgotten conceptions in crab-men's minds.

Long ago, so the legend says, six men and a boy were staying at our particular *cason*. The men spent each night fishing, and the boy remained in the house and cooked. One morning the fishermen, returning from work, found the corpse of a man floating in the water. Hoisting it aboard, they laid it in the bows of their boat, intending to take it, after breakfast, to the Ponte della Paglia in Venice, where the bodies of drowned people were exhibited for identification. The boy, coming out of the house to greet them, saw this figure in the prow, and asked why they did not bring in their guest to breakfast. It was all ready, he said, and there was plenty for an extra mouth.

The fishermen had a truly Venetian instinct for the macabre. Peeling off their coats and entering the house, they told the boy to invite the stranger himself. 'He's as deaf as a post', they said, 'and awful stubborn. Give him a good kick and a curse, to wake him up.' The boy did as he was told, but the man remained prostrate. 'Give him a good shake', the fishermen shouted, sitting down ribaldly at the table, 'and tell him we can't wait till doomsday for him! We're working men, we are!'

Again the boy obeyed, and presently he returned cheerfully indoors and began to ladle out the food. All was well, he said. The guest had woken up, and was on his way. The fishermen's flow of badinage now abruptly ceased. They stared at each other, say the story-tellers, 'pallid and aghast'; and presently they heard slow, heavy, squelchy, flabby footsteps on the path outside. The door opened with an eerie creak; the corpse walked in, horribly stiff and bloodless; and by the time he had settled himself ponderously at the table, all those six churlish fishermen had been struck with a lethal chill, and sat before their *polenta* as dead as mutton. Seven dead men occupied the *cason*, and only the boy paddled frantically away to tell the tale.

One day I determined to visit the House of the Seven Dead Men: but no *bricole* mark the channels, the charts are notoriously vague, and early in the morning I went to San Pietro in Volta to find myself a pilot. Fishermen from the littoral, I discovered, no longer much frequented that part of the lagoon. Several, pointing out an island in diametrically the wrong direction, swore that it was the *cason*, they had known it since childhood. Several others admitted they did not know the way. One took a look at my boat and said kindly that he had other things to do. It was an aged, hirsute and wrinkled fisherman, an Old Man of the Lagoon, who finally agreed to a price, stepped aboard, and came with me.

It would be, he said, quite like old times, quite a little outing. He hadn't been out there since the war, when he hid for a time from the Germans on a marshy reef near the *cason*. He was a talkative, jolly old man, wearing a slouch hat and geological layers of jersey: and he guided us merrily enough across the ruffled wastes of the central lagoon, the Vale of the Ditch of Low Water, the Small Vale of Above the Wind, where the seaweed lay only a few inches beneath our propeller, and swayed mysteriously with our passage. The day was grey and the wind cold, but as we voyaged the old man pointed out the landmarks – the Cason dei Mille Campi, a big stone lodge alone among the marshes; the distant white farmhouses of the mainland; the almost indistinguishable island of San Marco in Bocca Lama; Chioggia dim and towering to the south; the long line of Pellestrina growing vague and blurred behind.

The lagoon around us was deserted. The traffic of the big channels was far away, and only a few small shabby crab-boats lay at work in muddy inlets. Once or twice my pilot, who was not used to engines, ran us harmlessly aground: but presently we found ourselves in the deep water of the Fondi dei Sette Morti, the last stretch to our destination. Ah! what memories this stirred for the old man! Here his father had brought him as a boy, when he was first learning to handle a boat; and here, in the lean days before the war, he used to spend the long windswept night dredging the last possible mussel out of the mud; and over there, on that dank and blasted marsh-bank, he had hidden from the Germans, crouched beneath a canvas shelter, while his wife rowed out each week with his provisions; and just around this corner, between these shoals – *port a bit here, it's shallow, now back into the stream again* – here, just around this corner, we would find . . .

But the old man's voice trailed away: for when we rounded that marshy point, the *cason* was no longer there. That predatory, dissatisfied, restless, rapacious lagoon had been at work again. The water had risen above the shoals, and all that was left of the house was a sprawling mass of masonry, a pile of brick and rubble, through which the tide was already seeping and gurgling. The old man was astonished, but even more affronted. 'Now why should a thing like that happen?' he asked me indignantly. '*Mamma mia!* That house was there when I was a child, a fine big house of stone, the Cason dei Sette Morti – and now it's gone! Now why should that have happened, eh? Tell me that!'

He was an urbane man, though, beneath his stubble: and as we moved away from that desolate place, and turned our prow towards San Pietro, I heard a rasping chuckle from the stern of the boat. '*Mamma mia!*' the old man said again, shaking his head from side to side: and so we chugged home laughing and drinking wine, until, paying insufficient attention to his task, that fisherman ran us aground and broke our forward gear, and we completed the voyage pottering shamefacedly backwards. 'Like a couple of crabs,' said the old man, unabashed, 'though even the crabs go sideways.'

EMBARKATION

Perhaps you are a millionaire, and can maintain your Venetian palace the year round, with your gilded gondola behind its grille, your bright-painted mooring posts, and the vivid blue curtains which, drawn aloofly across your windows, proclaim your absence in Park Lane or New England. The chances are, though, that one day you must pack your bags, pay your bills, give a farewell kiss to the faithful (and touchingly sniffing) Emilia, and sail away to less enchanted shores. Then a curious sensation overcomes you, as you pass among the retreating islands of the lagoon – a sensation half of relief, half of sadness, and strongly tinged with bewilderment. Venice, like many a beautiful mistress and many a strong dark wine, is never entirely frank with you. Her past is enigmatic, her present contradictory, her future hazed in uncertainties. You leave her sated but puzzled, like the young man who, withdrawing happily from an embrace, suddenly realizes that the girl's mind is elsewhere, and momentarily wonders what on earth he sees in her.

For though there have been many scoffers at the Venetian legend, rationalists, sceptics and habitual debunkers, nevertheless the appeal of the Serenissima is astonishingly empirical. Nearly all its visitors seem to agree, when they leave Venice at last, that on the whole, and notwithstanding, it really is a very lovely place. An interminable procession of the talented has made the pilgrimage to St Mark's, and been received into the Venetian state of grace. An army of visiting admirers has written its paeons – Goethe, Stendhal, Gautier, Hans Andersen, Musset, Charles Reade, Wagner, Taine, Maurice Barrès, Thomas Mann, Mendelssohn, Henry James, Rilke, Proust, Rousseau, Byron, Browning, Dickens, Dante Gabriel Rossetti, Hemingway, Ruskin, Dante, Wordsworth, Petrarch, Longfellow, Disraeli, Evelyn, Shelley, Jean Cocteau – not to speak of George Sand, Ouida, Mrs Humphry Ward, Freya Stark and George Eliot, whose husband once fell, with an ignominious plop, from their hotel window into the Grand Canal beneath. Corot, Durer, Turner, De Pisis, Bonington, Dufy, Kokoschka, Manet, Monet, Renoir, Whistler have all painted famous pictures of Venice, and there is hardly an art shop in London, Paris or New York that will not offer you a sludgy prospect of the Salute by some less eminent practitioner.

Nietzsche, of all people, once said that if he searched for a synonym for music, he found 'always and only Venice'. Even Hitler thought the city beautiful: he stayed at Stra, on the mainland, but he particularly admired the Doge's Palace, so I was told by one of the custodians who escorted him around it, and legend maintains that he broke away from protocol to range the city by himself in the small hours of the morning (some say at a half-demented jog-trot). Garibaldi liked the Doge's Palace, too, though not a man of artistic yearnings: he thought he saw a satisfying resemblance to himself in the image of the heroic Admiral Veniero in Vicentino's *Battle of Lepanto*. More slush has been written about Venice than anywhere else on earth, more acres of ecstatic maiden prose. Venice is paved with purple passages. But as John Addington Symonds once remarked, she is the Shakespeare of cities, unchallenged, incomparable, and beyond envy. Stockholm is proud to call herself the Venice of the North, Bangkok the Venice of the East. Amsterdam likes to boast that she has more bridges than Venice. London has her own 'Little Venice', in Paddington, where a notice on one irreverent householder's gate warns visitors to 'Beware of the Doge'. Venezuela was given her name by the *conquistadores* when they saw the amphibious villages on the Gulf of Maracaibo. Churchill himself did not object when an Italian admirer, trying to evolve a worthy translation for his title 'Lord Warden of the Cinque Ports', dubbed him the Doge of Dover.

All this strikes me as odd, for though Venice is obviously lovely, you might not expect her appeal to be quite so universal. The city undeniably stinks, for one thing; it can be disagreeably grasping of temperament, for another; its winters are cruel, its functions coarsened; its lagoon can be unpleasantly chill and colourless; its individual buildings, if you view them with a detached and analytical eye, range downwards from the sublime by the way of the overestimated antique to the plain ugly. I myself dislike most of the grandiloquent Grand Canal palaces, with their pompous façades, florid doorways and phallic obelisks. Many of the city's celebrated structures – the Dogana, for instance, or the old prisons – would look undistinguished if deposited in Clapham or the Bronx.

Ruskin, who hated half the buildings in Venice, and worshipped the other half, wrote of San Giorgio Maggiore that it was 'impossible to conceive a design more gross, more barbarous, more childish in conception, more servile in plagiarism, more insipid in result, more contemptible under every point of rational regard'. Charlie Chaplin once remarked that he would like to take a shot-gun and knock the figures off the Sansovino library in the Piazzetta, deity by deity. Evelyn thought the Basilica 'dim and dismal'. Herbert Spencer, the philosopher, detested the 'meaningless patterns' of the Doge's Palace, the tesselation of which reminded him 'of nothing so much as the vertebral spine of a fish'. D. H. Lawrence, taking a first look at the buildings of Venice, called it an 'abhorrent, green, slippery city': and I know just how he felt.

The allure of Venice, though, is distinct from art and architecture. There is something curiously sensual to it, if not actually sexual. 'Venice casts about you', as a nineteenth-century Frenchman put it, 'a charm as tender as the charm of woman. Other cities have admirers. Venice alone has lovers'. James Howell assured his readers, in the seventeenth century, that if once they knew the rare beauty of the Virgin City, they would 'quickly make love to her'. And Elizabeth Barrett Browning expressed some of this libidinous or perhaps narcotic rapture when she wrote that 'nothing is like it, nothing equal to it, not a second Venice in the world'. Today the place is loud with motor boats, tawdry with tourism, far from virginal: but when I lean from my window in the early morning, when the air is sea-fresh and the day unsullied, when there is a soft plash of oars beneath my terrace, and the distant hum of a ship's turbines, when the first sun gleams on the golden angel of the Campanile, and the shadows slowly stir along the dark line of the palaces – then a queer delicious yearning still overcomes me, as though some creature of unattainable desirability is passing by outside.

I think this is partly a matter of organic design. Venice is a wonderfully compact and functional whole: rounded, small, complete, four-square in the heart of its sickle lagoon like an old golden monster in a pond. Corbusier described the city as an object lesson for town planners. The variegated parts of Venice have been mellowed and diffused, like the two old palaces on the Grand Canal whose roofs intimately overlap above a minute alley-way. Her architecture is a synthesis of styles – eastern and western, Gothic, Renaissance, Baroque – so that Ruskin could call the Doge's Palace the central building of the world. Her canals and streets fit neatly into one another, like the well-machined parts of an engine. Her symbols are simple but catching, like advertisers' images – the sleek winged lions, the golden horses, the Doge in his peaked hat, the twin pillars on the Molo, the ramrod Campanile, the lordly swing of the Grand Canal, the cobra-prows of the gondolas, rearing in the lamplight. Her slogans are exciting and memorable – *'Viva San Marco!' 'Lord of a Quarter and a Half-Quarter'*, *'Pax Tibi Marce'*, *'Morto o Vivo'*, *'Com' era, dov' era'*. Venice has the feeling of a disbanded but still brilliant corporation, with the true ring and dazzle of capitalism to her ambiance. You feel, as you stand upon the high arch of the Rialto, that you can somehow capture the whole of her instantly in your mind – the whole of her history, all her meaning, every nuance of her beauty: and although her treasures are inexhaustible, in a way you are right, for Venice is a highly concentrated extract of her own reputation.

It is partly a matter of light. The Venetian painters were pre-eminent in their mastery of chiaroscuro, and Venice has always been a translucent city, a place of ravishing sunsets and iridescent mornings, monochromatic though its long winters can seem. Once it was vivid with gilded façades and frescoes – the Doge's Palace used to glow with gold, vermilion and blue – and here and there, on decomposing walls or leprous carvings you may still see faint lingering glimmers of the city's lost colour. Even now, when the Venetians hang out their flags and carpets in celebration, put up their gay sunshades, light their fairy-lamps, water the geraniums in their window-boxes, sail their bright pleasure-boats into the lagoon – even now it can be, at its sunlit best, a gaudy kind of place. The atmosphere, too, is remarkable for a capricious clarity, confusing one's sense of distance and proportion, and sometimes etching skylines and façades with uncanny precision. The city is alive with *trompe-l'oeil*, natural and artificial – deceits of perspective, odd foreshortenings, distortions and hallucinations. Sometimes its prospects seem crudely one-dimensional, like pantomime sets; sometimes they seem exaggeratedly deep, as though the buildings were artificially separated, to allow actors to appear between them, or to give an illusion of urban distance. The lagoon swims in misty mirages. If you take a boat into the Basin of St Mark, and sail towards the Grand Canal, it is almost eerie to watch the various layers of the Piazza pass each other in slow movement: all sense of depth is lost, and all the great structures, the pillars and the towers, seem flat and wafer-thin, like the cardboard stage properties that are inserted, one behind the other, through the roofs of toy theatres.

It is partly a matter of texture. Venice is a place of voluptuous materials, her buildings inlaid with marbles and porphyries, cipollino, verd-antico, jasper, marmo greco, polished granite and alabaster. She is instinct with soft seductive textiles, like the silks that Wagner hung around his bedrooms – the velvets, taffetas, damasks and satins that her merchants brought home from the East, in the days when all the ravishing delicacies of the Orient passed this way in a cloud of spice. When the rain streams down the marble façades of the Basilica, the very slabs seem covered in some breathtaking brocade. Even the waters of Venice sometimes look like shot silk. Even the floor of the Piazza feels yielding, when the moonlight shines upon it. Even the mud is womb-like and unguent.

The Venetian allure is partly a matter of movement. Venice has lost her silken dreamy spell, but her motion is still soothing and seductive. She is still a dappled city, tremulous and flickering, where the sunlight shimmers gently beneath the bridges, and the shadows shift slowly along the promenades. There is nothing harsh or brutal about the movement of Venice. The gondola is a vehicle of beautiful locomotion, the smaller craft of the canals move with a staccato daintiness, and often you see the upper-works of a liner in stately passage behind the chimneys. There are several places in Venice where, looking across a canal, you may catch a momentary glimpse of people as they pass the openings in an arcade: their movement seems oddly smooth and effortless, and sometimes an old woman glides past enshrouded in black tasselled shawls, and sometimes a priest strides silently by in a liquefaction of cassocks. The women of Venice walk with ship-like grace, swayed only by the gentle wobbling of their ankles. The monks and nuns of Venice flit noiselessly about its streets, as though they had no feet beneath their habits, or progressed in a convenient state of levitation. The policemen of the Piazza parade slowly, easily, magisterially. The sails of the lagoon laze the long days away, all but motionless on the horizon. The chief verger of the Basilica, when he sees a woman in trousers approaching the fane, or a short-sleeved dress, raises his silver stick in a masterly unhurried gesture of dismissal, his worldly-wise beadle's face shaking slowly to and fro beneath its cockade. The crowds that mill through the narrow shopping streets do so with a leisurely, greasy animation: and in the winter it is pleasant to sit in a warm wine shop and watch through the window the passing cavalcade of umbrellas, some high, some low, manoeuvring and jostling courteously for position, raised, lowered or slanted to fit between one another, like the chips of a mosaic or a set of cogs.

And in the last analysis, the glory of the place lies in the grand fact of Venice herself: the brilliance and strangeness of her history, the wide melancholy lagoon that surrounds her, the convoluted sea-splendour that keeps her, to this day, unique among the cities. When at last you leave these waters, pack away your straw hat and swing out to sea, all the old dazzle of Venice will linger in your mind; and her smell of mud, incense, fish, age, filth and velvet will hang around your nostrils; and the soft lap of her back-canals will echo in your ears; and wherever you go in life you will feel somewhere over your shoulder, a pink, castellated, shimmering presence, the domes and riggings and crooked pinnacles of the Serenissima.

There's romance for you! There's the lust and dark wine of Venice! No wonder George Eliot's husband fell into the Grand Canal.

Chronology

date   *page*

During the last four centuries of her history, despite periods of astonishing artistic fertility, Venice declined in power and virility, her power whittled away in constant defensive wars against the Turks and by the rise of new commercial rivals in the West. By the middle of the 18th century her Empire was almost gone, and she subsided in carnival and garish excess towards her end as a State.

	date		*page*
For nearly a century Venice has formed part of the Italian State. She is now a prefecture, the capital of a province, and the third port of Italy.	1866	Venice joins Italian Kingdom	13
	1902	Collapse of Campanile	151–3
	1915	Operations against Austria	96–7
	1931	Road causeway built	107
	1945	British Army enters Venice	97, 242–3
	1960	Construction of Marco Polo airport	228–9

Index

Map indices refer to the plan of Venice at the beginning of the book